JUN 1 5

A GAME OF THEIR OWN

A GAME OF THEIR OWN

VOICES OF CONTEMPORARY WOMEN IN BASEBALL

Jennifer Ring

UNIVERSITY OF NEBRASKA PRESS

LINCOLN AND LONDON

Portions of the introduction originally
appeared as "Invisible Women in America's
National Pastime . . . or, 'She's Good. It's History, Man,'" by Jennifer Ring, in *Journal of Sport
and Social Issues* 37, no. 1 (2013): 57–77.
Portions of chapters 1 and 3 originally appeared
as "America's Baseball Underground: Invisible
Women in the National Pastime," by Jennifer
Ring, in *The Cooperstown Symposium on Baseball
and American Culture, 2011–2012*, ed. William
M. Simons, pp. 160–78. © 2013 and reprinted by
permission of McFarland & Company, Inc., Box
611, Jefferson NC 28640, www.mcfarlandpub.com.
Portions of chapter 3 originally appeared as "American Women Play Hardball in Venezuela: Team USA
Battles Invisibility at Home, Is Celebrated Abroad,
and Faces Gunfire at the Women's World Cup," by
Jennifer Ring, in *The Baseball Research Journal* 41,
no. 1 (Spring 2012): 53–56. © 2012 by the Society
for American Baseball Research and reprinted by
permission of the University of Nebraska Press.

∞

Library of Congress Cataloging-
in-Publication Data
Ring, Jennifer, 1948–
A game of their own: voices of contemporary
women in baseball / Jennifer Ring.
pages   cm
Includes bibliographical references and index.
ISBN 978-0-8032-4480-1 (cloth: alk. paper)
ISBN 978-0-8032-6994-1 (epub)
ISBN 978-0-8032-6995-8 (mobi)
ISBN 978-0-8032-6996-5 (pdf)
1. Baseball for women—United States.
2. Softball for women—United States. 3. Women
baseball players—United States. I. Title.
GV880.7.R56 2015
796.357082—dc23
2014042618

Set in Lyon by Lindsey Auten
Designed by N. Putens

CONTENTS

ILLUSTRATIONS

PREFACE

There is a national women's baseball team in the United States. Team USA has medaled in every international competition it has played in for the past decade, but it is virtually unknown: one of the best kept secrets in American sports.

Where did the ballplayers on the USA Baseball Women's National Team come from? The story should not be mysterious: the national team in every sport comprises the best athletes in the nation in their sport. The stories of America's best athletes follow a fairly predictable pattern: The athletes begin to play their sport at a very young age, often influenced in their choice of sport by parents and siblings or an important coach or role model. They show precocious athletic ability. Their natural talent appears early in life and earns them admiration and encouragement, coaching, private lessons, participation in skills camps and clinics, and a rapid rise to highly competitive levels of play. Some are pushed to succeed by parents with hopes of wealth, fame, and college scholarships for their child; others push themselves, perhaps for similar reasons. But it takes commitment, hard work and discipline, and the sacrifice of some of the joys of childhood to become sufficiently accomplished by adolescence to compete for a place on the national team.

This path and its rewards have become amplified in recent years for all youth sports, but it has been open to girls only since 1972, when Title IX was passed.[1] Before then the few individual sports in which women might earn recognition were racially exclusive, upper-class, "country club" sports: golf, tennis, swimming, and perhaps gymnastics and ice-skating. They were sports that could be seen as "feminine" if the athlete was dressed appropriately.[2] There were a handful of prominent African American women track athletes in the mid-twentieth century, but for a long time track and field was not considered feminine enough to be an "acceptable" sport for middle-class white women. A few American women rose to prominence in individual sports, but team sports were almost completely unavailable to girls and women of any race.[3] Today's most visible women athletes are still clustered in individual sports, while very few female team athletes have an opportunity to earn a living at their sport, much less become wealthy. The women team athletes who try to play professionally after college find more opportunities in Europe than in the United States.

Debate about whether intense focus on one sport throughout childhood is physically and emotionally healthy for young athletes has received plenty of attention, although the phenomenon appears to be here to stay. Whether disproportionate wealth bestowed on male athletes is good for our culture and whether female athletes should aspire to that inflated celebrity are also issues for discussion. But even without opportunities for wealth and fame, athletic girls have embraced the opportunities to participate in team sports that were opened when Title IX passed.[4]

The stories of the USA Baseball Women's National Team diverge from the usual path of women athletes, even post–Title IX. Girls who play baseball have barely benefited from that pivotal piece of legislation. The women of Team USA have reached the pinnacle of their sport without encouragement or infrastructure. Indeed, most of the players whose biographies are included in this book were actively *dis*couraged from playing baseball. None had easy access to baseball teams after the age of twelve, most were the only girl on their team or in their league, and after age twelve, most battled to find a team to play on at all.

Still, there are some similarities with girls who are accomplished athletes in other team sports. The players on the USA Baseball Women's National Team are American girls from across the nation, of diverse racial, ethnic, and economic backgrounds. Most were exposed to baseball early in life and fell in love with the game immediately. All knew they were athletes as soon as they were aware of anything about themselves, and all had a bat and ball in hand before kindergarten. Some had a father or a brother or even a mother who introduced them to the game. Some had parents who signed them up for Little League without giving the specific sport much thought. There was no softball league in the neighborhood; or the local Little League was a safe place for a working mother to leave her kids on Saturdays; or baseball was simply the game all the kids in the neighborhood were playing, and their daughters wanted to play with the boys who were their neighborhood friends. Then baseball itself did the rest. The girls felt at home on a baseball diamond and discovered something important about themselves. This is not a mysterious process.

The mystery is why, no matter how good they were, all the girls who grew up to play on the USA Baseball Women's National Team were told to leave baseball at age twelve and to find another sport. Most obliged. A few refused to and continued with baseball for as long as they could. Baseball reappeared later for all of them, and they responded once again to its call and followed it to Team USA.

That's the surface pattern, anyway. Actually, the stories are more individual, nuanced, and compelling. I was familiar with the story of my daughter, Lilly Jacobson, who was a member of Team USA in 2006, 2008, and 2010. But I knew her story couldn't possibly be unique. I wanted to know how other girls who love baseball arrived at the top of the women's game, how they think about their baseball journeys, and what their goals are for continuing in the sport. I chose ten of the most outstanding members of Team USA to interview for this project. I was hoping to learn about their earliest experience with baseball, about how they persevered, sometimes lost, and then rediscovered their love of the game. My concept was to put the best team on the field for the purposes of this book: one player at each position and a relief pitcher. I first became acquainted with these women through their play on Team USA, and on a tournament team, the New England Women's Red Sox, which helps fill the need for baseball in the years when there is no international tournament.[5] With two exceptions, all the women I interviewed played on the

2010 USA team. Donna Mills, whom I chose for the third base position, retired from USA Baseball after the 2008 tournament to have a baby, born in August 2010, just as the team was getting ready to depart for Venezuela. Donna had been Team USA's starting third basewoman in 2006 and 2008, had been the tournament Most Valuable Player (MVP) in 2006, and had not been replaced with a regular at that position in 2010. The other exception, the eleventh player, is Meggie Meidlinger. She did not play on the 2010 USA team, although she pitched for the team in 2006 in Taipei and 2008 in Matsuyama. Meggie was interviewed by Lilly in May 2011, when they were at a baseball tournament in Baltimore that I was unable to attend. Theirs is the only private conversation between two teammates in the book, and because of that, it earned a place in the volume along with the other oral histories.

The two players I knew least well when I began these interviews were Jenny Dalton Hill and Jenna Marston, both of whom played for Team USA for the first time in 2010. I was not able to travel with the 2010 team because Lilly had been injured on the eve of their departure to Venezuela. Hill played first base in 2010, and Marston played shortstop and pitcher.

I chose the players for their established athletic excellence on Team USA and also because I knew they were articulate and self-aware and could tell a story well. I hoped they trusted me enough to feel comfortable discussing aspects of their athletic careers that might not be easy to talk about. I approached each of them individually by email or Facebook message, described the project, and asked if they would be willing to give an oral history interview about their baseball journey from childhood to Team USA.[6] All agreed to be interviewed. Nobody declined the opportunity to tell her story, and I didn't need to go to the bench for backup.

After each player had agreed to be included in the book, I scheduled an interview at her convenience, informing her it would take between one and three hours. The travel and lodging expenses were funded by a Scholarly and Creative Activities Grant from the College of Liberal Arts and research funds made available to me by the Political Science Department at the University of Nevada, Reno, as well as the generous donations of several individuals interested in women's baseball. I received from the Society for American Baseball Research (SABR) a SABR-Yoseloff grant and from the American Women's Baseball Federation a grant to help fund start-up and equipment costs.

When each player agreed to be interviewed, I sent her a list of questions to think about. I was hoping to establish some consistency in the oral histories, but I assured each player that she was free to focus on whatever aspects of her story seemed most important (see appendix A). For the most part, once the digital recorder that I brought to the interviews was turned on, each player addressed the questions I had given her, without direction from me. I prompted each player once with the questions she had not covered but did not pursue issues that she did not want to talk about. All had the option of remaining anonymous, but none wished to. All had the opportunity to read their chapters when they were written, to advise me of any statements or details they preferred to omit, or to add additional material. All were required by the University of Nebraska Press to sign an interview release. The recorded oral histories, transcripts, and photographs provided by each player are now housed in the National Baseball Hall of Fame Library as the Jennifer B. Ring Collection.

I interviewed the players geographically closest to me first: Tamara Holmes, in Oakland, California, and Sarah Gascon, in Santa Monica. I then traveled to the Midwest, where I interviewed Jenna Marston in Columbia, Missouri, and Jenny Dalton Hill in Lexington, Kentucky. My next trip took me to the South, where I interviewed Malaika Underwood at her home in Atlanta, Georgia, and Veronica Alvarez at her parents' home in Key Largo, Florida. Tara Harbert lived in North Carolina at the time, but I interviewed her in my hotel room in Baltimore at the Eastern Women's Baseball Conference Tournament, in which the New England Women's Red Sox were playing over Memorial Day weekend, 2012. Several weeks later, I returned to the East Coast one more time to interview Donna Mills in Boston, and Lilly Jacobson, also living in Boston. Finally, I waited until Marti Sementelli had finished her freshman year at Montreat College near Ashville, North Carolina, and returned for the summer to Southern California, where I interviewed her at her mother's home in Van Nuys. All the ballplayers were wonderfully gracious with their hospitality, welcoming me into their homes and generously talking with me for several hours, in several cases an entire day and part of the following day, wherever our conversation led. All, including myself, experienced intensely emotional moments during the course of these interviews. Tears were shed by strong women.

The stories in this volume are oral histories. They are not meant to be "objective" in the conventional sense of scholarly distance. They are "objective" only in the sense that they are the players' own stories, in their own words, based on transcribed oral recordings. Where facts and statistics were verifiable, I verified them and cited the source of verification in a footnote. I accepted the players' narratives at face value. These are memories and reflections of their young lives, and that is exactly what I asked the players to share with me. Their parents, siblings, coaches, and teammates may recall events differently, but theirs are not the perspectives I sought in this book. Whatever they have shared *is* the story and perspective that I wanted.

There are hundreds of other girls and women who play or have played baseball, and I was obviously not able to talk to all of them. The eleven players I chose for this book have earned their places on the USA Baseball Women's National Team, but that does not mean they are the only women in the United States who can play on this level. Selection for the national team is not an objective science and is no less subject to politics than anything else. Appendix B provides a more comprehensive (but still not exhaustive) list of girls and women currently playing, coaching, or administering women's baseball in the United States.

The book begins with an introduction setting the historical context of American women's baseball, a history of exclusion and perpetual invisibility. Flying under the radar is the USA Baseball Women's National Team. My familiarity with the team is through my daughter's experience, which I describe at the beginning of the book. That chapter is Lilly's story from my perspective as her mother. The final oral history chapter is Lilly's story in her own words.

The ballplayers' collective description of the dramatic 2010 Women's World Cup Tournament in Caracas, Venezuela, sets the stage for their oral histories. Then each player tells the story of her own baseball journey from childhood to the national team.

Each woman's oral history is presented individually as its own chapter. The eleven chapters of players' stories are organized into three groups, roughly by age and also by whether the ballplayers played softball or baseball, or both, before being selected for Team USA. The groupings are somewhat overlapping, and I debated other means of presenting the oral histories before settling on organizing by generation and childhood sport. I considered presenting the players by baseball's conventional position numbering order (starting with pitcher first and ending with right fielder), but that made no scholarly, literary, or narrative sense, other than adhering to that baseball convention. I didn't presume to select a batting order for this team, but that would have been another option for organizing the chapters. I decided, after having deliberated about the order of presentation, to begin with the senior players and end with the younger ones. My intention was to present a narrative sweep that would provide perspective on what has changed for women baseball players who are now nearing forty, and those who are a decade or two younger. Overlapping that arrangement was consideration of whether each player's path to Team USA had been primarily through baseball or softball. The stories are thus organized both by age and pathway to baseball. The diversity of experience of the eleven women speaks for itself; the common thread is love of the game.

Three concluding chapters identify common themes in the players' stories; describe the context of race and sex segregation in sports; and document the current state of women's baseball in the United States at the grassroots and the elite levels. The grassroots chapter contains interviews with two men who have spent decades organizing and coaching women's baseball in the United States. The USA Baseball chapter contains interviews with the chief executive officer (CEO) of USA Baseball and the director of the Women's National Team. I conclude with suggestions for strengthening the baseball infrastructure for American girls and women at both the local and national levels and making the national pastime accessible for all Americans.

ACKNOWLEDGMENTS

This book is a work of love. I thought I had fulfilled my need to write about women's baseball in the United States when *Stolen Bases: Why American Girls Don't Play Baseball* was published in 2009. But it was just the beginning. At a book signing at the Eastern Women's Baseball Conference Tournament in Baltimore, Memorial Day weekend of 2009, ballplayers approached me emotionally, thanking me for writing a book about "their stories." I was grateful for their kind words but aware that my first book had just scratched the surface of girls' and women's baseball stories in contemporary America. Here were more than a hundred women playing baseball whom I had not written about at all. What were their stories, and how did they arrive at this tournament?

I realized my work was not done. My first book had only increased my desire to tell the "whole" story of women's baseball in twenty-first-century America.

My friends Joan Burton and Dave Stinchcomb, who live near Baltimore, regularly accompany me on my annual pilgrimage to the Eastern Women's Baseball Conference. Before that 2009 tournament was over, Joan and I were sitting at her kitchen table, planning my next book. I would interview as many women as possible currently playing baseball in the United States and write a comprehensive book about the women's game. Joan helped me to distribute questionnaires to all the ballplayers in the tournament, asking if they would be willing to be interviewed about their baseball careers.

The response was overwhelmingly positive and I was quickly overcome by the enormity of the task. How naive I had been, to think I could document and interview "all" the women currently playing baseball in the United States! As I worked, I realized that I really sought oral histories: detailed narratives that could be acquired only in person. The book project became focused on a few players, of acknowledged excellence, whom I knew well enough to ask for oral history interviews and who knew me well enough to trust me with their personal thoughts about their athletic lives. The stories of the hundreds of girls and women who currently play would have to wait for another volume or for pursuit by other baseball historians.

I gratefully acknowledge the women and men who, in that very first stage of my research, took the time to talk to me about their involvement with women's baseball. They include both players and coaches: Adriane Adler, Sierra Barton, Ila Borders, Megan Borgaard, Laura Brenneman, Tiffany Brooks, Don Freeman, Angela Hill, Richard Hopkins, Lindsay Horwitz, Renee Hudson, Jennifer Hughes, Anna Kimbrell, Irina Kovach, John Kovach, Ed Kurakazu, Melanie Laspina, Jennifer Liu, Janet Miller, Julie Mills, Clarissa Navarro, Judy O'Brien, Tim O'Brien, Sam Ostrom, Ashley Pirani, Ghazaleh Sailors, Loren Smith, Mary Jo Stegeman, Ashleigh Vargas, and Jen Zilke. I also owe thanks to members of Team Australia—Kathy Welsh, Katie Gaynor, and Taylah Welsh—and Coach John Gaynor for taking the time during a tournament to talk to me about Australian women's baseball. I am grateful to Coach Andre LaChance of Team Canada, who shared his perspectives and insights about Canada's baseball programs for girls and women.

As the project began to take shape, a number of individuals, organizations, and institutions offered financial support that enabled my work to continue. The College of Liberal Arts at the University of Nevada, Reno, generously awarded two Scholarly and Creative Activities Grants that provided funding for travel, equipment, and transcription of interviews. The Society for American Baseball Research awarded me a SABR-Yoseloff grant for baseball research. Jim Glennie and the American Women's Baseball Federation provided funding for recording equipment. Rob Conatser at Sierra Strength and Speed in Reno distributed a letter to individuals who might be interested in supporting the project. Dixie May, Joan C. Wright and Gregory Hayes, Patricia Ann Tripple, Charles and Jane Johnson, Albert Anderegg, and Carol Ann Carroll responded with financial contributions to permit me to travel to interview the women whose oral histories are told in this book.

Eric Herzik, chair of the Political Science Department at the University of Nevada, Reno, supported my research, encouraged me to take full advantage of the slim but essential resources made available by the University of Nevada and added crucial advice: "Write fast, Jenny!" Kristen Kabrin, administrative assistant in the Political Science Department at Nevada, was there to facilitate this project from beginning to end. With good cheer and extraordinary competence, she oversaw everything from travel arrangements to manuscript preparation to research for an appendix. Her sense of calm was contagious (even if my sense of calm was only fleeting), as she provided both administrative expertise and baseball wisdom.

Samantha Swing, undergraduate and later a graduate student at the University of Nevada, was my first research assistant for this project, helping with the initial organization and transcribing the interviews about the 2010 Women's World Cup Tournament. Several years later, Erin Lewis, an undergraduate at Nevada, was a tenacious and enterprising research assistant, who compiled the list of suggestions for further reading.

I am grateful to the scholars of the Beatrice Bain Research Group (BBRG) at the University of California–Berkeley, 2010–11, for giving me an intellectual home while I was on sabbatical leave from Nevada. Their scholarly interests and expertise focus on global gender issues and feminist theory, but they gamely listened to my talks about American women playing baseball and offered astute and encouraging insights at our regular meetings. The BBRG gave me the opportunity to present this work publicly for the first time. Jack Citrin, director of the Institute of Governmental Studies (IGS), offered office space in the IGS, included me in IGS events, and took me to lunch many times, evoking an era when I was his graduate student. Martin Sanchez-Jankowski, director of the UC Berkeley Institute for the Study of Social Issues (ISSI), provided a venue to lecture about the book in progress at the ISSI.

I am grateful to my friends at the NINE Spring Training Conference every March in Tempe, Arizona. I met Rob Taylor, of the University of Nebraska Press, at a NINE conference, and his early interest in my research presentation led to the publication of this book with Nebraska. In addition to Rob, I appreciate the expertise and efficiency of Courtney Oschner, Sabrina Stellrecht, Tish Fobben, and the entire editorial and artistic staff at the University of Nebraska Press. I am also grateful to Julie Kimmel, whose copyediting was precise and delicate and painless for me.

The Cooperstown Symposium on Baseball Research gave me a venue for presenting my research on Team USA and enabled me (finally!) to visit the Hall of Fame. Jim Gates, Bill Simons, Tim Wiles, and John Odell expressed an enthusiastic interest in my work on women and baseball. The Hall of Fame's invitation to submit the oral histories of the ballplayers in this volume to the Hall of Fame Library was one of my proudest moments as a researcher and author.

Ashley Bratcher, director of the USA Baseball Women's National Team, generously granted me two interviews, read and offered feedback on the earliest chapters on the 2010 Women's World Cup in Venezuela, and has provided photos of the players and whatever other details and information I have asked her for. Ashley also put me in contact with USA Baseball CEO Paul Seiler, who took time from his busy schedule to speak with me for over an hour about the operation of USA Baseball and the Women's National Team.

Pat, Stephanie, and Kira Wagar supplied wonderful photos of the New England Red Sox in action. Several people read this manuscript at different stages and helped shape its outcome. Thank you to David Block, Steve Simrin, Lilly Jacobson, Suzie Schwartz Jacobson, Monica Miller, Bonnie Freiberg, and Rachel McFarland.

To my daughter Johanna Jacobson: my gratitude and love, not only for understanding and tolerating my writing a book about her little sister and her baseball teammates, but for giving it its working title: "The Shutout." Although the title was changed late in the game, in my mind it was "The Shutout" for all the years I worked on it. JoJo's inspiration reflects her generous spirit and genius for always finding the right words, whether written or spoken, to capture the occasion.

My heartfelt gratitude to my baseball family: the players from Team USA and the New England Women's Red Sox who agreed to share their life stories for this book; their parents who have become my close friends as we watch our girls play; and Jim Glennie and Kevin Marden, for their tireless commitment to making competitive American women's baseball a reality. To Ofelia and Julio Alvarez, Terri and Rick Meidlinger, Roger and Joanne Harbert, Gary Sementelli, Dave Gascon, Cindy and Bill Marston: thank you for your companionship, your input for this project, the Little League photos of your girls, and the shared understanding of why we're still thrown into nervous apoplexies every time we watch our grown daughters step into the batter's box or onto the pitcher's mound at an amateur baseball game. Thank you for holding me up both physically as well as spiritually while watching Lilly bat and for allowing me to support you while your daughters were in the spotlight.

To Tamara Holmes, Donna Mills, Jenny Dalton Hill, Tara Harbert, Veronica Alvarez, Sarah Gascon, Jenna Marston, Malaika Underwood, Marti Sementelli, Lilly Jacobson, and Meggie Meidlinger: I dedicate this book to you. It has been an honor and a pleasure getting to know you, not only by watching you play, but through your hospitality as you welcomed me into your homes and graciously shared your time, trust, and emotional energy with me. Thank you all for carefully reading and commenting on your chapters; correcting the details, spellings, and quotes; and contributing your favorite baseball photos. You are heroic for your strength, your goodness, your optimism, and your perseverance. I hope this book does justice to your baseball journeys and serves to inspire young girls to follow in your footsteps.

INTRODUCTION

"Baseball is war!" said Albert Spalding.[1] He was referring to the game's new identity as the "national pastime," suitably masculine, a young man's game for a young nation with ambition for power and global expansion. Spalding was emphatic about the game's unsuitability for the nation's women. "A woman may take part in the grandstand, with applause for the brilliant play, with waving kerchief to the hero . . . loyal partisan of the home team, with smiles of derision for the umpire when he gives us the worst of it. . . . But neither our wives, our sisters, our daughters, nor our sweethearts, may play Base Ball on the field. . . . Base Ball is too strenuous for womankind."[2]

Spalding's description of baseball as war has always seemed far-fetched to me: a wish or a fantasy on the part of a baseball man who hopes that what he loves is the equivalent of history's ultimate descriptor of masculinity. In spite of its record of exclusive masculinity, baseball seems much less warlike than, for example, American football. It's not a contact sport, its goal is not primarily to penetrate and possess an opponent's territory, and in spite of American passion for power, those purist fans who really know baseball will tell you stories of great moments that involve finesse, speed, artistry, and subtle deftness. The base runner who turns an infielder's slightest hesitation into an opportunity to steal or score, the speedy outfielder who reaches over the fence to rob the slugger of his home run or lays out in a diving catch to prevent a run from scoring—they are as much admired as the ballplayers who display the strength and power to hit "bombs."[3] A squeeze bunt, the virtual opposite of the home run, is one of the most daring and exciting plays in the game.

Yet Spalding's sentiments have been honored. In the United States, baseball has become so exclusively male that the picture of a girl playing baseball is confusing, calling for explanation. A girl with a bat in her hand swinging at a ball is perceived to be a softball player. Invisible to the public imagination are the generations of women, from the late eighteenth century, when baseball first arrived in the United States, to the U.S. national women's baseball teams of the twenty-first century, who have refused to relinquish the nation's diamonds. Women have played for nearly two centuries in the United States yet still are greeted with astonishment and disbelief, as though they are eternally the first girls ever to play baseball.

This attitude was exemplified by the media coverage of a baseball game in Van Nuys, California, on March 5, 2011. Marti Sementelli and Ghazaleh Sailors, two pitchers who had been teammates on the U.S. women's national baseball team of 2010, were now in their senior seasons on the baseball teams at their high schools, Birmingham High of Van Nuys and San Marcos High of Santa Barbara. They were scheduled to be the starting pitchers in a game between their schools. For the first time in American history, two high school baseball teams played a game in which the starting pitchers were girls. It didn't hurt that the game took place in media-obsessed Los Angeles, between two highly rated large urban schools. More than a thousand girls in the United States play high school baseball on "boys' teams," but the story would not have had such impact if it had been a game between two small-town schools.

The stands filled an hour before the game started at 11:00 a.m., and spectators stood when there were no longer seats available. Media trucks from ABC, NBC, and ESPN jammed the spacious parking lot adjacent to Birmingham High's athletic fields. Prominent reporters from Southern California newspapers, including a nationally known sports columnist from the *Los Angeles Times*, and representatives from network news and online webcasts were busy interviewing parents, siblings, friends, and teammates before and during the game. After the game both pitchers were kept busy for over an hour, answering questions for reporters and television crews.

Even the Birmingham junior varsity team, sitting in the bleachers waiting for the press to clear so they could play their game, were asked, "How do you feel about this? What's it like to have a girl on the team? Is it okay?" They responded with positive grunts, well representing all fourteen- and fifteen-year-old American men: "Uh, yeah. Fine. She's good. It's history, man." The reporter who asked the questions seemed oblivious to the fact that the girl on the pitcher's mound was playing on a higher level than these boys. They *aspired* to play on varsity, as she was doing.

The questions put to Sementelli and Sailors seemed to me startlingly naive: "Isn't the overhand throwing motion dangerous for a girl's arm? That's why they play softball, isn't it?" "Do you think a girl will ever play college baseball?" "Do you think there will ever be a time when a woman can play in the Major Leagues?" "What does it feel like to strike out a boy?" "I noticed that you wear your hair tucked up under your hat. Isn't that uncomfortable?" "Do you think this game will end prejudice against girls playing baseball?" The journalists asking these questions had just witnessed the girls playing successfully with and against boys' teams but seemed incapable of believing their eyes. Marti Sementelli, pitching for Birmingham High, had gone the distance, giving up only one run and two hits. Ghazaleh Sailors, pitching for San Marcos High, had pitched superbly, opening the game with a three-up-three-down first inning and allowing only two runs off three hits in three and a half innings. After she came out of the game, the boy who relieved her surrendered the walks, hits, and runs that allowed Birmingham to break open the game.

Both girls pitched beautifully, but the attitude of the press with whom I sat was the same bewildered astonishment that characterized news stories about girls playing baseball in the early twentieth century and still dominates news coverage of girls who play baseball today. When I mentioned the existence of the U.S. Women's National Team, to which both pitchers belonged, the seasoned sportswriters were caught by surprise. After a moment of silence, one asked, "Wait! There's a women's national *baseball* team?" When I asked why there was no American press coverage of the 2010 Women's World Cup Tournament in Caracas, Venezuela, the reporters responded that they didn't know about the tournament.

I mentioned that the games had been attended by tens of thousands of Venezuelan fans and that the tournament had included an incident in which the shortstop from Team Hong Kong had suffered a gunshot to the leg while fielding her position in a game against the Netherlands. She underwent emergency surgery in Caracas, and the incident nearly ended the tournament, to which twelve nations' teams had traveled. The sportswriters were unaware of both the international tournament and the violent incident that had nearly canceled it.

Shooting or not, a World Cup tournament in which the American national team competes is news that should be reported. The U.S. Women's National Team has medaled in every World Cup tournament in which it has played, which includes gold medals in 2004 and 2006 and bronzes in 2008 and 2010. Not knowing about or acknowledging their existence amounts to an American media blackout. Media from the eleven other nations were present and attentive in 2010, as they had been in previous women's World Cup baseball tournaments.[4] Yet the American journalists to whom I addressed the questions merely shrugged and remarked that they hadn't heard about it. One asked, "Was the player all right? I mean . . . did she die?" Another observed, "Venezuela is a violent country." The reporters and I were engaged in the sort of slow-paced conversation that occurs in the bleachers at a baseball game. Our eyes were focused on the field as we watched a pick-off play, a long fly ball that was caught, a strikeout, and our discussion was interspersed with admiring remarks about the play. After a routine grounder had been fielded, I said, "No, she didn't die. She had emergency surgery, and her team withdrew from the tournament to accompany her home." Another pause in the conversation to observe the fate of a pop foul and I answered the other reporter: "Sure, Venezuela is a violent place, but still, you don't expect a baseball player to have to deal with getting shot while playing. And you shouldn't have to get shot to get noticed by the American media." A brief pause to watch a throw to first, and the reporter responded, "You're right. You don't usually have to worry about being shot while playing baseball."

I was describing a highly dramatic international baseball tournament that had been entirely overlooked by the American media. The shooting incident, it turned out, had nothing to do with the fact that the event was a women's baseball tournament. But if this had been the men's U.S. national baseball team playing in Venezuela and dodging bullets while on the field, it would have sparked outrage and been the lead story on every media outlet in the nation. If the headline had been "Bullet Narrowly Misses Derek Jeter during World Baseball Classic in Venezuela," the response of the press would not have been to explain it by noting, "Venezuela is a violent country."

To my surprise, and perhaps indicating some real change in the making, the stories that were submitted about the game were uniformly supportive and serious. They avoided the trivialization and patronizing attitude that often accompanies news about effective female athletes and that I had expected from the game-time questions. A front-page article by Bill Plaschke in the *Los Angeles Times* Sports Section on Sunday, March 6, was accurate and respectful. Mark Saxon's ESPNLosAngeles.com article was equally admiring and raised the question of both girls moving on to play college baseball, and perhaps Minor League ball.[5]

I was caught up in the excitement at Birmingham High, happily witnessing the event and the attention it garnered, but I was also amazed that it was such big news. I have written a book on the history of the exclusion of American girls and women from organized baseball that begins with the story of the resistance my younger daughter faced when she wanted to continue playing baseball beyond Little League.[6] It was legal for her to play Little League in the 1990s, but the cultural barriers she faced weren't very different from those I had faced when I had wanted to play baseball as a girl in the pre–Title IX era. When my daughter was twelve years old, the age limit for Little League, she was expected to give up the sport she loved and switch to softball. She was pressured to change games "for her own good," with the counterintuitive argument that she was so good at baseball she shouldn't squander her talent on a sport in which she had no future. She could expect to earn a college scholarship if she played softball. There is no college baseball for women, so what was the point of continuing to play the sport? The rationale occasionally took the form of astonishing responses to her finest moments on the baseball diamond:

the better she played baseball, the more forcefully she was urged to play softball by "concerned" parents, umpires who voiced their opinion to her in the middle of games, and coaches at the local high school.

My daughter refused to give up the game she loved. Her baseball journey took her from Little League, through high school and college baseball, to the virtually unknown USA Baseball Women's National Team. Her story has attracted more attention than any other aspect of *Stolen Bases*, even though it is only the prologue. The ten chapters that make up the scholarly core of my previous book trace the history of women and baseball from fourteenth-century England, through the nineteenth-century American college and barnstorming teams, to the lawsuits in the 1970s to allow girls to play in Little League, to the continuing and current exclusion of girls from high school and college baseball in the United States. But the story of one girl playing baseball on a high school team, and later on a college team, is what surprised readers and became the focus of attention.

The appeal of stories of American girls and women who play baseball in Little League, high school, and (very rarely) college became especially apparent to me at a 2009 book signing at a women's baseball tournament in Washington DC. Players approached me tearfully and thanked me for writing the book, claiming that I had told *their* story. I had not. Their struggles resembled my daughter's, but each one also had a unique tale. When told together, they add up to systematic and disturbing discrimination. The women who have achieved recognition at the highest level of their game tell stories of persistence, fortitude, and heart and are true to themselves, even in the face of public neglect and derision. The stories are worthy of sheer celebration in their own right. But they also share themes that provide theoretical coherence to the struggle of half the population to gain access to the "national pastime."

Baseball wasn't invented on American soil, although Americans laid claim to it.[7] Baseball historians agree that early forms of baseball, called "stool ball," "rounders," or "base ball," were spontaneously invented children's games, with references dating back to the fourteenth century in England. Girls as well as boys played, and indeed the games were often regarded as "girls' games." Britain's more "manly" sport was cricket. "Stool ball" was a version of early baseball invented by milkmaids. Four milking stools were placed in a circle, and the girls played with either a rock or a cricket ball and a stick, or perhaps a rolling pin. A ball (or rock) was served to the hitter, who after hitting the ball, was to run to base before the player who fielded the hit could put her out by plugging her with the thrown ball. Rounders is a schoolyard game still universally played by English boys and girls, with a ball identical to an American baseball only smaller. Its name reflects the rule that the batter, after hitting the ball, must attempt to run around all four bases before being put out by a fielder—no stopping at base.

Baseball met with immediate popularity when it emerged on the American continent in the early nineteenth century. It was beloved by both men and women, but two major factors appropriated it as a "manly" game by the end of the century. Spalding's 1911 proclamation that baseball is too strenuous for womankind reveals a need to associate the "national game" with military prowess and masculinity. American global expansion and the growth of industrial capitalism provided the impetus for making baseball a lucrative profession. At the time women were excluded from all professions, including professional sports, and from the access to revenue sports generated.

One development besides baseball's new potential for profit ensured that the game stayed out of reach for women: the invention of softball. Created in the late 1880s and early 1890s by men in Chicago and Minneapolis who wanted to play baseball during the frigid northern winters, softball was intended to be played in a gym, with soft large balls and small bats. The first softball was actually a rolled up boxing glove secured with its own lace. It was fashioned in Chicago in 1887 by a group of young men who had gathered at the Farragut Boat Club on Thanksgiving Day to follow the Harvard-Yale football game on ticker tape. In high spirits after the game, one lobbed a boxing glove at his friend, who grabbed a broomstick and batted it away. Softball was born in the spirit of spontaneous good fun. It was found to be so entertaining that a set of rules was developed by one of the young men in that first game. It was originally called "indoor baseball" but moved outdoors when the weather warmed. Then, to ensure that the smaller, safer game not be confused with the more manly national pastime, it was given sexualized derogatory nicknames such as "sissy ball," "panty waist," "kitten ball," and "nancy ball."[8]

In 1887 Spalding took a team of white professional baseball players (and a black mascot named Robert Duvall) on a world tour to spread baseball as an Americanizing influence on the "less civilized" parts of the globe and to drum up business for his sporting goods company.[9] The tour began in Hawaii and continued west to Asia and North Africa before visiting Europe and returning to New York. In 1889 a banquet was held at Delmonico's restaurant to celebrate the "victorious" tour. The banquet was a male-only gala, with a celebrity-studded guest list that included Theodore Roosevelt and Mark Twain. During the evening Henry Chadwick, a major figure in early American baseball and an immigrant from England, mentioned that baseball had derived from the English girls' game of rounders. He was shouted down with the chant, "No Rounders! No Rounders!"[10] Spalding determined to settle the issue of baseball's origins and called together a commission with explicit instructions to find the American origins of the game. Eight years later, in 1907, Spalding's commission finally submitted a report containing the story that Abner Doubleday, an army general with a distinguished record in the Mexican War, the war against the Seminoles, and the Civil War, invented baseball in 1839 in Cooperstown, New York, by drawing a diamond in the dirt with a stick. The report was pure fiction, but the myth stuck in the American popular imagination, somewhat like the story of George Washington and the cherry tree.

It was at nearly the same historical moment that softball inadvertently sealed baseball's exclusive masculinity. The feminized sport was institutionalized as "girls' baseball," and it has created social and cultural roadblocks that continue to deprive American girls of the choice to play the national pastime. These two related developments—the professionalization of baseball and its symbolic significance as our national game during an era of American imperialism, and the segregation of girls and women into the "equivalent" sport of softball—closed the door on American women's baseball.[11]

A few decades later, in 1939, Little League Baseball was created for boys only, to promote the qualities of "citizenship, sportsmanship and manhood."[12] The gender segregation of baseball and softball was embedded in mid-twentieth-century culture. Individual girls continued to play baseball, but it was difficult in the absence of girls' teams and leagues and with softball becoming increasingly entrenched as the girls' equivalent of baseball. Still, a handful of girls continued to battle their way onto America's diamonds.

In 1973, after Title IX had been passed, the National Organization for Women (NOW), on behalf of eleven-year-old Maria Pepe, brought suit against the Hoboken, New Jersey, Little League, with the claim that it was illegal to exclude girls. The lawsuit was successful, although it resulted not in the actual integration of girls into youth baseball, but in the establishment of Little League Softball for girls. Passage of Title IX provided the impetus for the lawsuit, but the new legislation was inadequate as a legal basis for integrating Little League. Guidelines put in place for Title IX made a distinction between contact and noncontact sports and exempted contact sports from sex integration. Little League Baseball seized on the distinction as a pretext for excluding girls. Instead, attorneys for Maria Pepe and NOW utilized the equal protection clause of the Fourteenth Amendment to the constitution, which provides that "No state shall . . . deny to any person within its jurisdiction the equal protection of the laws." The Fourteenth Amendment was intended to protect freed slaves after the Civil War and makes no reference to sports of any kind, contact or not.

The New Jersey Little League exploited the argument that baseball was a contact sport and insisted it was too rough for girls. Girls' bones break more easily than boys, the League argued, and girls might get breast cancer from contact with a baseball. As one advocate of protecting Little League from girls, or protecting girls from Little League, worried, "If girls played, the league would 'get sued if they [females] get breast cancer from getting tagged out on the boobs.'" All these arguments were challenged by expert medical witnesses and ultimately dismissed in the hearings. Little League also argued that it would inconvenience (male) Little League coaches, as well as violate the privacy of little girls, if they were injured and needed to be touched or undressed by a concerned coach.[13] Advocates for excluding girls fretted that the individual rights of male coaches were violated by the discomfort they would feel patting a girl on the backside to congratulate her on a good play. Ironically, the concern assumes that a girl might actually be capable of making a good play.

When it became illegal to exclude girls in New Jersey, more than *two thousand* Little League teams in the state chose to shut down for an entire season rather than let girls play with boys. "Pony Tail" or "Bobby Sox" softball was soon created, and girls who wanted to play baseball were urged to take that more acceptable route for a girl. No statistical records are kept by Little League Baseball on how many girls play baseball, as compared to segregated softball.[14] The creation of organized softball for girls preempted any impetus to organize baseball and helped to cement the post–Title IX segregated masculinity of baseball.

Sex segregation is based on assumptions about male physical superiority, much as race segregation was based on assumptions about white superiority. Little League Baseball attempted to exclude girls with the assumption that girls can't play contact sports with boys. The persistent line of rhetoric is that boys are always going to be bigger, stronger, more aggressive, and better able to "take a hit." But baseball is less dependent on size for excellence than many other sports. Its most celebrated Major Leaguers include David Eckstein and Dustin Pedroia as well as Albert Pujols and Pablo Sandoval. Size is not the only determinant of toughness, a fact that can be attested to by any of the smaller-statured world-class competitors in the history of sport, dating back at least to David and Goliath. Bigger, faster, stronger athletes usually have an athletic advantage, although not necessarily a definitive one. Studies have shown that differences in ability have as much to do with encouragement and training as with inherent biological factors.[15]

Segregating sports by gender rather than ability is not a response to "nature" or biology. Rather, it is a political statement.[16] Eileen McDonagh and Laura Pappano argue that Title IX missed an opportunity to create true equality in sports by drawing a distinction between "contact" and "noncontact" sports, thereby institutionalizing the prejudice that girls and women are weaker, more prone to injury, and that it is immoral for men and women to have physical contact with each other on the sporting field. By enforcing a distinction between contact and noncontact sports, Title IX assumed a paternalistic and protectionist stance toward female athletes and may have done a disservice to gender equality, resulting in sex-segregated competition where it is clearly unnecessary. Sports such as bowling, riflery, curling, and golf are currently segregated. McDonagh and Pappano conclude, "In effect, Title IX reinforced, rather than challenged, assumptions of male superiority and female weakness."[17]

Baseball is not the only male institution to claim that letting women play with men will ruin the game.[18] However, of the major American sports, it is the only one for which the segregation is so complete that girls are directed to another "equivalent" sport. Softball is a sort of parallel universe that precludes the choice to play baseball. Girls' and women's participation in many other sports has increased dramatically since Title IX.[19] Basketball and soccer are two examples of sex-segregated sports that have large female contingents. Referred to by many as "girls' baseball," softball recruits girls from a young age, trains them, creates a pool of elite softball players for college and university play, and sends them down a path that is not baseball, but a different sport. Nowhere is the consequence of this double segregation more dramatic than in the virtually invisible U.S. women's national baseball team.

The journey of Team USA 2010 from USA Baseball's National Training Complex in Cary, North Carolina, to the site of the fourth biennial Women's World Cup Tournament in Caracas, Venezuela, reveals the challenges that have been faced by American women baseball players. USA Baseball's sponsorship of a women's team since 2004 has the potential to be a major development in American women's baseball history. A team of twenty women wearing the uniforms of the United States of America reflects both the progress women have made and the challenges they still face: invisibility at home; the absence of an infrastructure—teams, leagues, camps, coaches, tournaments—for girls' and women's baseball; and the power of organized softball to siphon girls away from baseball at an early age.

A GAME OF THEIR OWN

PART 1

Baseball and
American Women

1

The Dream and Its Challenges

In August 2010 I accompanied my daughter, Lilly Jacobson, to the USA Baseball National Training Complex in Cary, North Carolina, for tryouts for the women's national baseball team. She had been a member of the 2006 and 2008 teams, achievements that I hoped would calm her nerves about the 2010 tryouts. That maternal wish for calm and confidence was in vain: with each successive tryout Lilly seems to feel that she must prove everything about herself as ballplayer all over again. Anxiety about the tryouts and Lilly's desire to make the Women's National Team for the third time dominated the summer of 2010.

Access to baseball had been a challenge for Lilly since Little League, as it is for most American girls who want to play the national pastime. Not a year went by between Little League and college when Lilly could rely on playing the following season. The availability of a team to play on was so fragile it seemed as though baseball would simply disappear on her. From the time she was twelve years old, adults had been urging her to switch to softball, trying to entice her with visions of the college scholarship to follow high school if she would play the preferred game for girls. But she didn't like softball, and the more she was pressured to drop baseball, the more fiercely she dug in. Her unwillingness to play softball became a matter of principle with her: she would not succumb to cultural pressure, nor be forced out of the game she loved. She was, and would continue to be, a baseball player.

The battle was joined in earnest when she began playing Babe Ruth baseball, the continuation of Little League for children age twelve to fifteen. She went from being the starting first basewoman and a prolific hitter on her Little League team to being a marginalized player who played only the minimum required innings on her Babe Ruth team. The coaches and the players at that middle school level take themselves much more seriously than do those in Little League, believing that their play will prepare them for high school baseball, then college scholarships, and the possibility of professional baseball. The slim statistical likelihood of this career path is no deterrent to the baseball fantasies of even the most mediocre players and their parents. The swaggering environment of boys and their fathers preparing for a future in baseball did not leave much room for "wasting" a place on a team for a girl who was regarded as having no future in the game. One parent volunteered to my husband and me that Lilly "should be playing softball. No girl will play high school baseball in this town as long as I live here." We didn't know if he had the power to make the threat stick, but he probably didn't need to; plenty of people in town agreed with him.

Throughout her youth baseball years, Lilly's goal had been to play high school baseball. This was not a particularly original thought; the majority of her Little League and Babe Ruth teammates shared the same ambition. By the time she showed up as a freshman on the first day of Reno High's fall prep baseball season, it was clear that she faced a tougher battle than the boys did. Reno High School had perennial ambitions of winning the state championship and had the wealthy parental support to provide the best of everything in the way of equipment, facilities, and budget. It was one of the good teams in northern Nevada, but not quite the state powerhouse it aspired to be. Nonetheless, the coach, who had been a star catcher at the same high school and whose son was now on the team, took the team's success seriously, as did the parents whose donations funded it. This school, along with the other wealthy schools in the district, attempted to recruit the "best" players in youth baseball with zoning variances. High school sports is a high-stakes game in the United States, and it does not reflect the spirit of democratic public education my husband and I naively believed in at the time. The four months of daily preseason training throughout the fall were run like a boot camp, until final cuts for the junior varsity (JV) and varsity teams were made in February.

Lilly held her own during the preseason. She was trying out with the same boys she had played baseball with since she was seven years old. She knew that some boys were bigger and stronger than she was, but some were slower and less skilled, and she was confident that she had performed well enough to make the JV squad. To her surprise, as well as that of her teammates, she was cut. Tears of heartbreak and bewilderment streamed down her face as she left the meeting during which the coaches told her she needed to get "bigger, faster, and stronger." She knew that. So did the boys. That's what fourteen-year-old baseball is about. The coach offered no precise measures of evaluation. Although he referred to the "five baseball tools," his evaluation of the players was not objectively quantified. The only Hispanic and Asian boys trying out for the team also failed to make the cut, but with no objective measurements of where they fell short, there was no way to prove that any discrimination had occurred. The coach probably believed he was basing his decisions purely on baseball criteria, with no thought to the players' race or their sex or the size of their parents' donation to the program. It was the first adult betrayal of Lilly's life and was particularly destructive because it was received as an authoritative dismissal of her ability to continue to play and grow in the game she loved more than any other.

For the first time in her life, Lilly did not want to go to school. The implied lesson to Lilly, as well as her classmates and teammates, was either that she wasn't as good a ballplayer as she knew she was or that a girl could be excluded simply because she was a girl. My husband and I refused to validate either message with inaction. We are an academic family, with education a key value, and we never envisioned transferring from a good academic school because of sports. But we began looking for a high school Lilly could transfer to and found one in the district with an academic magnet program.

Wooster High School in Reno is a less well-heeled school than Reno High, with a less well-endowed athletic program. Coach Ron Malcolm welcomed Lilly to baseball practice and tryouts and was grateful that she could contribute to the team. The boys on her new team followed his example. Coach Malcolm was teaching open-mindedness along with baseball. Lilly's three years of high school baseball, one on JV and two on the varsity team, were an unmitigated joy to her. Her teammates became her brothers and best friends at school, and she was respected and admired as the first girl in the state to play varsity boys' baseball. Her baseball skills flourished in the supportive environment. She was a gifted natural hitter—a lefty with a sweet swing—but Malcolm and his assistant coaches recognized her potential as a pitcher and taught her to pitch. During her second season at the school, she earned a spot on varsity as a middle reliever with a nasty curve ball and change-up, which Coach Malcolm used to great effect behind his two heat-throwing starters. Good coaching helped her to become the player she needed to be to compete in high school, validating the concept that teaching, rather than recruiting and parental wealth, has a place in high school sports.

As she was preparing to graduate high school, Lilly was invited to try out for the 2006 USA Baseball Women's National Team. She hadn't know of its existence before Jim Glennie, president of the American Women's Baseball Federation, a man with his fingers on the pulse of women's baseball, emailed her about June tryouts. They were to be held at Phoenix Municipal Stadium, spring training home of Lilly's beloved Oakland Athletics. The invitation was an unimaginable thrill, although Lilly was stunned to see so many other girls at the tryouts who were also accomplished baseball players. She had been so isolated as "the only girl" playing baseball in Nevada that she hadn't been aware of other girls at her skill level. It was the first time she had been on a baseball diamond with other girls. Equally thrilling, and also somewhat intimidating, was the opportunity to play for Coach Julie Croteau, a modern-day women's baseball legend.[1] Lilly made the team and returned from Taipei, Taiwan, with the gold medal they won, ready to attend college.

Lilly chose Vassar College after high school. Vassar's long and celebrated history in women's athletics was certainly in the back of her mind, and it was an added bonus that Vassar had, in 1869, been home to the Resolutes, the first collegiate women's baseball team in the United States. However, her primary attraction to Vassar was academics, as well as the allure of the East Coast to a West Coast native. Reluctant to be defined as "the woman baseball player" from the minute she set foot on the intimate campus, she decided to take a year away from baseball. Her high school baseball years had concluded on such a high note that she preferred to savor the memory rather than shoulder the burden of proving herself all over again with an entirely new men's baseball program. The pressure of being "the only girl on the team" was weighing heavily on her, in spite of her unquenchable love of the game.

Shortly after she received her acceptance letter from Vassar, the coach of the golf team invited her to visit the campus. Lilly had learned to play golf at Wooster High at the urging of the school's athletic director. He wanted her to play a fall sport and suggested either football or golf. She chose the stick and ball game, as usual. She lettered in golf at Wooster (as well as baseball and skiing) but was still a beginner at the game. She was flattered by the opportunity to become a college athlete, but it struck her as odd that she should be invited to try out for a sport about which she knew so little, while collegiate baseball seemed out of reach. She made the Vassar golf team, but by the end of her freshman year in college, it was clear that she missed baseball too much to give it up, no matter what the challenges. She nervously approached the golf coach and told him she had decided to try out for baseball when she returned to Vassar in the fall. He quickly assuaged her fear that she was letting him down and responded with encouragement: "Of course you should try out! After all, this is the home of the Vassar Resolutes!"

But Vassar Baseball was no longer for women; it was now a National Collegiate Athletic Association (NCAA) Division III men's team. There was no softball team at Vassar, but if there had been, Lilly would not have been interested. She had avoided softball all her life and regarded it as an insult both to her baseball skills and to the game of softball itself to assume that she could simply pick up softball and play at the college level. Baseball was her sport, but always, the challenge was to find a team and the playing time to be able to continue to grow as a player.

Lilly returned to the San Francisco Bay area for a summer job after her

Vassar freshman year. She trained intensely all summer for fall Vassar Baseball tryouts, enlisting the help of local junior college coaches for pitching, hitting, and baserunning practice. They invited her to practice with their summer league teams, to ensure that she had access to game time during their scrimmages. She also played on one of the three teams that made up the California Women's Baseball League, organized by Melanie Laspina, who had played women's professional baseball during the brief existence of a league in the 1990s.[2] Laspina had recruited a few serious women ballplayers to the amateur league and also some recreational enthusiasts. Play was good-natured but inconsistent—not an environment for elite training, although Lilly enjoyed being on a baseball diamond every weekend.

Lilly also spent part of the summer in Reno, to continue working with the fitness and baseball coaches who had helped her during high school. She consulted her strength and speed trainer, Rob Conatser, and resumed private batting lessons with her beloved batting coach from the University of Nevada, Reno (UNR), Jay Uhlman. She asked Jay to teach her to play outfield. Together they would spend an intense hour in the batting cage early in the morning and then go outside to Peccole Park, the Nevada Wolf Pack's varsity diamond, where Uhlman would hit hundreds of fly balls and teach her the intricacies of tracking a ball off the bat from several hundred feet away. They quit each day only when it was too hot to continue. Finding access to adequate training resources to prepare for men's collegiate baseball at Vassar took two states and many hours on Interstate 80, leveraged around Lilly's full-time work schedule. The hardest challenge was finding a summer team to play on.

Lilly wanted to learn to play the outfield because she was conflicted about pitching. She knew that being a left-handed pitcher gave her the best chance of being needed on a men's team. A pitcher with an accurate arm and good control of off-speed pitches is always an asset, and pitchers are not expected to hit or run well. For a woman seeking a place on a men's team, being a pitcher eliminates the need to be as fast as a man on the base paths and to possess the strength of a man when throwing from the outfield or batting. But as a left-hander who *wanted* to be an everyday player, the only positions available to Lilly were first base and the outfield. She wasn't as tall as the men who are preferred at first base, but she could work on speed and arm strength to become an outfielder.

Lilly simply enjoyed hitting too much to give it up for pitching. She often remarked that hitting was what she loved most about baseball: both the feel of hitting the ball well and the mental duel of each at bat. Jay Uhlman had taught her to be smart and patient at the plate. She had a great eye for the strike zone, knew which pitch she was looking for in each at bat, and possessed the patience and discipline to wait for it.

Good outfielding is a beautiful skill that appears effortless when it's done right. But that apparently effortless grace requires knowledge of where a pitch is going, the ability to track a ball from the moment it leaves the bat, unhesitating bursts of speed to the right place, and a strong arm. The fielder must recognize immediately where the ball is going, sometimes turn her back on a hit as it leaves the bat hundreds of feet away, sprint to where it's headed, and at the last second, turn back to face the ball, with her glove ready to receive it. Shorter hits require racing full speed toward a pop fly with perfect timing so that the momentum of the run is transferred to the throw to the infield that follows the catch. Or racing in toward a pop fly and diving to get a glove beneath the ball before it touches the ground. Lilly learned to hurl herself, "laid out" and parallel to the ground, to snatch a line drive from its trajectory. She practiced wind sprints and speed drills for outfielding as well as baserunning. She lifted weights and played "long toss" with whomever she could find, to strengthen her throwing arm.

By fall Lilly was ready for everything except the curve ball that life threw her. A week after she had returned to Vassar for her sophomore year, and about a month before Vassar Baseball tryouts, Lilly's father died. She was shocked and devastated as she flew to California for the funeral. She chose to return immediately to Vassar to resume her classes and continue with her quest to make the baseball team, knowing that was what her father would have wanted her to do. Withdrawing from any part of her life would have deepened the depression that plagued her for the rest of the year.

Personal tragedies strike athletes just as they do anybody else and occasionally call for extraordinary emotional fortitude on the eve of the most important contest of their lives. Some athletes choose to carry on rather than withdraw, but many pay a price in terms of performance. Lilly did not want to withdraw from school, or from baseball, even in the midst of her grief. Her life was school and sports, and they seemed to provide the comfort zone she would need to begin healing from her loss. She immersed herself in her studies, continued to excel in her classes, and resumed training with the baseball team. After a month of fall practice and scrimmaging, baseball cuts were made, and she survived; she was the first woman to play NCAA baseball in over two decades.[3] But unbeknownst to her, she had been playing on an undiagnosed stress fracture in her foot. She had been fast enough to make the team while ignoring constant pain. Only when she returned home to Nevada for winter break did Rob Conatser, her strength and speed trainer, notice something amiss and send her to an orthopedic clinic for X-rays. A stress fracture had turned into a regular fracture and then begun to heal itself. The orthopedist in Reno fitted Lilly for a boot, which she would have to wear for about six weeks.

Lilly was deeply upset that her ability to train had been disrupted. She worried that she would lose credibility with the coaches and players on her new team when she returned to Vassar in January. Being the only woman to play baseball at Vassar in a century and playing on a men's team were pressure enough. The challenge of accomplishing this with a broken foot was over the top.

By the time her foot healed, she had become close friends with the players on the team, who admired her grit and determination in attending every practice and doing whatever she could to train: one-handed bat swings at soft-tossed balls to keep her eye sharp; keeping her throwing arm limber; working out with weights and cardio equipment that avoided putting stress on her broken foot. But as she feared, the coaches had not maintained their confidence in her. The Vassar pitching coach who had previously described her curve ball as "wicked" now ignored her. The coaching staff seemed uninterested in helping her to find a rhythm to enable her to resume pitching practice. But she had the affection, respect, and encouragement of her teammates, who voiced their incredulity to her that she was not given more of a chance by the coaches.

Lilly spent her season with Vassar Baseball practicing with the team and sitting on the bench. She was depressed and grieving the loss of her father. It was a miserable year. Still, her closest friends at Vassar were her baseball teammates. Once again she had a team of brothers. One of them became her close confidant and most sympathetic listener about all the sadness she was dealing with. Finally, toward the end of what had been a terrible season for the Vassar team, with but a handful of wins, the coach gave Lilly a chance to hit in the final innings of an inconsequential game. She made solid contact with the ball and drove in a run. It was the only hit by a woman in NCAA college baseball in nearly twenty years. The other woman to do it was the legendary Julie Croteau, the first woman to play NCAA baseball. Coincidentally, Lilly had played under Croteau, who had coached the Women's National Team to the gold medal in Tapei in 2006. Croteau was not only the first woman to play NCAA college baseball, but she was the first woman to coach a baseball team to a gold medal in international competition. She was a role model for Lilly, who admired her greatly. That she and Croteau stood alone in NCAA baseball made Lilly's first college hit all the more personally significant.

The men of Vassar Baseball 2008 had witnessed Lilly's perseverance in the face of a coach who seemed determined that she fail and recognized the significance of her hit against a men's college team after she had been benched all season. They cheered boisterously, stopped the game, retrieved the ball, and presented it to Lilly. Her coach remained silent while Lilly's teammates made it possible for her to accept this moment of vindication, amid all the discouragement and trauma of the year.

Baseball always provides a new season of hope. After the sadness and discouragement of Vassar Baseball in the spring of 2008, renewal presented itself in the form of tryouts for Team USA 2008. If Lilly were selected for the team, she would travel to the Women's World Cup Tournament in Matsuyama, Japan, to face Japan, Australia, Canada, and four other teams from around the globe. Her usual summer scramble for training and playing time was the prelude for her making Team USA 2008. The final tryouts for Team USA were held at the Youth Baseball Academy on the campus of Compton Community College in Southern California. The academy had been founded by Major League Baseball to encourage inner-city boys to learn about baseball. It made for a striking irony that the Women's National Team, having played ball in the shadow of neglect and lack of acknowledgment, held their trials at a facility designed to attract another underrepresented demographic to the national pastime.

Lilly made the starting lineup for Team USA 2008. After only two full days of practice in Los Angeles, capped by two games against the visiting Team Canada, Team USA traveled to Matsuyama, Japan, for the Women's World Cup Tournament. The Japanese people were welcoming and helpful to all the players in the tournament, and there was more commotion and attention paid to women's baseball than any of the American players had ever before experienced. The tournament was held in Matsuyama's major league baseball stadium, housed in an impressive athletic complex with facilities for world-class competition in several sports. Japanese television filmed every move the Japan team made, and Japanese media were a presence at every game. The stadium was packed with noisy, supportive crowds and a brass band blaring music. Japanese teenage boys who attended the tournament passed scribbled fan mail from the stands to their favorite American players, and Lilly was flattered to receive several messages written in English saying, "Lillian Jacobson, you are my favorite player!" When she turned to see where the notes had come from, the boys in the stands above grinned and waved at her. Three American players were honored with selection to the All-Tournament team: Malaika Underwood, for her play at second base; Marti Sementelli, as right-handed pitcher; and Lilly, as outfielder.

The team as a whole, however, was disappointed in its third-place finish. The Americans struggled unsuccessfully against Canada and Japan, teams that enjoy a more highly developed infrastructure than the U.S. women's baseball program. Disappointment did not undermine the joy of participating, however. Lilly and her teammates basked in the privilege of living, breathing, and thinking exclusively about baseball for the short period they had together. Many of the players longed for the luxury of devoting their lives full-time to baseball.

Lilly rejoined the Vassar baseball team for its fall practice season and tryouts, finally feeling confident and strong, much better than she had the previous, traumatic year, and fresh from the glow of the international tournament. Was this the year she would feel supported and able to relax, not having to prove something as a "the girl baseball player"? The climax to Vassar Baseball's fall training season was its annual doubleheader against another local college team. Lilly played well in the outfield and compiled several hits to add to her record in college baseball. She called me after that afternoon, glowing. She was finally feeling relaxed and confident on the Vassar team and pleased with her performance.

So she was stunned the next day when she received a call from the coach telling her that she had been cut from the team. She was the only returning player to be cut. I could barely understand her words when she called me Sunday afternoon and, before even saying hello, sobbed, "He cut me!" I wasn't expecting this phone call. I wasn't even thinking that her being cut was a possibility. The nightmare of the moment she was cut from that first high school team flooded back.

When she told her best friend, Vassar's center fielder, that she had been cut, he assumed she was joking. None of the players on the team believed the news was real, but it was. And the damage was irreversible; nobody could question the coach's prerogative. Lilly's letter of protest to Vassar athletic director Sharon Beverly went unanswered for weeks, until after Beverly had summoned a few members of the team to ask if they thought the decision was fair. One of her teammates who had been vociferously supportive to Lilly's face admitted that he had been invited to offer his perceptions to Beverly and had said nothing critical about the coach's decision. He told Lilly he was worried that Vassar would fire the coach and they would lose their season or that the coach would learn he had been critical and he would lose playing time. He asked Lilly if she thought he was a jerk, and she replied, "No. Just a coward." Lilly was never called in to discuss her perception of the matter with the athletic director.

In cutting Lilly, Coach Jon Martin had cut a starter on the U.S. national women's team who had been recognized as one of the best woman outfielders in the world for 2008. The implication seemed to be that a dominant player in international women's baseball was not good enough for Vassar's mediocre Division III team. Vassar had not distinguished itself at baseball in recent years. Cutting Lilly seemed unnecessary at the least: she was "good enough" by almost any athletic measure, she contributed positive energy with her work ethic and team spirit, and her presence was a tribute to Vassar's revered tradition of enabling women to break boundaries in sports and higher education. The team, which had won but a handful of games each season for years, was hardly in danger of being hurt by her presence. When the father of one of her teammates learned that Lilly had been cut, he remarked to his son, "How stupid! What a bunch of damned fools."

But there was no going back from the coach's decision, and as far as Lilly was concerned, there was no continuing on as a student at Vassar. In what was all too reminiscent of her first experience with high school baseball, she felt she could not live with the humiliating injustice. The coach told her she didn't have what it took to play college baseball. But she had hit and fielded well in every game he had allowed her to play in. Had she received any encouragement at all, she undoubtedly would have accomplished still more. The Vassar baseball team played their spring 2009 season without Lilly and won only two league games, compiling an overall season record of six wins and twenty-nine losses. A starter on the USA Baseball Women's National Team was judged inadequate to play on that weak Vassar team.

Lilly withdrew from Vassar College after having completed the fall semester and returned to Berkeley, her hometown. She rented a room, found a job, and applied for admission to the University of California for the following fall. She wanted to complete her undergraduate education where her father had taught for many decades. When her application was accepted, she sent an email to the president of the University of California men's club baseball team to introduce herself and ask about the team.[4] He responded enthusiastically and urged her to try out for the team, telling her, "I haven't had so much fun playing baseball in years." When Lilly learned that he was also the University of California student body president and a pre-law student, she marveled that he had time to play baseball at all.

In Cal Club Baseball Lilly found her third band of brothers since high school. The relaxed and accepting atmosphere of the club enabled her to enjoy baseball again. The team comprised former high school players who had chosen to attend a great academic university rather than play NCAA baseball and a couple of former Division I players whose injuries had forced them to leave NCAA play. The Cal team played other club teams throughout the West, including those from Pac-10 schools and others from both Northern and Southern California, every weekend during the season. They held practice one or two afternoons a week, at a time agreed on by the players according to their class schedules. Games were held at a municipal field in Oakland shared with high school and youth league teams. The team members carpooled for away games. A trip to Southern California required almost a full day of driving each way and sleeping on the floor of somebody's parents' house. The lack of pretension, easygoing attitude, and academic seriousness of the players suited Lilly, and she was pleased to be able to participate in competitive-level baseball that provided an opportunity for her to grow as a player. The team members pooled their modest resources and hired Nate Oliver to coach them. Oliver is a former Dodgers, Cubs, and Mets second baseman and an Oakland resident. He was as positive and responsive to Lilly's presence as her teammates were and offered his Major League expertise to all the players. Lilly was at home on a baseball field again, and her contagious baseball grin was beginning to make a reappearance.

The team's major rival was, of course, Stanford. Indeed, the only taunts Lilly heard all year were from Stanford players shouting to their own pitchers: "Blow it by her! She can't hit your fastball!" The first time she heard that she let it get to her. But she vowed not to let it happen again and made it her personal mission to practice hitting faster pitches. By her second year with the Cal baseball club, she had caught up with Stanford pitching. During that year's Cal-Stanford three-game series, she got a hit every time she was at bat, driving in several runs and scoring. This led to an exchange of unpleasantries between the Stanford team on the field and Lilly's teammates in the dugout. In keeping with the historic rivalry and her lifetime of loyalty to the Cal Bears, she was delighted to be at the center of Stanford discomfort and insults traded between the two teams.

Lilly had found joy in baseball again after soul-numbing discouragement. Her resilience and fortitude were unrelenting, but they should have been unnecessary in the pursuit of amateur baseball. Every time she was pushed off the field and out of the dugout, she called on inner reserves, picked herself up, and got right back in the game. While Lilly's story would be highly unusual for a man, it is a fairly routine description of the paths of the women who want to play. Only once did I ever see her give in to sadness and frustration. We drove all over the San Francisco East Bay one summer afternoon after I had picked her up at work, looking for an empty field on which to practice before the 2010 USA Baseball tryouts. We finally found a batting cage that was not being used at a Little League park, and I threw her some batting practice. I can get the ball over the plate, but I'm no pitcher; she needed to see a variety of pitches, thrown much harder than I can throw. It was so far less than she needed and so outrageous that a member of the U.S. national team, on the eve of tryouts, should have to wander from field to field for a chance to swing a bat, waiting until the local Little League was finished for the evening. Lilly finally broke down and tearfully said, "It's not fair. Every boy in America who wants to play baseball can find a team to play on and to train. I shouldn't have to do this to keep playing."

The regional preliminary tryouts for Team USA 2010 were held in six cities across the United States. Lilly and two USA teammates, Marti Sementelli from Los Angeles and Tamara Holmes from Oakland, would try out at the University of San Francisco baseball field over July Fourth weekend. Marti, who was on her first visit to Northern California, stayed with Lilly for the event.

I took the girls out to dinner the night before the two-day tryout began and was regaled by their war stories as "the only girls" on their baseball teams until they discovered Team USA. Both girls had proved themselves as athletes and good teammates on every team on which they had played. Still, both had vivid memories of what they referred to as "The Silence":

the first moment with a new team when the boys suddenly notice a girl in their midst. Marti described one tournament team that her father had encouraged her to join. She was a freshman in high school at the time and was enjoying the respect and camaraderie of her teammates at their daily practices. She was reluctant to join a new team of boys who played together only at weekend tournaments.

"There was no chance to get to know them as friends during practice every day, like on my high school team. We just showed up and played. I didn't want to. My dad told me to try it. So he brought me to the ballpark in the middle of a doubleheader. The guys on the team I was supposed to join were sitting in the dugout. I walked in, put my equipment bag down, and began putting on my game socks and cleats. Everyone in the dugout was watching me. There wasn't a sound. I wanted to say to them, 'Okay, here I am, taking off my socks. Now I'm putting my game socks on. Now I'm putting my cleats on and tying my shoelaces. Are you happy? Isn't this thrilling?' Total silence, everybody watching me. Finally one guy came over and introduced himself. That was really nice. Then another guy did. Then it was time to play. Things felt a little better when I struck out the first batter, but I still didn't really like playing on that team."[5]

Both girls had laughed when Marti described "The Silence." It resonated with Lilly as a description of every boys' and men's team she had joined in her life. For her, as for Marti, most of the boys on most of the teams had quickly become supportive good friends. There were always one or two who objected to her being there and wouldn't talk to her. But that first moment when nobody knows what to say and nobody believes you can really play was difficult. Most recently, Lilly recalled, when she had attended the introductory noontime campus meeting of the Cal men's club baseball team, she had walked into the meeting room in the student union, dressed in street clothes (as the men were) and carrying her backpack, having just come from class. Even though she had been encouraged to attend by the club president, the other players weren't expecting a woman on the team. "When I opened the door and entered the room," she recalled, "everybody stopped talking and turned and stared at me. I was sure they thought I had come into the wrong room by mistake. I must be looking for the introductory meeting of some other club on campus. I couldn't be there for the baseball club team!" The men on that team quickly adjusted when the president introduced her with "This is Lilly. She's an awesome player and some sort of superstar from the U.S. Women's National Team."[6] It was good-natured teasing, and it broke the ice. Later, at the first practices, the open-mindedness of this particular group of men enabled them to express their admiration for Lilly's international baseball experience and ask questions about it. None of them had ever played baseball on an international level. Still, the first response when a girl walks into a room or a dugout with a team of baseball players is invariably a difficult and unnerving silence.

2

Cary, 2010

USA Baseball has provided the possibility of escape from invisibility and of high-level competition for America's best women baseball players. The U.S. Baseball Federation Inc. (USA Baseball) is the governing institution for elite amateur baseball competition, overseeing the teams that will represent the United States in international competition.[1] Its mission is to act as the national governing body for amateur baseball in the United States, to maintain membership with the U.S. Olympic Committee (USOC), and to be a member of the international federation that governs baseball (the International Baseball Federation [IBAF]). USA Baseball's duties are "to develop, foster and encourage interest and participation in baseball throughout the United States" (Article V, Sec. 1). Its charter also requires the organization "to provide equitable support and encouragement for participation by women where separate programs for male and female athletes are conducted on a national or international basis" (Article V, Sec. 7).[2] USA Baseball has sponsored the Women's National Team since 2004, when the first international women's baseball tournaments were held, creating the venue for an American team. The women's team is selected and sent to the Women's World Cup Tournament, held every two years, after a four-day tryout and four-day training period. After a preliminary round of six regional tryouts held earlier in the summer, in August 2010 thirty-two ballplayers from across the United States were invited to attend tryouts at the National Training Complex in Cary, North Carolina.[3] They were culled to a team of twenty players in four twelve-hour days in ninety-five-degree August heat. The twenty women who made the final cut traveled, after those few days together as a team, to the Women's World Cup Tournament, where they faced twelve teams from around the globe. The most challenging teams were perennial rivals Japan, Canada, and Australia. In 2010 the tournament was held in Venezuela, the first Latin American country to host the event.[4]

The women's team is not a priority for USA Baseball. The organization sponsors and showcases a range of boys' youth teams, including the elite NCAA collegiate baseball team, comprising the nation's most promising draft picks for professional baseball. It also sponsors Team USA in the professional World Baseball Classic. The boys and young men chosen for its amateur teams are brought to Cary for trials lasting up to two weeks (the 2010 trials for the eighteen and under [18U] team ran from June 23 to July 3), and then they travel to tournaments from July to September, facing national and international competition nearly every day all summer long.[5] The promising young ballplayers who play under the auspices of USA Baseball usually play only one season in this venue and then move on. Team USA is but one showcase for them, a stepping-stone in what they hope will be a future in professional baseball and the possibility of wealth and fame.

Team USA holds a very different meaning for the women. It is a brief interlude of baseball lasting a little more than two weeks every two years and is the only nationally validated elite-level baseball available to them. Far from the full summer of competitive baseball that nurtures the boys' development as ballplayers, the girls have trouble finding teams to practice with and play on as they prepare for the national trials. There is no professional or even collegiate future for them in their chosen sport and no anticipation of financial rewards for their baseball skills. Whether or not they make this team, they know they face two years of trying to find a team to play on and access to coaches to develop their skills, before trying out again against younger contenders and experienced veterans. Because USA Baseball provides the most prestigious team and the best international competition for these girls, they tend to return to play on Team USA over and over again. They have become a tight-knit group of friends and welcome new talent to their midst each season.[6] This may be a blessing compared with the cutthroat, high-stakes politics of boys' and men's baseball, but it also reflects neglect, indifference, and outright hostility to women's baseball in the United States. For the women, playing on Team USA is akin to being in the Olympics—the highest achievement available in their baseball careers in a rare and fleeting moment. Except that nobody in the United States knows about them.

USA Baseball's National Training Complex in Cary, North Carolina, is a jewel. Carved from the lush North Carolina countryside outside of Raleigh-Durham, it comprises eight stunning and meticulously groomed baseball diamonds, including a showcase stadium, Coleman Field, which holds several thousand spectators in stands and on grass berms down the foul lines. Workers groom the fields, which are maintained to MLB standards. The entire lavishly equipped complex is designed to showcase Major League Baseball's future superstars. Far from representing Spalding's image of baseball as the hell of war, these are Elysian fields, a piece of baseball heaven, all about hope and dreams of a glorious future for the players who are lucky enough to be chosen to compete on one of the USA teams.

As visitors walk into the complex, they are greeted by a Team Shop displaying six larger-than-life photos of recent alumni, framed by an enormous placard that reads, "Our Pastime's Future." One of the six players is a girl, Marti Sementelli, who in 2008, when only fifteen years old, was a standout pitcher for Team USA, winning the trophy for the best right-handed pitcher in the tournament. The five boys whose photos flank Marti's at the National Training Complex gate are all expected to be future Major League stars. Some, including Bryce Harper, Stephen Strasburg, and Justin Smoak, are already young millionaires in the Major Leagues.[7] Neither Marti nor her teammates have any hope of wealth and fame through baseball.

Watching the women ballplayers at these national tryouts is no different than watching a team of accomplished male baseball players of the same ages. The best demonstrate brilliance at the five baseball "tools": speed, hitting for average, hitting for power, a good glove, and a strong arm. But a team of young men at this level would have been drawn from hundreds of high school, college, and privately sponsored teams and divided into teams by age groups of no more than two years each (twelve and under, fourteen and under, fifteen and under, seventeen and under, eighteen and under, and collegiate). In contrast, this is the single national team available for girls and women of all ages. With an age range from seventeen to thirty-seven, some women players are still in high school, and others are the mothers of children not much younger than the teenaged players.

Contradictions are built into the core of the U.S. women's team's existence. There is no infrastructure for women's baseball, yet there exists a national team. Indeed, even the single opportunity provided for American girls and women by USA Baseball comes with a loss of other playing opportunities. The "regular" women's season is limited to a few tournaments held over major holiday weekends and coordinated by various haphazardly organized leagues. But scheduling for the Team USA tryouts and World Cup tournament in 2010 usurped the July Fourth and Columbus Day tournaments that are regular fixtures in the women's short season. Women who did not make the final cut for Team USA 2010 actually lost two of their three opportunities to play in women's baseball tournaments that year.

The obstacles they face reflect nationwide resistance to including girls and women in the national pastime, yet the ballplayers do not view themselves as political activists. Far from seeing themselves as feminists, rebels, or civil rights activists, they are all deeply moved by the honor of wearing the uniform of America's team, donning the USA jerseys, and representing the nation. They are more patriotic than rebellious. The image of a young American woman playing baseball in a Team USA uniform hardly strikes one as radical. Rather, it seems to make a claim for inclusion in a revered American institution. The women are aware that gender bias has interfered mightily with their lives and professional choices, but most articulate it in terms of "just wanting to play ball." When Jackie Robinson broke the "color line" in Major League Baseball in 1947, he and the African American community of the mid-twentieth century were consciously challenging racially segregated sports as part of the larger civil rights movement. In contrast, the embattled women baseball players are barely visible as a group and not championed by any civil rights organization.

The very existence of softball as a gendered "equivalent" to baseball takes sex-segregation a step further than in other sports.[8] Soccer, basketball, hockey, tennis, and most other major American sports segregate men and women into separate teams and leagues. Only baseball, the sport with the longest historical association with American national identity, attempts to isolate girls and women into an entirely separate sport. That "equivalent" sport is a point of contention for many of the girls who want to play with a ball and a bat. Softball represents "settling" to some, but to others it is the sport that has allowed them to attend college and to continue playing a sport with a bat and ball in a challenging competitive context. The women who play only baseball claim that even the best softball players have sacrificed time needed to develop "baseball instincts" and game experience. In their view, if women's baseball is to be successful at the international level, girls must play the game from youth to adulthood, just as American boys do. Softball is simply a different game, with different dimensions, a different pace, and different moves. Advocates of baseball for girls argue that recruiting even the best American softball players for Team USA will not enable Americans to develop a competitive world-class women's baseball team.

Jim Glennie, president of the American Women's Baseball Federation, former scout for the Women's National Team, and a lifelong supporter of women's baseball, believes that the segregation of girls into softball is directly undermining the ability to develop girls' baseball in the United States. "Lurking in the background in all this, and the one thing that makes baseball different from every other sport that's played in the Olympics, is softball, an alternate sport resembling baseball, but not baseball. And baseball is the only sport that has this. It's not men's baseball and women's baseball, like men's soccer, women's soccer or men's basketball and women's basketball. It's men's baseball and women's softball. And until we defeat the bogeywoman, we will not develop women's baseball."[9]

USA Baseball's purpose, however, is not to develop women's baseball, but to showcase it, along with boys' and men's amateur baseball. This puts the organization in a paradoxical situation: How can you showcase a championship women's baseball team without developing women baseball players? In recent years USA Baseball has drawn more heavily on NCAA softball players to represent the nation in baseball competition, hoping to be able to teach them enough baseball in the short time the women's Team USA is together every two years. This is a dubious project for those who know baseball. It is not a sport that can be learned quickly. Paul Seiler, CEO of USA Baseball, observes that the mission of Team USA is to win gold medals, not to develop ballplayers. The organization is looking for the most efficient way to put together a championship women's baseball team. "What's our responsibility in terms of fielding a national team? To put the best team on the field to win the gold medal. So where do those athletes come from? A lot of girls playing baseball had a softball start." The situation, Seiler notes, puts USA Baseball in a "chicken or egg" position.[10] With so little girls' baseball in the United States, the only way to field a national team seems to be to draw from softball. But this puts Team USA at a continual disadvantage when it faces Japan, Canada, and Australia, countries with highly developed girls' baseball programs. USA Baseball often puts the best pure athletes in the tournament on the field, but in recent years they have not been the best baseball players.

Some of the players who came to Team USA Baseball via softball played baseball for as long as they could—even into high school—before making a change to softball. They may have sacrificed some baseball experience, but they gained the opportunity to play softball at the highest level with other girls. In contrast, the women who have never "given in" to the pressure to play softball are a distinct minority, and while they have acquired more years of baseball experience, they have likely paid a steep price for sticking to it. Most have sacrificed playing time in high school to their male teammates, who are often given preference and taken more seriously by their coaches. Being the only girl on a competitive boys' team brings unique pressures and challenges in terms of athletic confidence and gender identity, especially during adolescence. The crucible of being the "only girl on the team" throughout their adolescent baseball careers forges a special bond between the girls when they finally meet each other in the context of the national team.

So isolated are the girls who play hardball that many are unaware of each other's existence. The younger players trying out for the first time have never before been on a baseball diamond with another girl. The amazement of one seventeen-year-old high school baseball player captured the exhilaration of discovering a group of peers: "Well, it was pretty amazing because I have never really set foot on a baseball field with another girl before. It's always been me with a whole bunch of boys. I have never, ever played softball; I've never picked up a softball; and I've never played baseball with girls. You have a lot of stuff you have to go through, a lot of hardship and disappointment and broken hearts. And there is no one better that can relate to you. No one can relate to you better than another girl who has been through the same stuff that you have. So that was pretty thrilling."[11]

Another teenaged rookie on Team USA played youth baseball with boys and a year of high school baseball before switching to high school softball. She now has a college softball scholarship but marveled at finally being able to play *baseball* with other girls: "Oh my gosh, it was extraordinary. I have never had an experience like that in my life. I've never played with a group of girls who have the same passion for baseball—*not softball*—as me."[12]

One of the fathers watching the team members go through their paces in Cary remarked on how good the level of play is and how outrageous it is that nobody in the United States even knows this team exists.[13] Donna Mills, an All-Star who played in 2004, 2006, and 2008 (and who took 2010 off to have her first child), told me she believes "nobody *wants* to know we exist."[14] Echoing that sense of invisibility, two players, after having been cautioned about security concerns for Americans in Venezuela, joked about the probable consequences of being the victims of crime during the tournament. "If a busload of American women baseball players gets kidnapped in Venezuela it will solve our publicity problems!" one noted. Her teammate retorted, "Oh yeah? If we get kidnapped, nobody will pay our ransom . . . they'll just say, '*What* U.S. women's baseball team? There are no women baseball players in the U.S.! Did they kidnap the Easter Bunny too?'"[15]

The American conviction that a competitive national team can be readied for international competition with no institutionally supported infrastructure is baffling. Japan has won four consecutive gold medals in this tournament and has a feeder system for women's baseball that begins with girls' Little League and continues through high school. The women on Team Japan play all year long and are divided among A and B national teams. The veterans on Team USA who have faced Japan in previous tournaments refer to them as "The Japanese Machine." Japan, the country that boasts the best women's baseball teams in the world, is successful because their girls have regular access to baseball beginning in childhood.

Australia, also always a medal contender, has mixed-gender baseball for children up to age fourteen, when the girls and boys have their own separate leagues that play for state championships. If a girl prefers to continue playing with boys after age fourteen, she may. The Australian state champions compete for the national championship each year, and the women's national team is then selected from the best players in the national championship tournament. Australia has an A team and a "shadow," or B, team, which assures regular opportunities for competitive play for all the players.[16]

The Australian women's national team doesn't receive funding as the men's team does, which means that the Australian women have to pay their way to international tournaments. There is plenty of grumbling about that from the Aussie women. But in Australia there are also many more opportunities for girls and women to play baseball than there are in the United States. Team Australia player Kathy Welsh, thirty-two, described the system she has played in for ten years: "I didn't even know baseball existed in Australia until I was twenty-two. A girl I knew played and one day rang me up and said, 'Hey, do you want to play baseball? We need someone to fill in.' And I said, 'Excuse me? Baseball? Do we play baseball here?' So I went and played and had a great time. I thought it was fantastic and decided to play and started playing and found out we actually have quite a big league in Victoria. We have our serious league in the summer season. And in the winter we have a not-so-serious league and a smaller group of girls that play, and then every Easter we have our national championships.

And each state has trials, as people [in the United States] would have trials in each state for the team."

I reminded Kathy that there are no state teams at all for girls in the United States. She paused, looked puzzled for a moment, and then offered a sympathetic "Oh. Okay, yeah." She then continued to describe Australian women's baseball: "So every Easter we have our national championships, and they go for eight days with Victoria, New South Wales, Queensland, and Australian Capital Territory, and sometimes South Australia. And West Australia, of course, the capital, has a team. Victoria has two teams, and the same with New South Wales. From the national championships they select the team to come to the World Cup."

Each of the Australian states has its own women's baseball program, some larger and some smaller. In the states with fewer resources, the women play on men's teams during the regular season and then come together to form the women's state team to compete at the nationals. "In New South Wales and Victoria there are women's leagues. In Queensland, the girls play with the men and then come together for the national championships, and I think that's the same in South Australia. New South Wales and Victoria have quite strong women's leagues. We have three different grades in Victoria with between six and eight teams in each, in each grade. I think New South Wales has two with six teams and then five teams."[17]

Two other members of Team Australia spoke with me about women's baseball in their country. Katie Gaynor, thirty-two, is married to Team Australia coach John Gaynor. She's been playing baseball for ten years. "I was originally a softballer. I got into baseball through Johnny [her husband]. I had finished up with softball, and there was a women's league starting in New South Wales. I definitely prefer baseball. I can't really compare the two sports. I just like the dynamics of baseball. I'm done with softball. It just wasn't for me. When I started out, there wasn't much women's baseball, but now in New South Wales we have a pretty good women's league and a high-performance program going."[18] Taylah Welsh, seventeen, a young member of Team Australia, has been playing baseball since she was four. "I never played softball. My two older brothers and my dad played baseball. I've been around baseball all my life." When asked to compare softball to baseball, Taylah remarked, "I can't. I have no interest in softball."[19]

Canada has a similar system, with each province holding an annual championship to send a team to the yearly national championship. There is very little softball in Canada, and Coach Andre LaChance of Team Canada remarked that girls are simply not interested in playing softball. Softball does not serve as an "alternative sport" to siphon girls away from baseball. In Canada teenage girls can choose to play on either girls' or boys' baseball teams, although LaChance observed, "What's becoming very trendy at home is all-girls teams playing in the boys leagues. All-girl teams play against boy teams. We see that there. The social aspect for girls is very important. Being surrounded by a bunch of girls is what they're looking for. I think mixed competition before the age of fourteen is appropriate. After that it becomes more difficult. The girls play together in the boys' eighteen and under league in the summer. It's called the Midget League. It's a perfect match for them. We see that also with the young ones [that they want to play on all-girls teams against all-boys teams]. You can do both. It is not a problem. You can play with boys or girls."

Not all the provinces in Canada are equally well organized for girls' and boys' baseball. "The bigger provinces have teams that compete for the national championship, and the national championship feeds this team [Team Canada]. We have that every year. We have two divisions. The Open Division and another division called Bantam, which is sixteen and under. Both divisions, sixteen and under, and sixteen and up, go to the national championship, and the coaches go there and scout at the same time. Every year we have a camp for the sixteen and unders in Cuba. So every February, I go down with thirty girls, sixteen and under, and we play the Cuban team for a week. It gives the coaching staff an opportunity to see them play in an international environment. So when they move up, we've seen them before."

Andre is French Canadian, from Quebec. He speaks English with a French accent, and there often seems to be primarily French banter coming from the Canadian dugout. But Andre noted that there is a "good mix of English and French players. That's the nature of our country."[20]

By comparison, the United States is home to a paltry and disorganized infrastructure for girls' and women's baseball. Compared with the others among the perennial top four nations, the U.S. feeder system is virtually nonexistent. Japan nearly always wins the gold, and the United States, Canada, and Australia are always in the medal round. Given the better organization of the Japanese, Canadian, and Australian programs, it is admirable, if surprising, that the American team has stayed as competitive as it has. The United States' lack of support for player development between the biennial tournaments may explain why, after having won gold medals in 2004 and 2006, Americans have since that time finished behind Japan, Canada, and Australia. Ed Kurakazu, assistant coach with the Women's National Team since 2006, saw the Americans handle the Aussies decisively in 2006 and 2008 and get crushed by a score of 19–6 in 2010. He observed, "Australia has passed us by. Their program is so much more developed than ours they've passed us."[21]

Jim Glennie, long active in American women's baseball, laments its state of neglect compared with the programs in Canada, Australia, and Japan. "Canada has much more developed girls' and women's programs than the United States. They've got lower divisions, and different provinces play. They have a national championship for different age levels. That's more than we have, much more. Australia has somewhat the same thing. They believe in the men's teams having a counterpart to women's teams, and they have a national tournament. That's much nicer than ours. And they have state teams and state tournaments." Japan, said Glennie, is more difficult to describe: "Japan has girls playing baseball in high school on girls' teams and on boys' teams. And they have some universities which give scholarships and they have baseball teams. And in fact some high schools give scholarships for baseball. Baseball is big in Japan." When I asked Glennie if *girls'* baseball was also big in Japan, he said, "Yes, baseball has replaced sumo wrestling as the main sport over there. They have a developing softball program, but the girls mainly play baseball. Softball struggles like girls' baseball does here. Japan is the leader for women's baseball now. They come with teams so well trained that it is frightening."[22]

After four marathon days at the National Training Complex in Cary, the final cuts were made, bringing exhilaration to the players selected and devastation to the players cut. Lilly was selected for Team USA. But her season ended in heartbreak: in the final intra-squad scrimmage before facing Australia for a few practice games, she broke a bone in her hand while diving back to first base on an attempted steal. An X-ray revealed a fracture, and the emergency room doctor recommended Lilly return home to see a hand specialist. With a temporary cast and her arm in a sling, she refused to leave her teammates until they were ready to depart for Venezuela, cheering them on from the dugout in Cary. Witnessing this was certainly one of my most difficult moments as a parent. USA Baseball did its best to help my daughter over the first moments of heartbreak, by including her in all the final preparations and giving her the USA jersey she had earned. I handed my camcorder to her teammate Tamara Holmes and received promises from players and parents alike to record the tournament and share their observations with me when they returned. Lilly and I returned to Berkeley, where she was diagnosed with a spiral fracture in her hand and underwent surgery the following day.

3

From Cary to Caracas

The following account is based on the reports of the
players, coaches, and parents of Team USA 2010. All of
the members of Team USA and all of the coaches were
contacted and invited to contribute their observations.

Team USA 2010 was loaded with talent and split almost evenly between
veterans in their late twenties and thirties and teenagers. Three former
Colorado Silver Bullets were in the lineup: Tamara Holmes, left fielder,
who had played on Team USA 2006 and is the most powerful hitter in
American women's baseball, and first basewomen Jenny Dalton Hill and
Laura Espinoza-Watson, who had been teammates at the University of
Arizona.[1] Returners from 2008 included the charismatic catcher Veronica
Alvarez; star second basewoman Malaika Underwood, who was the RBI
leader in 2008 and a member of the 2008 All-Tournament team; center
fielder Tara Harbert, whose breathtaking speed (and unorthodox swing)
earned her the nickname "Ichiro"; power-hitting shortstop Sarah Gascon;
and two formidable young players: Marti Sementelli, the seventeen-year-
old star who has earned national recognition in boys' high school baseball
and was named All-Tournament right-handed pitcher for Team USA in
2008 at fifteen years old, and Alex Hebert, an eighteen-year-old catcher
with a canon for an arm. Pitcher-catcher Anna Kimbrell, pitcher Christin
Sobeck, and outfielder Karen Costes completed the lineup of returners.
Missing veterans from the 2008 team were thirty-six-year-old MVP third

basewoman Donna Mills, who took the year off to have a baby, and twenty-two-year-old Lilly Jacobson, All-Tournament 2008 right fielder, who was injured in the final intra-squad scrimmage before the team was scheduled to leave for Caracas.

New players included nineteen-year-old pitcher-shortstop Jenna Marston, recruited by Team USA for her talent as a Division I softball shortstop for the University of Missouri;[2] fireball-pitching Clarissa Navarro, eighteen, who also played shortstop and third base; sixteen-year-old pitcher and third basewoman Wynne McCann, the youngest player on the team; Nicki Holt, a former Division I softball player in the outfield; seventeen-year-old Ghazaleh Sailors, a talented high school baseball pitcher and infielder; pitcher-outfielder Ashley Sujkowski; and pitchers Loren Smith and Lindsay Horwitz, college freshmen who have played both softball and baseball.

During the four days before departure to Venezuela, the twenty members of Team USA continued rigorous daily practice sessions and nine-inning games every evening against Team Australia, which had joined them in Cary to get acclimated to the time zone before journeying to Venezuela. The intense practice schedule squeezed into four days appeared necessary to allow the Americans to cohere as a team. But the intensity of twelve-hour days of drills and games in the Carolina summer heat also ran the risk of wearing the athletes out before the real competition began. The dramatic age differences on the 2010 team also presented particular challenges. Some players had vast baseball experience but aging bodies; others had less baseball experience but the strength and resiliency of youth.

Adding to the American problem of fielding a competitive national team, there have been different coaches for Team USA for each of its tournaments. Although revolving-door coaches are probably an inevitable by-product of only playing every two years, the inconsistency means that the coaches must get to know a diverse set of players in a short time, while the players get to know each other and the coaches. Compare that challenge to the familiarity with players described by Coach Andre LaChance of Team Canada or Coach John Gaynor of Team Australia.

All of the American players had endured lifelong battles to play baseball, making for inconsistent or incoherent career stats and further undermining the coaches' confidence that they really knew what their players could do. Add to that mix the fact that some of the girls were elite softball players, while others refused even to touch a softball, and you have the unique challenge of American women's baseball. Was it possible in four days to mold this team into a unit that could turn double plays, run down a base runner attempting to steal, and execute a suicide squeeze? Choices had to be made, and the consequences were significant: not enough practice was an invitation to failure, but too much would wear the team out before the tournament began.

Malaika Underwood, who has played second base on Team USA in three Women's World Cup Tournaments, noted, "It's a tough task to get a team together in such short time, and there is a fine line between preparing a team in a week and a half, and overtraining a team. You don't want to look back after a loss and say, 'We took this day or that day off and so we were never able to cover this defensive scheme . . .' It doesn't matter who the coach is, it's going to be a challenge to balance that."[3]

The meager time allotted would never be sufficient to prepare for international competition against teams that had been playing together for months. It was the most dramatic problem created by the lack of a women's baseball infrastructure in the United States. The coaches sought to compensate in a few days for what should have been years of consistent baseball experience. The result, at least in retrospect, was predictable. Players and coaches alike wanted to win. But making up for so much lost time and lack of institutional support was nearly impossible.

Nonetheless, all set off for the World Cup tournament with high expectations, great excitement, and eagerness to take the field. They brimmed with pride as they accepted Team USA jerseys with their names displayed in block letters over their numbers on the back, USA emblazoned across the chest. They were the best women baseball players in the nation, bound to prove they were also the best in the world.

The players uniformly described the 2010 Women's World Cup Tournament as the most important experience of their lives. After having practiced all day and played an evening game against Australia in Cary on August 9,

Team USA awoke at 3:30 in the morning of August 10 to travel from Raleigh-Durham to Venezuela. As the players exited Customs in Caracas, they were greeted by television cameras, paparazzi, lights, and microphones. Nearby, a brass band burst into song, and they were showered in American flags, presented with flowers, and ushered into a press conference. Treated as interlopers all their lives, Team USA was greeted like a Major League team arriving for the World Series. The Venezuelan press quickly descended on Veronica Alvarez and Laura Espinoza-Watson, both fluent Spanish speakers who were pleased to address the Venezuelans without translators. The boisterous welcome lasted almost an hour and a half, with none of the Americans feeling their fatigue.

Baseball-crazy Venezuela welcomed each of the women's teams as they arrived. The press conference for the Americans ended only when Team Cuba, the next to arrive, emerged in the reception area. The Americans were directed onto a bus waiting to drive them to Maracay, one of the two venues for this twelve-team, ten-day tournament.

Leading the bus were a police motorcycle escort and members of the Venezuelan National Guard, armed with AK-47s and wearing bulletproof vests. An ambulance completed the motorcade. Everywhere they went, the players were accompanied by an interpreter and two private security officers sent by USA Baseball. The team bus never went anywhere without this motorcade, and while at the hotel the players and coaches never went anywhere unaccompanied by armed guards. When one of the coaches wanted to make a phone call to his wife in the United States, it took him ten minutes to assemble enough guards to cross the street to an Internet café.[4]

The bus windows were tightly covered with thick drapes. The interpreter cautioned the players not to even attempt to look out the windows, and players wondered if it was because Venezuelans might be tempted to shoot at a bus full of Americans. As the bus pulled away from the airport, the motorcycles fanned out, surrounded the bus, and roared into action, screaming sirens forcing traffic off the road so the Americans could pass. Maracay is less than eighty miles from Caracas, but dense traffic made the ride several hours long, even with the military escort. Half the teams in the tournament were scheduled to stay in Maracay for the first round of play, and the other half in Caracas. All the teams would move to Caracas for the medals round.

With the bus windows covered, the players could not catch a glimpse of Venezuela. Seventeen-year-old Ghazaleh Sailors really wanted to peek, security risk or not: "We got on the bus, and . . . our translators and our bus driver said we weren't supposed to look out the windows so nobody would see who we were and try to shoot us. I wanted to look out the window because I've never been to South America before, but they told us that this is the kind of place where people just get shot for no reason."[5] Sailors took all this in stride, since the thrill of being on the Women's National Team made any danger seem worthwhile.

After a three-hour drive in the blacked-out bus, the players arrived in Maracay and wrestled their bags up to their rooms in the hotel's tiny four-person elevators. After a quick team dinner, they finally had an opportunity to sleep. Wednesday was a practice day, and Thursday morning, USA would open the tournament against its toughest opponent, Japan. The tournament's gala opening ceremonies would be held Thursday evening in Caracas.

Attendance at the first game between Japan and USA was estimated at eight thousand, more than any of the American players had ever played in front of, but far less than the capacity crowd of about sixteen thousand that would turn out for their game against Venezuela. The Venezuelans not only showed up in greater numbers, but also made more noise for women's baseball than any other fans in the world. Unlike the ebbs and flows of cheering over a background hum typical at a Major League Baseball game, this was nonstop screaming, more like an international soccer match than a baseball game. Ofelia Alvarez traveled to Venezuela with husband Julio to watch their daughter, catcher Veronica Alvarez. Although both parents had watched Veronica play ball throughout her life, neither had experienced anything like this before: "The parents would sit behind the USA dugout, with guards and other security people watching and protecting us throughout the games. The stadium was packed. We could hardly hear ourselves think while sitting in the stands so I can't imagine how it must have felt for the girls on the field. There was music (sometimes sounding like noise) being played by several live bands, thousands of people chanting (usually against us), microphones blaring encouragements to their team, helicopters flying (guarding air space), and the natural excitement of the games themselves. The girls held it together incredibly well."[6]

Marti Sementelli drew the honor of pitching the first game of the tournament. She held off the Japanese for four innings, while Japan played its patient and practiced brand of small ball, using every possible opportunity to draw walks and advance the runners with bunts and steals. Left fielder Tamara Holmes described Japan's start in that first game: "It was a really good game on their part, where they were laying down those close bunts, just ahead of the catcher."[7] The American coaches drew their outfielders in close, anticipating the Japanese penchant for short singles. But in the fourth inning, with Holmes pulled in behind third base, the Japanese connected for two solid base hits over her head. Pitcher Marti Sementelli dryly commented, "They played smart. And that's Japan. We all know that Japan bunts. But how did they win the gold medal last year? You can't win a gold medal just by bunting. What no one got is: they can hit the ball. Nobody could even get close to the ball because we were playing so off. . . . And then we played Japan again, and they beat us again. I mean, they hit the ball. They did hit the ball."

An added threat was Japan's catcher, Tomomi Nishi, the first and only player to hit a home run in the 2008 Women's World Cup. Sementelli was fully aware of Nishi's power: "She is strong. I mean, she's the biggest girl in women's baseball."[8] Holmes might have disagreed with that statement, but she too respected the Japanese ability to hit the long ball. Holmes herself is a power hitter and a contender for the honor of being the strongest woman ballplayer in the world. In Venezuela she had Nishi in her sites, hoping to outdo her by being the first player in the history of the women's tournament to hit an out-of-the-park home run.[9]

Coach Don Freeman replaced Sementelli after the fourth inning because he believed her off-speed pitching so closely resembled the Japanese style of pitching that the Japanese batters were reading her pitches too well.[10] Marti noted that she didn't think she was throwing her best stuff in that first game, but the two Japanese hits that did the damage would have been routine fly balls if the outfielders had been positioned at normal playing depth. While Holmes and Sementelli were frustrated with coaching decisions that contributed to playable fly balls being hit over the outfielder's head, both showed character, claiming full responsibility for the missed plays. Sementelli insisted the responsibility was hers: "Holmes kept saying it was her fault, and I said, 'Well I pitched the ball.'"[11] But Holmes was annoyed with herself for not following her instincts and playing deeper: "They [the coaches] were having us play shallow because [the Japanese] were getting their typical drop shots, but I think we just made a stupid mistake and myself in particular. [The Japanese] got the bases loaded, and [I was] still trying to play for that close shot. They finally connected just enough. I mean, it was literally just enough to go over my head. Both [Japanese hits] had runners on and one out with bases loaded. You know, that was a mistake on my part. I should know better. When runners are on, you're going to have to give it up, if it's in front of you." Holmes thought it would have been wiser to concede one run if the ball fell short, playing deeper to prevent multiple runs from scoring if the ball was hit over her head.

It was the first game in a long tournament for a team that had played together for one short week. It's not surprising that Team USA struggled in the opener, but it was unfortunate that they had to face their toughest opponent in that first game. Holmes noted, "I think everybody got a little tensed up. And we just weren't hitting enough to recover. Had we been able to hit, we could have gotten some momentum. But that was the end of it."[12] First basewoman Jenny Dalton Hill went two for two, driving in rookie shortstop Jenna Marston (who had doubled), scoring the team's only run, but the Americans were unable to respond to Japan's big fourth inning. The team hoped to learn from its mistakes and beat Japan in the gold medal round.

Opening ceremonies were held that evening in Caracas. All the teams housed in Maracay were supposed to caravan to Caracas for the event. But miscommunication about scheduling left the Americans waiting on their bus while the teams that had returned from afternoon games showered and changed. Finally, Tony Novoa, the head of the security delegation from USA Baseball, declared that a bus full of American ballplayers sitting idle presented too great a security risk and pulled the Americans out of the ceremonies. A delegation of coaches and USA Baseball officials attended in their stead. The American parents were at the ceremony in Caracas wondering where their team was.

USA was not scheduled to play the next day, Friday, August 13. Many of the players lingered in the hotel lobby into the wee hours Friday morning, talking to fans and players from other teams. Team practice would be held at noon, which would allow the girls to catch up on their sleep. But at 6:30 Friday morning they were awakened with calls telling them that Venezuelan tournament officials had unexpectedly rescheduled their practice to the early morning slot: "Get dressed, bring your gear, and be at the bus ready to leave in fifteen minutes!" A five-hour practice followed. No sooner had they returned to the hotel than they were once again summoned, this time to the conference hall. Mystified, they approached the meeting room. The coaches' faces were not reassuring. Something bad had happened.

That second call to report downstairs immediately was not received enthusiastically by Tamara Holmes, who spends much of her time rushing when ordered to. The firefighter from Oakland, California, is accustomed to moving quickly and facing more physical and emotional challenges than most people ever encounter. She did not initially respond to the second call on Friday as though it were a three-alarm fire. However, when she encountered Team USA press officer Fumi Kimura on her way down, she knew something was wrong. "I was just kind of taking my time. And everyone was saying, 'Hurry up! Hurry up!' So I get rushed downstairs, and I saw Fumi in the elevator, and I asked, 'What's going on? Is something wrong?' And she says, 'Yeah one of the players got shot.' And my jaw dropped. When we first got [to Venezuela], they kind of freaked us out the whole time: 'You're not going to be able to go anywhere by yourself, there are high instances of tourists getting kidnapped, and you guys are Americans, and you know Americans are big targets.' At the time I was thinking, 'Man, is it *this* bad?'"[13] Now all the dire warnings appeared to be warranted. If the news was unnerving to the firefighter, how would it be received by the high school girls on the team?

The shooting had taken place earlier that day at José Casanova Stadium in Caracas during a game between Hong Kong and the Netherlands. Cheuk Woon Yee Sinny, the shortstop on the Hong Kong team, had been shot in the leg while she was on the field. Marti Sementelli described the shock they all felt at the meeting as the coaches broke the news to them. "The coaches looked at us and took deep breaths, and said, 'Okay, we don't know how to tell you this, but there was a game at Caracas, and the shortstop got shot in the leg.' And everybody was going, 'Oh my God! Oh my God! Somebody just got shot!' The coaches said, 'We don't know anything more right now. That's all we know. We're going to find more things out. Right now, you guys stick as a team. Don't go in the lobby. You are not allowed in the lobby anymore. We are in lockdown. You stay together tonight, do a lot of team bonding stuff. Stick together.'"

The games that night and the following day were canceled. Coach Freeman, USA Baseball Women's National Team director Ashley Bratcher, and Tony Novoa were on their way to Caracas to meet with Venezuelan officials and the representatives of the other teams. There would be no further games until the cause of the shooting had been determined and the safety of all could be guaranteed. Meanwhile, the Americans were in lockdown; they were forbidden to enter the public areas of the hotel.

The team responded with a combination of concern for the Hong Kong players, panic that the tournament would be canceled, and fear that they might also be targets if they took the field again. Sementelli captured the general sense of dread: "We played one game, and they're saying we don't know if we're going to continue. We worked so hard. My heart was like, 'I don't want to go home! We just started becoming a team. We just got here.'"[14]

A significant number of players, however, wanted to leave. The incident seemed the inevitable outcome of all the dire warnings, and the omnipresence of troops and guns did not make the women feel safe. Even Coach Freeman wondered, "If the place is so safe, why are there guns and guards everywhere?"[15] Sementelli recalled, "A lot of people thought, 'I just want to be out of here. I want to be safe.' The older ones were talking to us younger players and being really supportive. They were telling us,

'Don't freak out, don't get on the phone so fast, don't say, "Oh my god, there is a shooting here, I'm going to get killed!" like to your parents . . .' So we just bonded the rest of the night."[16]

The next thirty-six hours were spent in a state of apprehension. Some of the younger players fretted that their parents would insist that they leave the tournament; some of the older players knew this was their final tournament and were devastated to think of it ending this way. The younger ones worried about the older ones, and the older ones worried about the "kids." Ghazaleh Sailors remembered, "Some of the older players were crying. Because we pretty much knew we were going home; none of us thought we were actually going to stay."[17] Malaika Underwood, the veteran second basewoman, worried about the youngsters: "I know that for a lot of the younger players, it was just a totally shocking experience. . . . I was definitely shocked when I heard that somebody got shot on the field. But I resisted the urge to jump to too many conclusions, and at the end of the day, it's not like I felt very safe in the first place with a bunch of twenty-year-old national guardsmen carrying machine guns everywhere we went."[18]

Jenna Marston, one of the rookies, was stunned, but kept her cool. "I'll always remember a picture of the room and where everyone was sitting. . . . When they said the Hong Kong player had been shot, I really don't know how to describe my emotion. . . . I was definitely tense. . . . It was sort of a realization that what they've been talking about really can happen. I felt like the older players did a really good job of staying calm and letting the younger players feel whatever they felt. . . . I was never really freaked out."[19]

Ghazaleh Sailors was more worried about going home than being shot. "The first thing in my mind was 'Oh no, oh no, they are going to call the tournament off aren't they?' We all thought we were going home. The security guards said, 'If we don't get a good explanation from these people . . . we are going to go home.' And I thought: 'Are you kidding me? Do you know how hard I worked for this? Do you know how long I worked for this? You are going to send us home after one game? Really??'" Sailors declared she would prefer to stay and risk being shot than miss the rest of the tournament: "If I'm going to die, I don't want to die like an old lady in a hospital bed. I'll die doing what I love."[20]

Tamara Holmes was not so sanguine about dying with her cleats on: "I remember Ghaz saying, 'Well, if I have to die, at least it will be playing baseball.' . . . I'm looking at her, and I'm like, 'Later for you! I'm not going to get shot over this shit!'"[21] Holmes was, however, sympathetic when she saw sixteen-year-old Wynne McCann in tears, not from fear of physical danger, but because she feared her parents would insist that she leave when they learned of the shooting. A couple of other younger players were truly frightened at the prospect of sniper fire if they took the field again and wanted to go home to safety.

Veronica Alvarez, a Miami native who was accustomed to hearing news of random shootings in her hometown, was confident that this was a one-time incident that did not pose a threat to the ballplayers. After the players had been assured that the Hong Kong player would recover, she wisecracked, "If I knew it was only going to be a gunshot to the leg, I would have taken it. I'd take it if I got a little ESPN action."[22]

The Americans retreated to the two floors on which they were housed, talked all night, took a few straw polls to get the pulse of the team. All were respectful of those who wanted to leave and those who wanted to stay, a division that did not correlate to age in any way. Nor were the opinions of most set in stone. The team spent the night talking about it and "bonding," in part through group games introduced by Christin Sobeck, a veteran player and a teacher. She divided the players into two teams, "under twenty-fives" and "over twenty-fives," and pitted the youngsters against the older players. The result was rough-and-tumble hilarity and emotional release, with the younger players completely dominating their elders. The lockdown in the hotel rooms continued for nearly forty-eight hours.

The next day Ashley Bratcher, Don Freeman, and Tony Novoa returned from their meeting in Caracas with Venezuelan authorities, American diplomats, and representatives of the other teams. José Casanova Stadium, where the shooting had taken place, sits on a military base, with an impoverished neighborhood just beyond it. The Venezuelan authorities had determined that the Hong Kong ballplayer's wound came from a gun fired into the air from outside the stadium, either on the military base or in the adjoining neighborhood. It had been a freak accident. If the bullet had descended just inches to one side, nobody would even have known a shot was fired; inches to the other side and the player could have been killed. Cheuk Woon had been taken to a hospital in Caracas, had undergone successful surgery, and was recovering well. Her team had withdrawn from the tournament and would accompany her home. The Venezuelan authorities were convinced the players were safe but as a precautionary measure would move all remaining games out of Caracas, to Maracay, and provide helicopter surveillance over the two stadiums there. Tony Novoa, who was by now beloved and well trusted by the players, told them that he was as concerned about their safety as he would be about his own daughter and that he believed it was safe for them to take the field.

The actual decision about whether Team USA would stay or go was left to the ballplayers. The coaches left the room and told the players to call them when they had reached a decision. Veterans Malaika Underwood and Sarah Gascon opened the discussion. All agreed that the team should hold a vote to determine the course of action. But if the vote was not unanimous, what should they do? Gascon tearfully addressed her teammates and told them that she was "100 percent about the team." It was her opinion that if even one player wanted to leave, they should all withdraw from the tournament in solidarity with their teammate. Underwood disagreed; such a path would put too much pressure on the players who wanted to leave. She recalled, "I felt by saying that, you were indirectly putting pressure to actually suppress their fear and say, 'Okay, we'll stay' because they didn't want to be responsible for sending nineteen people home. So my perspective was, instead of doing that, if there are people who want to go home, we should support them, and let them. If you want to go home that's totally fine, let them go, and those people who want to stay should stay."[23]

Tamara Holmes then raised a problem with such a compromise: if enough players at key positions wanted to leave, it could jeopardize the team's ability to perform, and they might as well all go home.

In the end the players reached a unanimous decision to stay. The desire to play was stronger than any specific fear. Holmes noted, "You get back on the field, you don't know what is going to happen. But I think people just wanted to play in the end. They just really wanted to play."[24] Underwood agreed: "At the end of the day everybody, even those people who were afraid, weren't ready to go home, they just didn't want to go out on the field right away. But by the time we got back on the field, people were so ready to play, because we had been in the hotel for forty-eight hours. It was just like, 'Let's just do something.'"[25]

When the coaches were invited back to the room to hear the verdict, the players lightened up the somber moment with some playfulness. Underwood, as team spokeswoman, reported that the team was depressed and had decided to return home. The startled coaches had to readjust their expectations, responding slowly, "Okay, if that's what you've decided . . ." The team could no longer suppress their laughter as Malaika told the coaches that they had elected to stay.

With Hong Kong departing, the Australians waited to see what the Americans would decide. If the Aussies and Americans both left, Canada would follow suit. The American players knew that if they chose to withdraw, the tournament would end, and if that happened, international women's baseball would be in jeopardy, at least in the near future. Clarissa Navarro observed, "We had a heavy load on our shoulders. If we left, the whole tournament was off."[26]

The first moments back on the field evoked temporary jitters and hypervigilance, but baseball quickly reasserted itself, and remarkably, the shooting incident faded into the background. The teams would make up for the lost day by playing two games the first day back. The Venezuelan fans poured back into the park, and play resumed.

The Americans played two games on Sunday: in the morning against Korea and in the evening against Cuba. Korea did not pose a competitive threat to the Americans. Loren Smith blanked the Koreans for three innings and reliever Christin Sobeck completed the shutout, while the Americans, restless from two days in the hotel and eager to play ball again, teed off on the hapless Koreans. The Americans won 21-0. Under normal circumstances, the coaches would decline to run up the score in that manner, but under the rules of this tournament, the total number of runs scored could determine a team's placement in the medal round. The girls played flawlessly; hitting, pitching, and fielding were overwhelming.

In the evening game the Cubans couldn't touch Marti Sementelli's curve balls, and Tamara Holmes fulfilled her dream of being the first woman to hit an out-of-the-park home run in the Women's World Cup. Not only was that historic shot a grand slam, but she hit a longer two-run homer later in the same game. Team USA was playing Cuba in the secondary Maracay field, Aviacion Park, which had shorter distances down the foul lines than a Major League park. But Holmes's second shot went straight over the left fielder and easily cleared the wall. One of the coaches estimated that it went about 360 feet, a big league distance.

The Americans weren't done hitting home runs. In that same game against Cuba, Malaika Underwood also hit her first out-of-the-park home run. The Americans' two-day confinement resulted in a release of pent-up energy in the form of history-making baseball. In addition to those three home runs, the first day back was marked by stolen bases, clutch hits, suicide squeezes, and shutout pitching.

The winning streak continued the next day in the USA–Puerto Rico game, which the Americans won 9–0. That made three games without a run scored against the Americans, as they charged to the medal round.

Team USA had earned the day off that was scheduled between the preliminary and medal rounds and were treated to a trip to Hugo Chávez's private beach on a military base, under the watchful eyes of their envoy of Venezuelan national guardsmen. Parents, players, and coaches all enjoyed the beauty of the coastline and got to know the military men in a more informal setting. The team spent five hours melting out tensions in the sun, recuperating from an extraordinarily demanding week.

The medal round began on Wednesday with the games in José Pérez Stadium, home of Maracay's major league team. Team USA opened the final round against Canada. There is no love lost between the two North American rivals. Recently, the Americans have struggled against Canada, and every game has been played as though it were a grudge match. Canada knocked the United States out of the gold medal round in Japan in 2008 and celebrated boisterously on the field while the Americans waited silently on the foul line to shake hands. For the rest of that 2008 tournament in Japan, Americans and Canadians refused to make eye contact, and elevator rides with members of both teams on board were utterly silent. Canada has also consistently outplayed the Americans when the two teams have met between World Cup tournaments. This year in Maracay, the Americans finally got revenge, beating Canada 10–1. Still on a roll from their previous three games, the Americans enjoyed superb pitching by Jenna Marston, a triple by Malaika Underwood, and more displays of power from Tamara Holmes, who stepped up to the plate in a bases-loaded situation and hit another grand slam.

Although she had hit the two home runs three days earlier, doubters claimed that they had been hit in a small ballpark with short outfield fences. Holmes recounted the moment when nobody could detract from her crowning achievement:

> A few games later I got the ultimate redemption playing against Canada. This field's fences were 330 feet down each line. I couldn't see anyone hitting it out of there. I once again got up with bases loaded and hit a bomb to the left field bleachers. "Holy shit!" I thought. "Another grand slam!" And this time no one could say anything. [. . .] Here I was at 36 years old hitting 3 home runs, and 2 of them grand slams. Life does not get any better than this. The only thing that would top this feeling would be to take home the gold.[27]

The gold certainly seemed within reach as the women prepared to play Venezuela at José Pérez Stadium in the game all of Venezuela had been waiting for. Around sixteen thousand fans filled the stadium, and thousands more had been turned away. All the tournament games were televised, but USA-Venezuela was on prime time, at 7:00 p.m. Venezuela, a country that loves its baseball and has the highest number of Major Leaguers other than the Dominican Republic, had turned out to watch its *women's* team play. The noise level was overwhelming. Parents, players, and coaches described the deafening noise of the Venezuelan fans as one of the most gratifying aspects of the tournament. For American girls accustomed to the hollow sound of scattered cheers from a handful of friends and family sprawled throughout empty bleachers, taking the field before thousands of fans packed in a professional stadium was electrifying. It would either energize or paralyze the players. The women who had been on the 2008 team when it played in Matsuyama had some experience with playing before a large crowd. They remembered thousands of Japanese fans, along with television crews, journalists, and a noisy brass band. But the turnout in Venezuela dwarfed even Japan's support of women's baseball. Malaika Underwood tried to convey to the younger players how unique this much attention was, even for the Women's World Cup: "I thought the crowds were just amazing. I tried to tell some of the other kids that even in Japan it wasn't like this.... When we played Venezuela, there were over fifteen thousand [spectators], and none of us had ever played in front of that many before. And it was not just fifteen thousand sitting on their hands: they were all screaming and yelling the entire game. It was like playing in a bubble; you couldn't hear a thing. It was a great experience, and I'm not sure, unless we go back to a South American country, that we'll have that experience again. Especially in the games against Venezuela, I mean the local support was just astounding."[28]

Tara Harbert felt it was a moment of vindication in a lifetime of neglect as an American ballplayer: "They loved us. I mean they all knew our names, they all knew we played baseball. And then you come back to America and people are like, 'Oh, you play softball?' We had sixteen thousand people at our game versus Venezuela.... It was a dream come true, even though they were cheering for Venezuela, in my mind they were cheering for us. Because I've always played my entire life [in order to] to play in front of that many people.... Really I can't express how much it means.... Down there we were stars, and we come back here, and it's like you barely make ends meet, no one knows who you are. I feel like, 'Oh my god, I want to go back!'"[29]

Sementelli started the game against Venezuela and pitched three shutout innings. The Venezuelans couldn't touch her curve balls, and the Americans quickly cruised to a 5–0 lead. Coach Freeman had planned to take Marti out to save her for the semifinal game. Many of the players, including Sementelli, disagreed with that decision. Her teammates describe her as a "workhorse" with a "rubber arm." She throws every day of her life and has since she was a toddler. She was confident, as were her teammates, that she could have completed the game against Venezuela and still been ready to pitch again in the championship game. Veronica Alvarez had no doubts that Sementelli could have finished the game with Venezuela *and* started the gold medal game: "She was the MVP in the last tournament. She is a workhorse. She's going to get the job done today, and come back tomorrow and get the same job done."[30]

In the fourth inning Coach Freeman brought in curve-ball pitcher Anna Kimbrell, a collegiate softball player and star baseball pitcher and catcher. She got three straight outs in the fourth inning and struck out the first Venezuelan batter in the fifth. But then she gave up a hit to center field and walked the next batter. The Venezuelan fans had been uncharacteristically quiet, but they roared back to life when their team appeared to be rallying. The momentum of the game shifted as the crowd screamed and willed its team to rally against the mighty Americans. The vision of American might was somewhat misplaced on a team of women more accustomed to the echo of empty stadiums than the roar of tens of thousands of nationalistic fans.

The pressure mounted as Kimbrell walked the next batter and the decibels rose even higher. Then three batters in a row were hit by pitches—two of them, according to the Americans, because Venezuelan batters put themselves in the path of the ball—and were awarded first bases even though they made no effort to avoid being hit. Catcher Veronica Alvarez, a boisterous and irrepressible leader, both behind home plate and from the dugout, tried in vain to calm her team. Even her powerful voice could not reach the women on the field. She was helpless to stem the tide as the momentum slipped away: "[The Venezuelans] started to scream and cheer, and they started to blow on those horn things. . . . It sounded like a soccer match. As a catcher looking out . . . I saw our team crumble. I'm trying to calm them down, but what can you do? They don't hear each other, there's so much chaos. And in Anna's defense she didn't hit those batters. They got in the way. One was a strike down the middle of the plate, and the girl stuck her head out. She bent over and put her head into the ball. I immediately turned and yelled at the umpire, 'That's impossible!' But she gave her first base. Next batter, same thing: batter sticks her leg out in front and gets hit. I yelled, 'No, no, no, no, no!!' But the umpire let her go. The crowd went crazy, the bases were loaded, a run scored, then she walked another. Our team crumbled."[31]

Coach Freeman tried to change the momentum by calling in eighteen-year-old rookie Lindsay Horwitz from the bullpen. Horwitz recounted, "When I was warming up to relieve Anna, I was shaking so bad. Being right next to the Venezuela fans and trying to focus was difficult." When she got the call from the coach, bullpen catcher Alex Hebert told her, "This is your time, Lindsay. You have been waiting for this moment. So go get it."[32]

As Horwitz began her walk across left field to the mound, the decibel level in the stadium stopped her in her tracks. Holmes was in left field saying, "Come on, Lindsay! One foot in front of the other!" As Horwitz passed third base, Sarah Gascon also called out: "Come on, Lindsay, just get them to hit a grounder to me. I'll take care of it. Double play and we're out of the inning." Alvarez, waiting with Freeman on the mound, looked for something to say to calm the young pitcher: "I asked her if she had any annoying brothers. Pretend they're annoying you and ignore it."[33] Horwitz had her own technique for dealing with her nerves: "During my warm-up pitches I was shaking like no other. I was thinking, 'How am I going to do this?' I thought about the movie *The Rookie*. It actually worked. I found a zone, and the shaking went away. I was also able to clear out all of the screaming fans. I thought it was the sweetest thing ever to be able to pitch in front of seventeen thousand people, whether all of them were cheering for me or not."[34]

Horwitz pitched well, but the damage had been done. Even the most experienced, reliable veterans could not muster the calm they needed to play their usual game. Horwitz induced the batters to hit grounders, but errors were made by the usually unflappable Gascon and Underwood, and things got even uglier for the Americans. The Venezuelans got two more hits, making it a seven-run inning, before the Americans were finally able to end the nightmare with a double play. Sementelli, watching from the dugout, was devastated: "I had to watch from the bench. When you have a five-run lead and your team is looking sharp, and then you see it all unfold, it is so hard to watch. None of us once thought we were going to lose that game. It just slipped through our fingers. It seemed like we were in that inning, and we were never going to get out. . . . We just lost our composure . . . lost everything that we had, so much strength. It was nuts, seventeen thousand people are all cheering against you, and then everyone [on the team] got in their own head and played uptight, and [the Venezuelan] momentum just kept going. We couldn't stop it at all; we were just there watching."[35]

Alvarez sighed, "The fans are what made them win the game. I can't believe we lost that game. The fans really got them pumped and got them back into it."[36] On the field after their win, the Venezuelans celebrated as though they had won the whole tournament, dancing on the mound, circling the field with a big flag, fans going wild, while the Americans waited patiently to shake hands. The American locker room after the game was utterly silent.

Team USA did not recover their momentum after that loss. The next day, the deflated team played Australia and suffered a humiliating 19–6 loss. They had defeated Australia four times in Cary before the teams departed for Venezuela and had beaten them easily in 2008. But Australia had some big hitters and had since been building up their program. They were the sleeper team of the tournament; while everybody had their eyes on Japan, Canada, and the USA, Australia was hitting everything in sight and playing their way into the gold medal game. There was one highlight in the game for the Americans: Tara Harbert made a spectacular, full-speed, parallel-to-the-ground diving catch of an Australian line drive hit to the left-center gap. For that play she received a standing ovation from everyone in attendance and the trophy for the best defensive player of the tournament.

The United States lost to Japan in the semifinal round on Saturday, for their third-straight loss. The United States and Venezuela met again in the bronze medal game. This time the Americans won decisively, 15–5, before a somewhat quieter Sunday morning crowd. Japan defeated Australia 13–3 that afternoon, for their second-consecutive gold medal in the Women's World Cup competition.

PART 2

The Veterans

4

Tamara Holmes

LEFT FIELD

"The love brings you out there."

"Athletically, I always had some gravitation toward sports. We have pictures of me when I was little with a football I found in the backyard. But I don't remember playing any sports before I picked up a baseball. When I was seven, I remember seeing a neighbor of mine in his uniform, and I thought, 'Oh, that looks like the coolest thing ever.' Prior to that I had asked for a bat and a ball, and my dad had given me this little glove and a ball and a toy bat."[1]

Seven-year-old Tamara Holmes was moving back to her hometown of Albany, California. Her family had moved to Texas three years earlier, and now she was returning to California with her father, two sisters, and brother to her grandmother's house where she had lived before the move. Her mother had stayed in Texas. Her parents were divorcing, and her paternal grandmother, Essie Lofgren, would help raise the four children. "We moved back to my grandmother's house, and we all lived there. So I wasn't without a mom. I was raised mainly by my grandma, and my dad was always there."

The baseball player next door who dazzled Tamara with his new Little League uniform had been her best friend before they moved. "I saw his uniform and told my dad I wanted to play Little League Baseball." She was not the first American child to be drawn to baseball in order to wear the uniform, but her dad, Aubrey Holmes, had to make inquiries to find out whether his daughter could play. When he learned that girls were allowed to play in Albany Little League, Tamara's baseball career was launched.

Albany, California, is a tiny town wedged between the east shore of the San Francisco Bay and the city of Berkeley. The city was first incorporated in the wake of a political protest. In the late nineteenth century, Albany's larger and more celebrated neighbor, Berkeley, had routinely trucked its garbage through Albany to dump at the bay's edge, which was Albany's waterfront. In 1908, engaging in the direct-action politics that have come to define the East San Francisco Bay, a group of women armed with two shotguns and a .22-caliber rifle established a blockade to stop the horse-drawn garbage wagons at the Berkeley border. The confrontation worked. The Berkeley wagons turned around, and Albany filed papers of incorporation.[2]

Nowadays, the progressive community is no less militant about waste management, recycling, and just about everything else and is still a very small town. It has one library and community center, one high school, one police and fire station, and one Little League. Remarkably, the feisty town's single Little League provided the first baseball experiences for two little girls, separated in age by fifteen years, and destined to become teammates on the USA Baseball Women's National Team. Tamara Holmes and Lilly Jacobson both stepped onto a baseball diamond for the first time as seven-year-old rookies at Ocean View Park, Albany Little League's home field.

When her father signed her up to play, Tamara acquired a uniform as splendid as that of her friend next door. It had been legal for girls to play baseball in the United States since 1974, but there were no all-girls teams. In 1980 Tamara's right to play could still not be assumed. "It was no real problem, but my dad had to look into it to find out whether girls were allowed." Tamara is the second oldest of the four Holmes children. She and her older sister, Andrea, are the two athletes of the family. Andrea loved running and became a track star at Albany High. When the school cut its track program, Aubrey transferred Andrea to Berkeley High so that she could continue to develop in her sport. She went on to earn a scholarship at Boise State. Andrea and Tamara's brother, Aubrey Jr., played some Little League Baseball but fell in with a rough crowd of friends and did not pursue sports. Their youngest sister, Kjell, was not athletic, but like her older sisters and brother, she gave sports a try. Tamara chuckles at the memory of Kjell doing her best to be athletic: "My younger sister tried sports. I mean she was just a mess, but at least she tried."

Tamara began her baseball career in the Albany Little League with the Angels. She was not the only girl in the league: a friend of hers played on another team. As she recalls, "My first coaches taught me how to pitch. I did well and got drafted up the next year by Dave Krone, who ended up being a longtime mentor of mine." Krone was deeply involved with Albany Little League, taking care of the fields, helping with the tryouts, volunteering for whatever was necessary, and coaching his son's team, the Cubs. Even after Coach Krone's son gave up baseball, he would offer his time and expertise to Tamara whenever she needed it. She remembers that his generosity with his time was not always appreciated by his wife: "I know it used to drive his wife crazy because, when I asked him, we'd sneak out and he would say, 'Okay, I'll throw you batting practice.'" His mentoring paid off: she became the Cubs' cleanup hitter, pitcher, catcher, and shortstop and was elected to the 1986 All-Star team by a player vote. The Cubs won the league championship that year, and Tamara was credited in the local newspaper with leading them to victory: "Tammy Holmes hit cleanup and started the first championship game on the mound. In the second game, she started at catcher and finished at shortstop. She hit .369 for the season, and slugged .507, with five doubles and two triples. She was named to the 1986 All Star team by vote of the players."[3]

She continued with Little League through middle school, always "playing up" with boys a year older than she was. This is the age when baseball becomes more seriously competitive, as players prepare themselves for their hopes of high school, collegiate, and professional careers. At ages twelve to fourteen most of Tamara's teammates were also playing with the Albany American Legion team. Legion ball is private tournament baseball for middle school– and high school–age players. It provides daily play throughout the summer in a highly competitive venue. It is expensive, requiring money for uniforms, equipment, coaches, and travel. And unlike municipal Little League, its private status allows it to exclude players without fear of losing public funding. Here Tamara encountered the first roadblock of her baseball career. "In junior high I was playing up for my age, and [I] played up until high school. I wanted to play Legion because that is where the high school kids would play. I remember the coach already knowing I was going to try out and seeing me coming. He said, 'Oh, you know it's just for guys.' So I never made it to that, but freshman year I tried out for my high school for some reason."

Tamara didn't give much thought to whether she should try out for high school baseball. She just did it . . . "for some reason." She had a few more obstacles to overcome than many other high school baseball players. She was a girl trying out for a "boys'" sport, and she did not come from an economically privileged family. She was not a member of a private travel team, and although she had a supportive father, he had his hands full raising four kids. Tamara did not have expert adult guidance about her future athletic career and had to figure things out on her own, especially because she wanted to play baseball, which nobody expected she would be able to do beyond Little League. Her baseball teammates had been her friends since childhood, and now they were trying out for the high school team. It seemed natural for her to try out with them too.

Even the most confident and talented girls who play baseball through-out childhood often find themselves unexpectedly nervous when they try out for their high school team. They have usually played with the same boys all their life, and their sudden anxiety takes them by surprise. High school sports are a serious, almost sacred business in the United States, cultivating dreams—albeit slim ones for most players—of collegiate and professional futures. Girls who want to play high school baseball are usu-ally treated as interlopers, as though they are transgressing a boundary and in some way threatening the social order.

"This was the first time I got a little nervous, even though I grew up with a lot of these guys and started playing baseball with them and played with them in junior high. For a long time I was better than most of them, so I wasn't so intimidated. Then for whatever reason, coming into high school, I started getting a little unsure of myself, and I don't know why." Those nerves may have caused her to second-guess herself. For no good reason at all, she tried out as an infielder, at a position she hadn't played since childhood. It didn't work out. "I was trying to do something different, instead of just trying out for outfield where I probably would have made it. I missed a lot of balls trying out at third base and didn't make the cut."

The boys on her team couldn't believe it: "Everyone was in an uproar. It was like, 'Oh! She was one of our better players!' My dad talked to the coach, and the coach said, 'You know, it was just based on her tryout. She missed a lot of balls at third base.'" Reflecting on why she had tried out for an unfamiliar position, she mused, "I don't know. I think it was because I was nervous and intimidated and just not thinking and didn't have much direction. My dad was a good supporter of my baseball, but he never sat down with me and said, 'Hey, this is going to be hard. If you're a little nervous or whatever, it's okay.' I think I always assumed that I was mentally strong enough to do it. So the following year I tried out, and I made the team."

Tamara was athletically capable, but she was a fourteen-year-old girl and unprepared for the sudden feeling that she was all alone breaking some major social barrier that had never before presented a problem. She was hitting baseballs and also hitting the glass ceiling, moving beyond playing a child's game with boys into the exclusively male world of adult baseball. She felt alone and unexpectedly scared, and when she looked around, hoping for somebody to encourage her, nobody was there.

"I think being a young woman growing up, having someone to talk to about it would have been important. Having that discussion [that nerves and anxiety were inevitable] needed to happen. In hindsight, I didn't know—and my dad obviously didn't know—what it felt like. You need someone to tell you it's okay, no matter how good you are. Someone needed to say, 'Hey, this is just nerves. It's intimidating.' I think that would have helped."

Thinking back on what she faced as a teenager, Tamara's attitude toward herself is both demanding and compassionate: "If you are going to be a baseball player, you are going to have to learn to manage [the nerves], to suck that up, to know that it is a normal feeling. But at the time, you are the only one. There's no one to talk to; your female friends don't play. They are like, 'Why are you playing baseball? Why are you doing that?' They don't understand. So you are just all alone trying to figure it out." She expects herself to have been "tough enough" even without support. But another voice inside her acknowledges how lonely it is to be a path breaker.

She does not think her discomfort had to do with sexual identity at that point. "I don't think I was as aware of that then." Nor was it race. "I don't think I felt any problems racially or sexually." She simply did not, for the first time in her life, feel comfortable as a female athlete playing with males. "It was just about me being uncomfortable, even though the guys were [comfortable with me]. They were supportive, like, 'Hey, you are one of our better players; we want you on the team.'"

Tamara was tenacious and resilient enough to try out again her sophomore year. She made the team, but she still struggled with a sense of discomfort about being the only girl. She was not feeling at home with herself, and that led her to second-guess her decision to play baseball. Her father had always been the parent she turned to for help with important decisions, but during her high school years, he was distracted with problems of his own, trying to handle them without worrying his family.

Grandmother Essie Lofgren was loving but dubious. "She didn't understand it . . . my grandma was funny. She never stopped us, but I think if she could have had her way, she would have. I had asthma too, and she was real old school. She would always tell my dad, 'Oh, you know she's got asthma, and that stuff [sports] is going to kill her.' She would always complain about us ripping around the streets. I loved to be outside. I got grounded more times than I can imagine because I would never come home on time. The guys in the neighborhood and I were either playing strike out, tennis, Wiffle ball . . . I grew up skateboarding, racing bikes. I was an outdoor person, and I would never come home on time and stayed in trouble for that. Yeah, that used to drive her crazy."

But Tamara was also attuned to a hidden, more positive message from her grandmother. Essie was a dedicated athlete herself. "She was a bowler, my grandma was. In her eighties she held a 140 average, so she was an incredible bowler. But I guess the other stuff she didn't understand all that much, especially if I'd come home banged up."

During her first season on the baseball team, Tamara sought her father's reassurance that she was doing the right thing. She was a versatile multisport athlete, she needed a scholarship in order to attend college, and even though baseball was her preferred sport, it wasn't likely to pay for a college education. Plus, she was still struggling with feelings of doubt about being the only girl on the team. One afternoon while she and Aubrey were playing basketball together, Tamara expressed her doubts about baseball, albeit in a roundabout way that might have been difficult for her father to interpret. "I was talking to my dad—we were playing pickup basketball at the time—and I said, 'Oh, you know . . . what if maybe I just don't play anymore? What if I just get a job?' I just needed reassurance. He was going through a lot of issues in his life that we didn't know about at the time, and I remember he just got really mad and said, 'That's it! You got to quit!'" This was not the response Tamara wanted or expected, and she did some quick backpedalling: "No, actually I just want to play! I really want to play now, no, I do want to play!" But Aubrey Holmes was adamant: "He made me quit. And no amount of talking made him change his mind. I was really distraught."

She was playing volleyball as well as baseball and approached her volleyball coach for help, beseeching him to talk her father into letting her return to baseball. But her father held his ground: she could play volleyball but not baseball.

Aubrey never explained his sudden reversal about Tamara's participation in baseball. He had always been very supportive and attended all her games, no matter what sport she was playing. Tamara thinks he was just distracted and became impatient with her. He wanted his daughters to be athletes; athletic scholarships would pay for college. But baseball was more complicated, and it wouldn't support Tamara in college. What was the point of continuing with a sport that created emotional stress when she could play any number of other sports that were more likely to open doors for her future? For so many girls who play baseball, pure love of the game often doesn't seem to be reason enough to stick with it. Tamara's father never explained his thinking to her, and he now insists that he never meant to discourage her from playing baseball, but at the time she couldn't find a way around his edict. "So I quit and it hurt."

It wasn't long before the thought occurred to her, "Oh, screw it. I'll just do softball." Her father didn't necessarily prefer that; she simply didn't tell him about it. The Albany High softball coach failed to embrace Tamara as the answer to his prayers. "Oh, screw it. I'll just do softball" is a not an attitude likely to win the heart of a softball coach. Tamara had taught herself to switch-hit (bat both right- and left-handed) in Little League, and she had always been a power hitter. She was not circumspect about her belief that softball would be "playing down" for her: "I'm a baseball player, and I can hit a softball." The coach responded to her attitude by placing her on the JV team. Tamara responded to the affront with boredom: "It was boring as crap . . . ridiculous . . . like slow pitch. It was like someone soft tossing. I'm hitting right-handed home runs, left-handed home runs, just for fun, switch hitting, just killing the ball." She thought the coach had it in for her, and the coach thought Tamara had a bad attitude. Between the coach and her father, her high school softball career was short-lived. "My dad found out that I was playing softball and was mad and said, 'No, you can't do any of that,' so I had to quit softball."

That spring Albany High School cut its track program, and Aubrey transferred Andrea to Berkeley High so that she could continue to run. He decided to move Tamara too, wanting both girls to attend the same school. He was hoping Tamara would become interested in Berkeley High's excellent basketball program. Indeed, she was impressed with what she saw; Berkeley High had some of the best young basketball players in the country.

Tamara had grown up with a racially mixed group of friends in Albany and had played with boys all her life. "I grew up mainly hanging out with guys, and we had Native American, Indonesian, Black, mixed. . . . My parents had never really talked about race. You just were what you were. In Albany, I never felt discriminated against. Or maybe I was too ignorant to know the difference even if I were. But I never, to be honest, really felt it because I grew up with those people."

Berkeley High was different. Although Berkeley prides itself on being a multiracial community, it is polarized racially and economically, and its high school reflects that segregation. Tamara experienced culture shock when she transferred there. "Going to Berkeley High, all of a sudden I started learning all these things about African American history and Malcolm X, for literally the first time. It's weird that it took until high school to be exposed to it. So I learned what it was to be black, so to speak. And then it makes you hypersensitive. You become real skeptical of all white people and think, 'I didn't know these things . . .' Most of my basketball friends were black, although there were a few others mixed in. When I was playing volleyball at Berkeley High, one of my best friends was Filipino, and another one on my basketball team was Asian. But then the black girls on the team were saying, 'Why are you hanging out with those white girls?' I said, 'Who's white?? She's Filipino, and she's Asian. What are you talking about?' But that's how they were raised. To them, everything was black and white, and I didn't understand this. I was happy to learn more about my culture and myself, but I would hate to feel like I need to segregate myself. I didn't really buy into that."

Experiencing herself as something of an outsider all her life has made Tamara accepting of the differences between people and leery of group identities. "When people realize that the most important thing is human decency, a lot of things can be solved on that level. I won't be so naive as to say that there aren't cultural and racial differences, but half the problems people have are just from being humans; we're all going to have a lot of the same issues. I've always been in the position where I've never been 'black enough.' My black friends would say, 'Oh, listen to the way you talk!' And I would answer, 'What do you mean? I'm speaking English . . . maybe you should try it!' What does that mean 'to be black' or to 'sound black'? That's almost an insult to black people. If you've got someone who is barely speaking English, or speaking Ebonics, or some street stuff, and you want to say that's 'black,' why is that a compliment?"

Tamara bridged the racial divide at Berkeley with volleyball and basketball, but she couldn't scale the gender barrier to baseball. She still wanted to play, and that was a wall even an extraordinary athlete like Tamara couldn't get over at the time. She thought about trying out for the Berkeley High baseball team in the spring, but because her tournament-bound basketball team's season ran so late, she didn't. She was also discouraged by the baseball coach's attitude. "It was the same old thing: I heard some grunting, they had some old weird fat coach, and he was like, 'Oh, I don't know about women trying out.' So he kind of intimidated me." She stayed away from baseball spring of her junior year and played club volleyball after basketball season concluded with the state championship. In the spring of her senior year, Tamara's desire to play baseball returned. She tried out, and "the coach kind of gave me the spiel, 'I'd rather take a junior that is going to be here two years than you as a senior.' Which I understood, but it was also kind of the runaround, and he apologized for it after and told me, 'Yeah, I should have picked you up.' But it was what it was at that time."

Aubrey Holmes's belief that his daughter would thrive athletically at Berkeley High proved accurate. Tamara received scholarship offers from the University of California and every other Pac-10 school, except Stanford, in basketball *and* volleyball. She also received scholarship offers from the University of Tennessee and another university in the east that she doesn't even remember. She chose volleyball at Cal because it was her hometown school, she had a friend on the volleyball team there, and they knew the coach through their club team, Golden Bear Volleyball. She also hoped she could walk on as a basketball player and play both sports. "That was my plan: volleyball, walk on the basketball team." Jackie Robinson was a four-sport athlete at the University of California, Los Angeles (UCLA). Why couldn't Tamara Holmes play two sports at Cal? The two eldest daughters in the Holmes family had earned NCAA Division I athletic scholarships, which was a remarkable tribute to their talent and hard work and to attentive parenting.

During her first year at Cal, Tamara was expected to redshirt for the Cal volleyball team, meaning she could practice, but not play games or travel, to preserve all four years of her NCAA eligibility. The volleyball coach urged her to use that first year to concentrate on her education and acclimate herself to university life. He did not want her to play basketball. She liked and respected this coach and accepted his regimen.

The following fall, she was a starter on the volleyball team, but she became embattled with the new assistant coach, who had just arrived from the University of Washington. "She [the new assistant] whipped the team up in a way it needed to be, but nobody was having fun. I was always a very gifted athlete, and I didn't know how to push myself. So I was very combative and didn't get along with her. The team just didn't have a whole lot of respect for either coach, which I didn't like. I had one friend on the team, but most of them were sorority girls that I had nothing in common with."

Tamara was alienated and lonely. "I was starting and playing, but for whatever reason I still wasn't happy. I was doing really well, but it just went downhill. My roommate would always tell me, 'Get out of bed!' because I was missing a lot of school. Looking back, I realized I was depressed and just didn't know it."

The head coach reached out to her. "He said, 'I notice you're not having a good time in practice, and you seem real unhappy.' And then I just started crying and pouring it out, and all of a sudden, I didn't want it anymore. I ended up telling him I wanted to quit. He said, 'Okay, maybe you can not play the rest of the semester, and we'll give you the option to come back.' They were still going to pay for my school until the end of the semester. After that, unless I played volleyball I would have to pay for school . . . which I ended up doing, because I never came back to the volleyball team." The day she quit the team, she went to see her academic adviser, who immediately noticed that she looked happier. Tamara walked into her office, and her adviser greeted her with, "Oh, you look so much better! What's different?" It was then that Tamara realized how depressed she had been.

Tamara's grades had tanked during those first three emotionally challenging semesters at Cal. After she quit the team, she tried to improve her grades but couldn't pull them up fast enough to avoid academic probation. She was advised to attend a junior college for one semester to make up the work and then to return to Cal and the volleyball team the following fall. But before academic probation closed in on her, Tamara tried out for the Cal softball team. There, for the first time since high school, she found friendship and the possibility of a joyful athletic life. "When I tried out [for softball] at Cal, before I got kicked out of school, I actually enjoyed it. I loved it. One of the catchers ended up being the catcher on the Olympic team. When I first tried out, they had Michelle Granger, who was one of the top pitchers in the nation. I'm actually a ton more afraid of softball than I am baseball. You've got Michelle Granger who is six foot two, a lefty, firing the equivalent of a hundred-mile-an-hour fastball at forty feet. Yeah, screw that!" Laughing, she demonstrates her softball batting stance: "I remember when I was at bat, my ass would be sticking way out like this. Like, I don't want any part of that pitch! That is too close!"

Practicing with the softball team for that brief preseason, Tamara was finally having a good time in college sports. "So now I could finally respect softball because these women are throwing it hard. It was not baseball . . . it was a different game. I had a baseball swing. In softball they pitch to kind of rise up or something, so you need to hit more down. I had a total baseball swing. It was a challenge for me for the first time. And the cool thing was, for the first time since high school, it was a diverse group of women, and I was having fun. It was amazing: you could work hard, *and* you could have fun. In volleyball, the coach just lost sight of that, and I couldn't connect with my teammates. When I went to softball, I was outside in the sun and the grass again, and they were a great team."

The diversity of Cal's softball team was sexual and economic as well as racial. "It wasn't like in volleyball where a majority of the girls were sorority girls. It was a mixed group. It wasn't like they were all hard-core softball players; it just was a diverse group of people that were just nice, and each one different and great in their own way." When pressed to talk further about racial diversity in women's sports, Tamara observes that the sexual diversity on the team was as important to her as racial diversity. The isolation she experienced as a lesbian on a volleyball team of straight women seemed more intense than that she experienced as the only black woman on a volleyball team of white women. "I could see maybe how race would be an issue. I mean volleyball obviously is predominantly white, especially at the time I grew up. Basketball of course is more urban and predominantly black. Softball was a mix. And it was sexually balanced. In basketball and softball there is a higher chance of having gay members on the team."

Having teammates with whom Tamara had something in common helped her to relax and enjoy the team. For the first time in her athletic life, she was not "the exception." She was not the only girl on a boys' team, as she had been on the high school baseball team; and she was not the only working-class gay black player on a team of wealthier straight white women, as she had been on the Cal volleyball team. Tamara just wanted to play, and she wanted to minimize the intrusion of race and sexuality into team dynamics.

Unfortunately, her grades had fallen so low during those first three tumultuous semesters that she lost her athletic eligibility and could not play softball for Cal. She transferred to a local junior college, stayed there a year, and then made up her mind to return to Cal, even though she knew the academics would be a struggle. "I wanted a degree from Cal, but I was a terrible student." She still had an invitation to rejoin the volleyball team, but she declined. She was readmitted to Cal and worked at two jobs to pay for school. She was willing to pay her own way and master the academic rigors of the University of California.

She later learned that she had also been struggling for years with undiagnosed attention deficit disorder (ADD), which had contributed to her academic difficulties. "Even in high school, I was the kind of student who when I got it, I was fine, but if I didn't understand something, I didn't have the heart to step up and ask for help. I later found out that I have some form of ADD, where I can't concentrate for long periods of time. I'm only learning these things about myself in my thirties, and I'm still dealing with them. Like when I take my fire department classes, I think, 'All right, I'm going to sit here and concentrate!' But literally thirty seconds later I could be daydreaming about playing drums in the middle of Indonesia or some random stuff that comes over me, and I can't focus on things. I'm better now as I'm older, and I can focus on the things I want to learn more, but school was just so hard. I was a terrible student. I'm a better student now because I can focus my attention specifically on subjects I'm really interested in. I want to learn more and make up for things I have missed."[4]

In 1995, when she was preparing to reenroll at Cal, baseball reappeared, and this time she was determined to respond to its call. She saw the Silver Bullets professional women's baseball team on television and felt the same excitement she had experienced when she first saw her neighbor's Little League uniform all those years ago. "When I saw the Silver Bullets on TV, I said to myself, 'I'm going to try out for that team.' So I looked up the team online and figured out where they were having tryouts. This was '95 going into the '96 season. I didn't know anybody." She had battled with college academics and with a sport that made her unhappy. She had overcome academic probation and emotional depression and was dealing with ADD. Women's professional baseball offered a welcome break from those struggles and excited her, and she knew she owed herself the opportunity to try it.

She hadn't played baseball since her sophomore year of high school. She needed a coach and a place to practice. She needed to get her swing and arm strength back. She called on one of the few people she had ever been willing to ask for help: her old friend and Little League coach Dave Krone. "I told him, 'Oh hey, I'm thinking about trying out for this team,' and he said, 'That's great!' I told him, 'It's a wood bat league,' and he said, 'Well, check this out . . .' He had these super-old Louisville bats, and you know they are the older ones because Hillerich & Bradsby were producing those bats. So anytime you see Hillerich & Bradsby, you know that's an old Louisville bat. These things were like tree trunks: huge. One was a 44½-inch bat. Mind you, they were a little bit older, so probably not as heavy as they were in their prime, but two of them were super heavy. So, that's all I knew: he threw me BP [batting practice], and I was hitting really well with those big bats."

Dave and Tamara returned to Albany High's baseball field, which is in a public park. It has a short right field but an extra-high fence to prevent fly balls from hitting cars, pedestrians, and the houses across the street. But the high right-field fence was no match for Tamara, as she and Dave worked on her swing with those enormous old bats. Anybody sitting on their front porch across the street needed a baseball glove for protection. "Dave would leave from work and meet me there. He bought a net to throw into and a bunch of balls. He would throw me batting practice and fly balls, and then I'm hitting home runs over to somebody's porch. It was pretty funny. And then I went down to Loyola [Loyola Marymount University in Los Angeles] to try out for the Silver Bullets."

The Silver Bullets coaches were impressed with Tamara's hitting, and her arm was so strong that they asked if she could also pitch. Tamara hadn't pitched since Little League, but she was prepared to do whatever they wanted her to. Johnny Grubb, who had played on the '84 Tigers team that had won the World Series, was one of the coaches. "He was a real nice guy. He was a lefty, and he got into the batter's box with his southern drawl, and just said, 'Come on! Put it in there.' I thought, 'Okay . . .' And I reel back and just stick him right in the back![5] And I'm thinking, 'Oh God, this can't go well!!' And he just shrugged it off and said, 'Oh yeah, that's all right. But we probably won't have you pitching. You will be an outfielder.'"

She received an invitation to spring training in Fort Myers, Florida, where the Silver Bullets used the Red Sox's spring training facility. Meanwhile, she enrolled at Cal.

Her instructions from the Silver Bullets were to find a team to play on and practice with before spring training. But that was more easily said than done. Beneath her dramatic athletic prowess, her Major League switch-hitting slugger swing, and her charismatic swagger, Tamara is a private person who asks for help reluctantly. In response to the Bullets' request that she find a team to practice with before final selections were made, she demurred. "I was too nervous. At the time I was back at Cal, and I was too nervous to ask about a team. But I had Dave. Still, you know the limitations of one-on-one training . . . it would have been nice to see a little play action, but he pretty much got me ready." She was working on two dreams: to finish college and to play baseball. Dave Krone, the coach who had first spotted Tamara's baseball talent when she was an eight-year-old Little Leaguer, stepped in to help her prepare for the Silver Bullets of 1996.

Although she played only one year with the Silver Bullets, the team's third and final year before it folded, she made her mark, hitting a grand slam, the only home run in the team's history. The event was celebrated in an article in the *San Francisco Chronicle* on May 15, 1996:

CAL ROOKIE BLASTS HISTORICAL HOME RUN

SF Chronicle (May 15, 1996)—Rookie leftfielder, Tammy Holmes, a current Cal student, got hold of a high fastball and clouted the first home run in the three-year history of the Colorado Silver Bullets, the all-women's baseball team that plays all-male teams.

Her bases loaded drive in the top of the 9th traveled about 380 feet at the University of Georgia's Foley Field. Trailing the Atlanta Mustangs 11–4 going into the ninth, the Silver Bullets staged a huge rally, tied the score on Holmes' grand slam and completed a 10-run inning for a dramatic 14–11 win. "Their outfielders were disrespecting us," Holmes told the Chronicle. "I just wanted to put the ball in play."

Holmes added that she was happier that the Bullets came back to win than she was about her historic home run.

When the Silver Bullets folded, Tamara completed her bachelor's degree at Cal as a full-time student, graduated in 2001, and got a job as a fire-fighter for the City of Oakland, California, where she has worked since 2004. She discovered USA Baseball through the Silver Bullets and was a member of the first Team USA in 2004. In 2014 she was the only former Silver Bullet still playing on Team USA. She has achieved the status of a living legend among the younger players and is still the player her team relies on to deliver the timely extra-base hits and home runs. She has hit more home runs than any other woman in baseball history. In the 2010 Women's World Cup Tournament in Caracas, Venezuela, she hit three home runs, including two grand slams; won the home run trophy; and was named the Offensive Player of the Tournament. In the 2012 Women's World Cup Tournament in Edmonton, Canada, she was the only American player selected for the All-Tournament team. It is thrilling to watch her line drives bounce off the outfield walls and to see her obvious delight

FIG. 1. (*top left*) Tamara Holmes, Team USA 2010, Tournament Home Run Champion. Courtesy of Brian Fleming.

FIG. 2. (*top right*) Holmes coming to the plate, 2010. Courtesy of USA Baseball.

FIG. 3. (*left*) Lieutenant Tamara Holmes of the Oakland Fire Department with her father, Aubrey Holmes. Courtesy of Jennifer Ring.

when the ball pops off her bat. She is a crowd-pleaser equivalent to any Major League slugger. Ken Griffey Jr. is the player to whom she has been most often compared when she strides to the plate.

She still practices baseball primarily on her own. Her full-time sport these days is Olympic weight lifting, in which she is a nationally ranked competitor. She tries out for Team USA every two years, knowing that she will have to prove herself to new coaches each time. She takes nothing for granted. Her confidence in her talent as a ballplayer doesn't translate into cockiness about making any team. "I don't know . . . at some point you think you've gone through it enough times to make it a little easier. Still, each time I worry, 'What is it going to be like this time?' But the love brings you out there. As nervous as it makes you, somehow you still show up."

5

Donna Mills

THIRD BASE

"To fall in love again the following spring . . ."

On the occasion of her induction to the Athletic Hall of Fame at the Lynn Vocational Technical Institute in September 2007, Donna Mills paid tribute to her most beloved sport. She graduated from Lynn high school in 1991, excelling in softball and basketball. In her speech accepting the honor, she waxed poetic: "I met my true love when I was a little girl. It was a beautiful spring day. The sun was shining. The grass was green. The dirt was manicured. Even as a little girl, I could recognize that my love was something I couldn't live without . . . that I wanted to see every day . . . that I wanted to devote all my time to . . . that I dreamed about every night . . . that I thought about all day when I was away from it . . . that I could express myself openly to . . . that I could falter and my love would still be there waiting for me."[1]

Like so many love stories, this one had both heartbreak and innocence: "I was forced away from my love simply because I was a little girl . . . it broke my heart . . . it disappointed me . . . just to fall in love all over again the following spring. . . . My true love is baseball. I can't live without it. It's what drives me. The vehicle to express myself. My stage to perform. It's what I'm most passionate about in my life."

At a ceremony in which her softball achievements were being celebrated, why did she give a speech about baseball?

"I wanted to talk about my love, and that was my love. It was, you know, everything. It was baseball. It was baseball. It was baseball. I couldn't talk about softball like that because the love wasn't there."

Donna Mills played baseball as a girl, switched to softball in high school, and earned an NCAA Division II softball scholarship at the University of Massachusetts Lowell. After college she returned to baseball and was a starting infielder three times on Team USA: in 2004, 2006, and 2008. In 2006, when the team won gold for the second time, she was named MVP of the tournament. That recognition prompted the National Baseball Hall of Fame in Cooperstown to request an item for their exhibit on women's baseball. She gave them her batting gloves, which are now a part of the Hall of Fame's permanent display "Diamonds and Dreams." In 2010 she took time away from baseball to give birth to the new love of her life, her daughter, Gianna Marie Mills, born on August 9, 2010.

The second child and only daughter in her working-class family, Donna was born on July 13, 1973, in Lynn, Massachusetts. Her brother, Michael, is three years older. She has a sparkle in her eyes, speaks in a thick Boston accent, and has been an athlete all her life. Like many girls, she followed her big brother everywhere, and joining in his play with the neighborhood boys launched her into sports. When Donna and Michael were young, their father, David, worked for General Electric, made good money, and was trying to purchase a home for his family. But things went wrong. "On pay days he began to disappear. He'd get paid on Thursdays, and we wouldn't see him until Sundays. Then Sundays turned into two weeks, with no sight of him. That's when my mother made the decision to leave him. When they split, my father had a pretty significant drug and alcohol problem."

When Donna's mother, Josephine, took her children and left her troubled husband, she received no financial support and suddenly became the single parent of a nine-year-old daughter and a twelve-year-old son. Michael had been playing baseball in the Pine Hill Little League since he was nine, so Josephine signed up Donna too and scheduled her work around their school and baseball. Baseball came into Donna's life in the form of a child-care opportunity for her mother, but it introduced her to something she would love for life. "My parents were going through a divorce. My mother was like, 'I have to go to work. I'm signing you up for baseball.' It was much easier for Mom to go to work on the weekends and just drop me and my brother at the park. You stay there all day."

Donna played in Pine Hill Little League from ages nine to twelve. She was a left fielder, and it was tough being the only girl, but not as tough as what her family was enduring. The distraction of baseball helped Donna to keep her balance. The family was just plain poor: "Not only was I a product of a 'single parent' upbringing, we were also poor. My mom had zero support from my father. We lived in subsidized housing. My mother had to apply for welfare because she simply couldn't support us alone. That's when she went back to school. But we lived off very low means. Growing up, we had government cheese, peanut butter, and powdered milk. No joke! I never had cleats or batting gloves. Every glove I had was donated to me from a coach or teammate. I think that's why I attached myself to baseball. It represented the 'good' in my life. From very early on. I clung to it. Fell in love and devoted everything to it."[2]

She felt drawn to the baseball diamond: "Something drives you, even as a youngster, to go to the field every day, even though your mother signed you up, and she paid for you, so you have to go. I mean, I was always looking for rides to get to the field, and you know, my mother was always working. Something drove me there. Something motivated me to go to baseball."

Josephine Mills was the daughter of an old-fashioned Italian family, for whom girls' education was not a priority. She had been allowed to drop out of high school. When she was faced with responsibility for her family, she realized how important that diploma was. Working as a floral designer, she returned to school to earn her GED, then an associate's degree at community college, and ultimately, a bachelor's degree. She currently works for the Department of Transitional Assistance (the welfare department) for the Commonwealth of Massachusetts. She did not have the time to witness her daughter's athletic brilliance, and that is still a source of sadness for Donna. "In my entire career, I can count on one hand how many sporting events my mother came to. She was not very supportive. Plus,

FIG. 4. Donna Mills, Pine Hill Little League. Courtesy of Donna Mills.

she was very busy furthering her education, working, and trying to raise two children."[3]

In a childhood bereft of parental attention, Donna's support came from her grandparents, Josephine and Ralph Severino. "As a child, they came to every Little League game they could. They'd tell other parents in the stands, 'That's my granddaughter out there in left field, with the pony-tail.' They made sure my brother and I never went without. They would deliver bags of food to us. We lived on the third floor of a three-decker, and my brother and I used to fight over who'd go downstairs to carry up the bags of food. They didn't have much, but everything they did have, they gave to us. [. . .]

"My senior year in high school, once I had made the decision to attend the University of Lowell [it was the University of Lowell before it merged with the University of Massachusetts], I said to my grandmother, 'Nany, I'm going to go to the University of Lowell on a softball scholarship.' Her response was, 'Why? Why would you go so far away? I don't like that idea.' [Lowell is twenty-four miles from Lynn.] Then as soon as I left, she bragged to her entire apartment building, 'My granddaughter's going to a university.' My grandfather passed away in 2003, and my grandmother in 2005. There's not a day that goes by that I don't think about them. I truly believe they were with me in 2006, in Taiwan."[4]

Donna's father had been an excellent athlete who played football, bas-ketball, and baseball. Both of his children inherited his athletic ability, although troubled as he was, he could offer them little in the way of guid-ance. "He did introduce my brother to baseball. He even made a short stint as his Little League coach. But that was an embarrassing event in my brother's life. He would show up under the influence and then was a no-show. Nothing that an adolescent boy should endure. [. . .]

"My brother was a very talented baseball player, who could've done great things. He was the home run record holder in the history of Pine Hill Little League. But he went astray soon after my parents divorced. After they split, he began skipping school and experimenting with drugs. As he got older, his behavior escalated. My sophomore year in high school, my mother picked me up from work, where I was a part-time cashier at Stop

& Shop, and took me for a ride. She explained to me, 'Your brother was arrested today, and he's going away for a little while.' A little while would be two years, House of Correction, at the historic Salem Jail. He would continue challenging my mother, doing various 'bids' [short jail sentences], committing crimes, until his son was born in early 2005. Now he's dedicated to being a supportive father and steering his son in the right path."

Donna's relationship with her father was shattered. "I made the decision to stop all contact and communication with my father. After years of promises and attempts at having a relationship with him, I stopped contacting him. He never showed up for visits with me. He'd make arrangements for weekend visits, such as bowling, and then he'd never show up. Even as a child, I'd had enough. In the spring, I didn't need my father to interrupt my baseball journey. I'd seen the pain that he'd caused my mother and ceased all communication. It hurt that my father could be in the same city as me and not make the effort to see me. All through my entire career; Little League, high school, and college, he never stopped by."[5]

It is ironic, but perhaps not surprising, that with both her father and brother in trouble with the law, Donna has found work on the other side of it, in uniform, policing prisoners and taking care of their families. She is a court officer for the District Court of Massachusetts. It's dangerous but gratifying work, guarding and escorting prisoners between holding cells and the courtroom and helping their families when they are in court. "We are basically the police of the courthouse. We transport prisoners throughout the courthouse, we have a lockup facility that holds approximately forty custodies per day, we secure the courtrooms, and help the general public. Basically, we're social workers and psychologists and peacekeepers. I love it. Every day it's knowing that the little things you did helped out, whether it was a coworker or a prisoner or a family member. [. . .]

"Back in 2002, I was at work, I was up in a courtroom, and I got a call from my chief. My chief said to me, 'I have a guy down in lockup who just told me he's your dad. He's asking to see you. He's asking if you'd come down to lockup and see him.' I said to my chief, 'He is my father, but I won't be coming down to see him.'" Her father later died in 2009 in a rooming house in New Hampshire.

In spite of her brother Michael's personal difficulties, Donna credits him with making her into an athlete. "It was hanging with my brother that made me an athlete. Plus, growing up I had all boys in the neighborhood. I mean, there were girls, but they played with Barbies and played house, and I wanted to be outside. . . . We had a Wiffle ball court set up in someone's backyard; we had bases painted in the street. We used to play half ball: you get a tennis ball, and you cut it in half, and you get a stick, like a broomstick. You could curve it, you know . . . it was really hard to hit. That is what we used to play as kids. We were never in the house, not like it is today. We never played a video game . . . it didn't matter the season, especially up here. If it was a blizzard, we were, 'Yes! We'll go sledding!' I grew up playing with boys. Of course we were competitive."

Baseball provided Donna with structure, order, pleasure, and a substitute family for three years. But it shut her out when she was twelve. She wanted to continue to play after Little League and was directed instead to softball. "When my age limit had run out for Little League, then it would have been Babe Ruth, and they wouldn't allow me to play Babe Ruth. Or Senior League. They referred me over to Babe Ruth Softball, and I said no. So I took junior high off from baseball. I guess I didn't think anything was wrong with it. Just they said, 'You go over there,' and I thought, 'Okay.'"

She found ways to compensate for the loss of baseball. The gap was filled in middle school by Catholic Youth Association basketball, where she met Linda Reyes. "She was my basketball coach. She was just a volunteer, and I was probably fourteen years old, so it was right around that time when I took time off from baseball. I was, you know, a teenage punk, and she took me under her wing, and we spent the summers together. Even after, she would take me to the mall or take me to the beach. We'd go play basketball for hours. She was kind of like my mentor, never let me veer in the wrong direction and was close to my family. She grew close with my mom and is still friendly with her today."

Another major influence was Donna's high school softball coach, Pati Kane. Donna could have attended one of four high schools in Lynn, Massachusetts: Lynn English and Lynn Classical are the academic high schools with Division 1 athletic teams; St. Mary's is the Catholic school; and Lynn

Vocational Technical Institute, or Lynn Tech, is intended to prepare students for a trade directly out of high school. Donna's mother believed that her daughter needed the security of learning a trade. "That's where she sent me to school, and I didn't have the opportunity of switching high schools because she didn't allow me to. I wanted to switch for more academics, to receive better academics so that I could go on to college, a better college, or to be seen by more colleges too."

On her first day of high school gym class, Pati Kane walked up to Donna and told her, "You're going to be my starting catcher on the softball team. You're going to college. Only pitchers and catchers get softball scholarships, so you're going to college." Donna was incredulous, as she'd never played softball (or catcher) before. Kane was insistent, and Donna was a quick learner. She became the starting catcher for Lynn Tech and then switched to shortstop. In spite of Kane's proclamation about catchers, shortstop was the position that would eventually earn Donna college scholarship offers. She excelled so quickly at softball that she tried out for the Softball Junior Olympics and was selected for the Peabody Raiders, a local team that qualified in 1990 and 1991 for the Junior Olympics Nationals held in Lodi, California. There Donna was recruited by Harvard University's softball coach. "Here he is shaking my hand and offering me his contact information. I was like, 'Listen, I go to a trade school, and I don't have the academics for Harvard.' I thought, 'This is a joke. I can't pass my SATs.' He asked me, 'Have you taken your PSATs yet?' and I was like, 'What are those?'" She laughs just thinking about it. "We really did not have the academics in high school. I went to school, and it emphasized trade classes, so I never wrote a paper in high school. I got to college, and my first assignment was in College Writing 101. The professor said, 'Write a paper on *Oedipus*.' And I was, 'What is that, like a book report?'"

Donna couldn't see herself at Harvard, and so it didn't happen. She was also recruited by a local coach from the University of Massachusetts Lowell (NCAA Division II). "I'd met her at softball camp my sophomore year in high school, and I just got to talking with her. She took a liking to me, and she recruited me my senior year, and that's how I ended up at Lowell. Also, it was a full scholarship."

The program that gave Donna the courage to attend college was Lowell's Equal Opportunities Program (EOP). EOP students were admitted on a trial basis and tutored so that they could succeed academically. The first semester was a struggle for Donna, but EOP saved both her college education and her athletic career. "I flunked out. My first semester I flunked out, but it didn't go against me further on academically after the first semester. I enrolled as an exercise physiology major. I tried, and that was what my interest was. But given my academic background, it was simply too hard. The cards were stacked way against me." Rather than actually flunking out of college, she was redshirted in softball, while her advisers worked to get her academics up to speed. They paired her with another student-athlete who was also in the EOP program but who had more academic experience. "I met a woman in the same program, Nora Baston. She was in the same boat I was, but she was a basketball player. She taught me how to study. When I wanted to go to bed, she woke me up and took me out of my dorm room and took me to a location where we could study all night for nights on end so that we passed."

After that first probationary year, Donna was allowed four full years of athletic eligibility to play softball. She graduated from UMass in 1996, a speedy five years after she entered, right on schedule for college athletes. Softball had enabled Donna to begin her adult life on solid footing, with a college degree and a happy college experience.

She has no regrets about playing softball and doesn't think she was forced into it, although she still prefers baseball. "It's a completely different game than baseball. It's apples and oranges. It's a complete different pace of the game. Softball is a much, much faster paced game. It's a different strategy, you know. It's different even from the coaching standpoint, the swing is different. Every position is totally different, especially hitting. I mean, hitting is so much closer. There is no rise ball in baseball, there is no ball that is going to come at you belt high and finish over your head. It's too bad that softball and baseball always get thrown into the same group. If you tell somebody you play on the U.S. women's baseball team they are like, 'Oh, you play with Jenny Finch?' 'No, it's hardball. I play baseball, smaller ball.' I've had this conversation with attorneys at the court who would ask about the World Cup, and I would tell them it's baseball, and we're going to play in Japan, and they'll say, 'Oh wow, that's awesome. Well, good luck with the softball.'"

In spite of her preference for baseball, she is glad to have avoided the difficulties she would have faced playing on the boys' team. "If through high school I had stuck it out and tried to play baseball, I think with those restrictions and boundaries I would have had a worse experience. But [switching to softball] happened naturally. There are some women out there who played high school baseball, and they had to deal with discrimination that I didn't have to."

Donna believes collegiate softball is the more difficult sport. "Softball is much harder. I mean, you've got balls coming at you from forty feet, forty-three feet, and some of the women are throwing sixty-five to sixty-seven miles an hour. That's the equivalent of a ninety-mile-an-hour baseball coming at you. But once you connect, it's an offensive game. All you have to do is connect, put your head down and connect, and if the pitcher is throwing sixty miles an hour, the balls are going to fly out of the park. As opposed to baseball, where you wait on a curve and then you've got some time to react. And you have so much more ground to cover in baseball. But I'm sure it's just a matter of time in baseball before women throw eighty, eighty-five, even ninety."

After graduating Lowell, Donna was invited to play professional softball on a team in Connecticut called the Raybestos Brakettes. But she declined, saying she was "burned out" with fast-pitch softball. Before long, however, she was looking for a way to play baseball again.

The return to baseball felt like coming home to something left behind, although there were some bumps on reentry. In 1999 in Boston, she was invited to join an all-women baseball team, the Boston Blue Sox, being organized to participate in an all-men's league. "They allowed us in to play, and it was just a horrible experience. A handful of guys on each team supported us and were like, 'Wow, this is great! I'm going to bring my daughter to this game. This is excellent!' And then there was another handful that would throw fastballs inside, would try to intentionally hit you, would try to take you out at second. Which is fine, it's part of the game, but over nothing: just because we're women. It's the ego thing. My opinion is that had we entered the league and they allowed us to separate and go to teams and play with men, it would have been the perfect experience, but we didn't get to do that. The Blue Sox wanted to enter the league as the 'exclusive' women's team in the men's league."

In 2001 she met Jim Glennie, who finally reunited her with her childhood game in a way that worked. Glennie was putting together a women's national baseball team to play in international tournaments. Three years later, this team acquired USA Baseball sponsorship and became Team USA, competing internationally under the auspices of the IBAF. Glennie's U.S. team played its first tournament in Toronto at the SkyDome, against Australia, Japan, and Canada. Not surprisingly, there were funding and organizational challenges in the first years of women's international baseball, along with jockeying for political power. "In 2002 Jim [Glennie] and another guy involved in forming the Women's National Team had a falling out, so Jim Glennie ran it on his own in 2002. It was down in Tampa, Florida. Australia, Canada, and Japan came over for it. It was disorganized, and we never received any funding. Jim gave us fliers to raise our own money." Glennie's American team came in third. "The team was just thrown together. We kind of felt that Jim Glennie was just trying to keep the ball rolling. He's always tried to keep it going, and he kind of has. We probably wouldn't be where we are if it wasn't for Jim Glennie. 2004 was the year that we officially were sponsored by USA Baseball. We finally got their backing, but what a price to pay."

The price women's baseball has paid, from Donna's perspective, is that while the women earned the symbolic honor of playing for USA Baseball, they lost control of their sport. USA Baseball, she believes, is not committed to the long-term project of developing a program that will sustain and promote the success of women's baseball in the United States. The organization's thinking is dominated by the short-term goal of recruiting a team to win a gold medal quickly. This creates a quandary: Where will the players come from if there is no effort made to develop them?

Donna was a member of the original USA Baseball Women's National Teams in 2004 and 2006. Those teams, coached first by Marty Scott and then Julie Croteau, won gold medals. They drew from an available pool of experienced women baseball players, both amateur and professional, that had already been brought together by Glennie. The women on the first USA teams were superstars of American women's baseball: former members of the Silver Bullets and women who had been playing baseball for years with men, coached by professionals. They included former professional players Bridget Veenema, Laura Purser, Kim Braatz, Tamara Holmes, Julie Croteau, and experienced amateurs Alex Sickenger, Kristen Mills, Keri Lemasters, Patti Raduenz, Sarah Gascon, and Judy O'Brien. "That team was loaded, and we won gold. We won the first ever World Cup. [In 2004] we went to Japan, and we played in the World Series, and then we came home and then went to Edmonton to play in the first Women's World Cup." Over the span of three weeks in 2004, the first U.S. women's national baseball team won a gold medal and a silver medal on two continents in two separate international tournaments.[6]

USA Baseball funded the team again in 2006, when the second Women's World Cup Tournament was held in Taipei, Taiwan. Julie Croteau, former Silver Bullet, first woman to play NCAA men's baseball, and first woman to coach an NCAA Division I men's baseball team, accepted USA Baseball's invitation to manage the Women's National Team. She invited retired members of the All-American Girls Professional Baseball League (AAGPBL, the real League of Their Own ballplayers), now women in their seventies and eighties, to be present at the tryouts and share their input with the coaches.[7] The team won gold again, and in Donna's opinion, it was the best organized and coached team in Team USA's short history. "2006 was my most relaxed World Cup or international experience that I ever had. There were no problems, no bickering, no off-field complaints. We just showed up and the tryout process was very fair. They held the tryouts; then they brought us to Arizona. The way they made the final cuts was very professional, and like I said, it was just relaxed. I think that was a huge factor in us winning in '06 too, other than luck."[8]

Croteau did not return to coach Team USA in 2008. Donna played again in 2008 at the World Cup tournament in Matsuyama, Japan, but she was becoming disenchanted with the leadership of Team USA and had other

FIG. 5. Donna Mills in action at third base, Team USA 2008 MVP. Courtesy of Donna Mills.

things on her mind. She decided to retire as a player. She was thirty-six, she had a stable income and a job she loved, and she wanted to have a child. Her daughter, Gianna Marie, born in 2010, eclipsed baseball as the love of Donna's life. Although the focus of Donna's life has changed with motherhood, she would still like to be involved with her sport as a coach.[9]

Donna was invited by USA Baseball to be one of eight coaches at the 2011 Friendship Series, a tournament held in August of that year at the National Training Complex in Cary. USA Baseball was using the tournament to decide on the coaches for the 2012 team and to evaluate thirty-six American women who were invited to participate in scrimmages with each other and in games against the visiting Team Canada. By the end of the tournament, it seemed as though USA Baseball had made a tactical decision to fill its 2012 squad with softball players and had chosen its coaches for their access to NCAA softball. Donna and Bridget Veenema were the only two women with extensive baseball experience in the group of coaches contending for a position with Team USA 2012. Neither was invited to be one of the four coaches on the 2012 team.[10]

USA Baseball was experimenting with the idea of taking a team made up primarily of Division I softball players to Edmonton, Alberta, for the 2012 Women's World Cup Tournament. To Donna, that decision demonstrated disrespect for the idea of a national women's *baseball* team and also for the women throughout the nation who had worked hard for years to excel at baseball rather than softball. Donna believes that the national women's baseball team merits an experienced baseball coach with elite-level baseball experience. She fears that coaches who are more interested in coaching boys and men are using the USA Baseball Women's National Team to build their résumés. "With all of the Division I baseball coaches that are out here, with all of them in the United States, Division I college, minor leagues, professional, retired, who are available, why are we getting what we're getting? Look at their baseball résumés. Look at their coaching and playing experience. I don't feel the coaches we're getting are truly acting in the best interest of women's baseball. We deserve quality coaches out there, who have already established their resumes."[11] She is saddened that softball and baseball expertise are regarded as indistinguishable for the Women's National Team and hastens to add that although she would like to be one of the assistant coaches, she doesn't think she is qualified at this point to manage the team: "I am not qualified to coach the USA Baseball Women's National team as a manager in the World Cup. I haven't been around the game of baseball long enough to manage a team that competes in the World Cup."[12]

Donna was outspoken about her belief that the coaches selected in 2012 were not the best qualified to coach the women's national baseball team, and she suspects that her outspokenness took her out of the running for an assistant coaching position. "Maybe I was too honest. It breaks my heart to sit here and have to be speaking of this stuff. [. . .]

"You know, you can only hang on and fight the battle for so long, and what's ignored is that we all share that love or else we wouldn't be playing. It's that love that drives you once you've reached the USA team and the quest for gold. It's what drives you every day to work out and to hit and to lift weights and to get yourself in shape for that level of play."

More recently, Donna has found refuge in women's slow-pitch softball, occasionally with tragicomic results. "It's been quite an adjustment, in terms of abilities. I remind myself before every game: 'This is not Team USA, and this is not the World Cup.' Three years ago, I had my first introduction to this league. It was my first game of the season. I was playing shortstop. In the third inning, there was a base hit to left field, and a runner on first who was trying to score on the hit. I was in shallow left field as the cutoff. I received the ball and turned and fired it home. The catcher put her glove up, and I guess she lost it in the lights or didn't get her glove up in time, and my throw hit her dead center in the forehead. The poor catcher paused and then went down. The ball bounced to first base. I've never seen anything like it. In my entire career, I've never hurt anybody like that! She had an egg out to here!! I was so sorry. As she was being taken away in the ambulance, the catcher said to me, 'Yeah, no problem. I'm okay. Oh, by the way, I'm a schoolteacher, and I'm just going to have to take tomorrow off.'

"I've made an adjustment. It's not about winning gold medals anymore. It's about being a mom now, taking it all in, and passing my knowledge on."

6

Jenny Dalton Hill

FIRST BASE

"Superman and Clark Kent."

Jenny Dalton Hill, the eldest child of Bruce and Patricia Dalton, was born in Glendale, California, on March 5, 1974.[1] She was a softball superstar at the University of Arizona from 1993 to 1996, and many of her national records still stand. She is the NCAA leader in RBIs; she was named as a first-team All-American three times (every year she played except her freshman year). Arizona won the NCAA Women's College World Series (WCWS) three out of the four years she attended.[2] In 1996, her senior season, Dalton won the Pac-10 Triple Crown for the highest batting average (.469), most home runs (25), and the most RBIs (109); she was the first player ever to do so. She was the NCAA's Most Valuable Player, made the first-team All-American, and was World Series MVP. Her number, 16, was retired at both the University of Arizona and at Glendale High School in Los Angeles, where she played high school softball.

Less than a month after Arizona won the WCWS in May 1996, Jenny married Marc Hill, whom she had met in the Arizona weight room while he was working there as a strength and conditioning coach. The couple was soon blessed with three children: Dalton, who is fourteen, Brookelyn, twelve, and Cogan, ten. The family now lives in Lexington, Kentucky, where Marc is associate athletics director at the University of Kentucky. Jenny is aware that her playing days are behind her and is still coming to terms with that loss. She grieves for the part of herself that was a star athlete.

Jenny Dalton Hill, raised Mormon, is a deeply religious woman who embraces the blessings of her beautiful family and loving husband. But her awareness of what she might have had is evident in her poignant remark, "If your name is Tim Tebow and you're at the top of your game, you get offered millions of dollars; if your name is Jenny Dalton and you're at the top of your game, you don't have that luxury." Her reference to Tebow is fitting: he is a devoutly Christian football star who finished a brilliant career as quarterback for the Florida Gators and became a highly paid starting quarterback in the National Football League (NFL) the following year. Jenny is a devout Mormon and star athlete who was raised to believe that "the right thing" for her was to have a career that allowed her to be a wife and eventually a mother. Her battle to embrace that part of her life, while relinquishing competitive athletics, is continuous and painful. She quickly recovers from her uncensored moment of jealousy about Tebow by remarking how blessed she is in her life.

The Hills' comfortable home is snug in a suburban neighborhood in the exquisite Kentucky bluegrass country. The drive from Louisville to Lexington winds through rolling pastures where the world's most celebrated horses live in equine heaven. The road passes stud farms and distilleries, the occasional roadside shop selling homemade candies, and fields where colts and fillies frolic in the spring morning. Life is good for both horses and people. The Hills' backyard is as green as the pastures, made even more idyllic because it is unfenced, shared with the neighboring yards. Children can visit each other as though they were an extended family and play any ballgame appropriate to the season in their shared yard. After school and softball practice, Jenny's twelve-year-old daughter, Brooke, crosses the yard to visit with a friend before beginning her homework. In front, three boys shoot hoops in the cul-de-sac, safe from traffic and visible to a half-dozen parents in their surrounding homes. Jenny loves the neighborhood, and remarks, "We've found Mayberry!" (She's referring to the quintessential mid-American small town of the 1950s portrayed on early television's *Andy Griffith Show*.)

FIG. 6. Jenny Dalton Hill, Team USA 2010. Courtesy of Brian Fleming.

Still, talking about the finality of her days playing ball at Arizona brings tears to her eyes, and she stops frequently to collect herself as she recounts her years of athletic glory. "I won the National Player of the Year for Softball and was the World Series MVP in 1996. After that championship game, I have never played another softball game in my life. I can't believe as I look back that I never put that big yellow ball in my glove again. It's hard to think about that."

Being both Jenny Dalton, the Arizona softball star, and Mrs. Hill, the suburban wife and mother, is "like being Superman and Clark Kent." Jenny Dalton was a famous and celebrated athlete. "Mrs. Hill" is like a secret identity; nobody knows who she "really" is. Jenny struggles to reconcile the two equally important parts of herself. She believes that all women who play sports at the highest levels face a form of the conflict. When your athletic career is over, "you go into a dark place in your soul, and you bear deep scars. You don't have to be female to experience that loss. Every athlete, whether pro or amateur, gets to a point where the lights go out and you don't get to take the field anymore. Coming to terms with life without your sport is where you really learn to find out who you are."

Baseball came into Jenny's life as a coda to her softball career. She was offered a contract with the newly formed professional softball league in the United States after she had graduated from Arizona, but the salary was too small to live on, and she would have lost her amateur status if she had played professionally, ending her hope of playing softball for the U.S. national team. So she turned to baseball, accepting an invitation to try out for the Silver Bullets professional women's baseball team, although she had never before played the game. "I played baseball as my secondary sport because it was a place I could go to feel alive. The Colorado Silver Bullets opportunity came along during a time when I still wanted to play ball, and it gave me a chance to use my skills in a new way. Baseball gave me a chance to be me, only reinvented. Years down the road, USA Baseball came along and was almost like a rising phoenix that allowed me to feel reborn and renewed and find a way to heal."

Jenny never even thought of baseball when she was a girl, although her father had been a college baseball player. But it was clear from early childhood that she was a natural athlete. "It was very obvious from the beginning. I didn't like to sit still, and anything that had to do with a ball, I was playing with it, throwing it, hitting it. We lived in a little townhouse in Glendale, California, and my mom and dad couldn't contain me. They finally bought me a Nerf tennis racquet and ball so I could hit it against the fireplace. I'd move the couches out of the way and count how many I could hit in a row over and over and over again."

While both parents were willing to move furniture to give their daughter room to play ball in the house, five days a week of that was enough to prompt her father to give his wife a break on Saturdays and take his daughter to the basketball gym at his school while he caught up on his office work. "I was probably seven or eight. My dad was the athletic director at the high school, and Saturday mornings Mom would need a break from me because she had me all week, and he'd take me down to the high school and lock me in the gym, and I would shoot baskets and kick balls and throw balls, and I was all by myself, but that's what brought me joy. He would say, 'Come get me if you need me.' I knew where his office was, it was just down the hall, and I'd go in and play ball. I mean, every ball imaginable was in there, plus birdies for badminton. So volleyball, basketball, softball, racquetball, anything I wanted was in there."

She was a solitary girl with a lot of athletic equipment at her disposal. "I don't want to say it was a lonely childhood, but it was a solitary childhood because my brothers and sisters weren't really old enough to play with, and Mom and Dad were busy. So they gave me this environment that allowed me to just be who I was. I found joy in being active."

Bruce Dalton had a family of six to support on a teacher's salary. To supplement his modest income, he ran sports camps during the summers, and Jenny was a regular camper. She was seven years old the first summer she attended and quickly put her father in an awkward position. Each weeklong session ended with a competition on Friday, with prizes and trophies given to the winners of contests in the various skills tests. Bruce had placed Jenny with the seven-year-old girls the first summer, and she won every competition all summer long. "I won it every week. I wasn't paying, and I was getting the trophies and all the accolades, and my dad thought, 'This doesn't look right. My kid's winning, and that's not how it should be.'" The next summer, he put her in with older girls, and she still won. He tried putting her with boys her age and then boys a year older. No good: she kept winning. Finally, her father made a decision: even though her scores were the best, he was going to give the prizes to other kids in the camp. Thinking about those summer camps, Jenny muses, "He didn't know it at the time, but he was fostering this competitive spirit in me that it didn't matter if you were a girl or a boy, I was going to win. I was going to give everything I had to make more baskets than you, swim the farthest, run the fastest, throw more balls in the hole. I was going to beat you."

When she was nine, she signed up for softball because "it was just the next sport on the list." All the girls in town that she knew played softball, so it seemed a natural fit. She began playing on softball city teams and soon was a Little League Softball All-Star. In 1989, when she was fifteen, her team went to Kalamazoo, Michigan, to the Little League Softball World Series. There she hit the first out-of-the-park home run in Little League Softball World Series history. She realized she might have future in the sport, but it was not the only sport she played. In high school she starred in softball but also played volleyball, basketball, and badminton and learned to shot put. She believes that children today should not overspecialize in one sport at too early an age and that the range of sports she played when she was young enabled her to become "an athlete, not just a softball player."

At fifteen she still wasn't thinking about a college scholarship. Although her father was immersed in high school athletics, Jenny wasn't groomed to be a collegiate athlete. From her perspective, she simply followed softball to higher and higher levels, buoyed by her talent and athleticism. "You ride the current. It takes you on a path, and you're simply trying to stick your rudder in and guide where you're trying to go. All of us can step off the boat at any time and go any direction we want, but we like the way it feels on the ride."

In her younger years, she never had private lessons. "My dad was a schoolteacher and my mom was a stay-at-home mom, so we didn't have money to spend on lessons and travel squads, and I didn't even know anything about it." Jenny played on a local softball team and one day accompanied two of her teammates to their private batting lessons. She watched both lessons, and finally, the coach asked her if she wanted to hit a few. She showed so much talent that the coach called her at home that night to ask her to join a travel team that was going to Nationals. Her dad gave his approval, and "it ended up that I was sixteen and this was a Women's Open team, which means nineteen and above. The people on this team were Michelle Granger from the University of California, Berkeley and Yvonne Gutierrez, the national home run leader from UCLA. These were big names in college softball, and I didn't even know who they were. I didn't even know what Women's Open was, and they took me with them to play on their team."

That tournament was life changing for Jenny. "While I was with that team, there was a girl who was playing at Arizona also on the team, and we were just taking Wiffle ball practice before one of the games, and I was shagging with her. After I hit Wiffles, I was standing by Suzy [the Arizona player], and she said, 'You know you have a beautiful swing. My coach would love it.' I said, 'Who's your coach?' She said, 'My coach is Mike Candrea. I play at Arizona.' That was enough to leave an impression, and I wanted to know more about who this coach was." Jenny was four years younger than most of her teammates that summer, but word got around about her ability, and she was invited to play on a travel team called the California Panthers. Meanwhile, she was also playing softball at Glendale High. The team played at a local park. When the school board finally did build a softball field at the school in 2005, it was named Dalton Field in her honor, and her number, 16, was retired.

Arizona recruited Jenny and so did some of the best Division I teams in the nation—certainly the best in the West, which was where she wanted to be. She was also recruited in volleyball and basketball, but she was a relative innocent about college sports. "I got [recruiting] letters for basketball first and then some for volleyball, and then the softball ones started. I had letters from three sports and from different schools. I remember laying out a basketball letter, a volleyball letter, and a softball letter. I did pros and cons. Like, 'All right, you run a lot in basketball. That is not as fun. Volleyball, that's a lot of fun. But I haven't played club volleyball, and there's a lot of things that I don't understand.' I didn't like that feeling because I didn't want to just go play ball; I wanted to win. That was more fun than just playing. To me, you play to win, you don't just play. So then I looked at softball. I was just riding the wave. The wind blew, and I set my sail. That's all it was. I mean, God had a path, and I didn't realize how blessed I really was. I never made a recruiting video. I never sent out a letter of interest. They all came to me. I felt important. I never had to try to sell myself."

She chose softball because "I thought, 'Well, I'm already kind of plugged in there. I know that one pretty well.'" But when asked if she really likes the game of softball the best, Jenny responds, "I just liked being me, and as I looked at the opportunities, I realized that was going to allow me to be me easiest." When urged to describe who that "me" was, Dalton responds, "You know, I think you reinvent yourself. I think you reinvent at the different stages of your life. At that point . . . who was me? I know I loved the attention. I know I ate up the success, and it bothered me when I wasn't good, and I would work to be the best."

She continues, "So I got recruited by my top choices. I grew up Mormon, so my mom and dad pushed for Utah. It was not where I wanted to go, but I felt I should give it a chance. I took recruiting trips to the University of Utah, Utah State, UCLA, and U of A. I took my trips to University of Utah and Utah State, and it was so stinkin' cold, I thought, 'I will never, ever go here,' because it hurts hitting on a cold day." She was too much a Southern California girl for Utah: "I can't imagine hitting on a snowy day, and so that was what did it for me. It wasn't the culture, it wasn't the people, it was the weather. I went home and said, 'Not going there.'"

She focused on UCLA and the University of Arizona, the two national softball powerhouses, both in warmer climes. UCLA had won the national championship in 1990, and Arizona had won it in 1991. UCLA was half an hour from Jenny's home in Glendale, so it seemed like a natural fit. But neither the coach's visit to her home nor her campus visit to UCLA felt right. "When [Arizona] Coach Candrea, came to my home and started his presentation, I knew. I just knew. As he gave his presentation, it felt like home."

It took a while for Jenny to actually feel at home once she arrived at

Arizona. She was a shortstop, and the team already had a shortstop, Laura Espinoza, who was only one year older than Jenny. Both Espinoza and Dalton were power hitters. "Well, I was the kid coming in, and she was the big hitter shortstop already there. In my first college at bat, I hit a grand slam in our brand-new facility. But that was her job, in her eyes. So from our first game I was stealing her thunder, and I knew that, and I was never trying to compete against her. She was my teammate. But it caused some tension, and she and I are both very different athletes."

The coach resolved the problem by moving Jenny to second base. But there was another first-year second baseman, and the two of them competed for the starting position. Even as competitors, the two remained close friends, but after so many years at shortstop, it was disconcerting for Jenny to have to switch her perspective to the right side of the diamond. "My body fought against it. There are two sides to the field. From this side [left side, or shortstop side], you move through everything and throw hard. Here, at second base, you still charge but not as aggressively, and you have to have touch because your throw is so short. I was pure grit and muscle from the left side. From the right side, it requires finesse. It's almost a ballet dance over there, where at shortstop, you're the football linebacker."

The pressure to learn a new position and wrest the starting spot away from another freshman was intense. "I had changed positions, and I was learning everything, and I was watching her and feeling inadequate, and I'd never felt inadequate. So I'm battling it personally, I'm battling it physically, and then I have this outfield behind me who's two years out of a national championship who just lost the championship a year ago, screaming at me: 'Get to your spot!'

"There was one day in practice, we were doing cutoffs and relays, and I went to the wrong spot again, and an outfielder yelled, 'How many times do we have to do this? Get it right!' But I'd taken it and taken it, and I finally turned around and said, 'Don't you think I'd be where I was supposed to be if I knew how to be there?' But she was a senior, and I was a freshman, and I knew you don't talk back to seniors. It was a tough moment realizing I was the reason we were doing it over and over again."

The center fielder called her out after practice, but Jenny held her ground.

Although Jenny would go on to dominate at Arizona, she had many challenges to overcome and personalities to learn to accommodate. "I was so different than everybody else. Usually, Sunday games started at one o'clock, so we had to be there about eleven. I went to church on Sunday mornings. I would wear my dress and heels and then pack a bag with my uniform and just change at the field. There was one day when I got there, and I was walking behind the outfield fence coming from church. One of the outfielders said to me, 'Did God tell you you're going to hit a home run today?' I said, 'You know what? He did.' I didn't think about it until after the game, but I did hit a home run that day, and she never said another word. I shouldn't have been so cocky, but I was grateful I didn't have to put up with the teasing anymore."

Arizona won the national championship three out of the four years that Dalton played there. Jenny Dalton's senior year at Arizona was 1996. Her teammates of the previous three years had graduated, and she was alone with talented but inexperienced younger players. The team struggled all year, which was not how Jenny had envisioned her final year at Arizona. "We had lost our assistant coach, our shortstop, our first baseman, our center fielder, and our catcher, and we had young pitchers, a new infield, and we were rough. I was mad. I thought, 'This is my senior year! What the heck? Where is everyone?' It felt empty because everybody was gone and playing out of normal position."

She was so disappointed and frustrated that she considered quitting and told her future husband, Marc, that she didn't think she could take it. "I went to him, and I said, 'I can't do this. I can't play on this team.' We went to our first tournament of the year, and we were losing. I mean, we're talking regular season games, and we're losing. That doesn't happen [at Arizona]. We don't lose. That's not an option, and this year we're losing. We look like jungle ball in comparison to the years before, and I'm devastated. I think, 'This is not how it ends! This is not how this picture ends! This is not what I fought my whole career for!' I missed the cut to the '96 Olympics in the fall of 1995. When I didn't make it, it was devastating, but I accepted it because why fight it? That's just how it was going to be. I'm done. And I'm getting married. It's time to grow up and move on."

Jenny felt she was at a crossroads during her senior year at Arizona. She was preoccupied with the end of her softball career and wanted to finish on a victorious note. She decided not to quit and instead grew into the role of team leader. She tried to infuse her younger teammates with the work ethic she regarded as necessary to win. She put together a stellar season for herself and pulled the young team along with her. Beyond her personal record-setting stats, she led Arizona to the NCAA Division I Championship and hit the home run that would prove pivotal as the game came to a close. But she was bereft that her athletic career was over. "So that's my last softball game ever, ever. I've never played again. I was named World Series MVP and National Player of the Year and won the Triple Crown, Pac-10 Medal of Honor, like all these awards that you aspire to. So the World Series was May 30, and on June 21, I became Jennifer Hill, and everything changed."

Jenny and Marc married three weeks after Jenny's senior season and stayed at Arizona for a year. She finished her degree in elementary education, and he worked as an assistant strength and conditioning coach. Jenny was student teaching but bristling at being addressed as "Mrs. Hill" by her students. "Mrs. Hill" just wasn't her. "It doesn't feel right because it's not me. I was still in Arizona. But that's not who I am. All my teacher stuff says Mrs. Hill. I can't even sign my name correctly. I'd signed my autograph on hats, balls, shirts, cups. I even signed my autograph on my shoes and gave them away at the World Series. That's my name, Jenny Dalton. And all of a sudden I'm writing 'Mrs. Hill' on everything, and it was this alter ego. There is no Superman anymore. You just had to stop. The season ends, you walk off, you get all the medals, and then . . ."

But she believes she was doing what God meant for her to do when she got married and started a family. "To me, that's how I was raised. You get married, you get a job, you move on. Like life has a course and a path you follow. I thought you [were supposed to] pick a path at the fork in the road, and whether you chose athletics or chose a family, you had to pick." She headed off down the road she thought she was supposed to take and tried to make peace with her life without athletics.

Within a year she had an opportunity to play ball again. The Silver

Bullets women's professional baseball team called Coach Candrea at Arizona to ask if Jenny might be interested in trying out. Coach Candrea didn't think she would. He knew that she was committed to the traditional path of marriage and family. But Jenny wasn't so sure. She thought, "Huh. Let's try." Her father was against it but not because it would mean leaving her new husband for the summer. As a Mormon, he didn't want her playing for a team that was sponsored by a beer company. He knew the women would have to make appearances in which they were representing Coors and trying to sell beer. "He's a perfectionist. To me, he demanded perfection without ever saying it, and the appearance of anything not good should be completely avoided. This team was sponsored by Coors Light, and I don't drink. To him that was endorsing something we didn't believe in, and so he was very upset by me choosing to play."

Trying out for the Silver Bullets was part rebellion against her father and part desperation to regain her athletic self. She had never played baseball, and here she was, trying out for the only professional women's baseball team in the United States. Marc encouraged the idea and was willing to throw her batting practice and work out with her to get her ready. Jenny found that she could hit a baseball just as well as a softball, but fielding presented a challenge. "The baseball was little. It was so teeny tiny, and I couldn't figure out how to hold it. In softball I grip it with everything [her whole hand]. So I picked up a baseball the same way then, and it didn't make sense. It didn't feel right. I could hit it. Hitting it was fun. It went a long ways, and that was really fun. But I couldn't grip it or throw it."

Her strong arm as a softball middle infielder didn't translate into a strong arm in baseball because she hadn't figured out how to grip the ball. "I couldn't hit the target! I had no clue. No clue." The Bullets moved her to first base, where throwing is less important than catching. Before that they had tried her at third base and hit groundballs to her. Her task was to make the throw to first base. "Everything was different. With softball bases being only sixty feet away, you can't take time to shuffle when you've received a ground ball. You field and release immediately. In baseball, you have so much longer to shuffle, get your feet under you, and let the ball get there."

Even more significantly, Jenny was stymied by baseball's mental and strategic aspects. Baseball required that she think for herself on the field, and since she knew little about the game, she did not know what to think. "The culture of baseball is different than the culture of softball because the culture of baseball is get them on, move them over, move them around, score or get them in. In softball Coach had the luxury of allowing the big hitters to swing away all the time. There was no thinking. There was no strategizing. There was no planning. It was just, 'Hit.' [. . .]

"The thing I hated about baseball was there was so much time to think. I was raised not to think because my job was to see the number [on the jersey] and beat the player, not come in and think about what he's thinking about. That messed with me to the point that I'm like, 'Take it all away. Just tell me what to do, and I will do it. Don't make me try to figure out what she's going to do.' Coach Candrea had learned early on that I did better if I didn't think and just allowed my ability to take over. He called it playing 'unconscious and competent,' but at this point in my baseball career, there was simply too much I needed to learn, and I didn't have the correct instincts yet. The Bullets coaches would say, 'Watch the spin.' Well, as soon as I watched the spin, I was analyzing that more than I was worrying about my timing. I just wanted to hit the ball. The learning curve to go from softball to baseball was a comedic process. My tryout had to have been comedic relief for the coach. He hits a ground ball, and I field it, and I let it go. He says, 'Slow down.' I'm thinking, 'Slow down? How do you slow down?' I don't know how to slow down. I don't know what that means. So I field it, and I let it go slower. He says, 'Slow down!' But the problem is we have two different worlds. So I have to say, 'What do you mean?' He says, 'Shuffle through.' Okay, that I understand. So I field it, and I shuffle once, then I throw.

"He says, 'More shuffles.'

"I say, 'Okay.' But in my mind, I'm thinking, 'Is he crazy? The runner is going to be there.'"

The batting part of the tryout was equally mystifying.

"We went to the cage, and he said, 'Hit opposite field.'

"'Okay.'

"'Hit up the middle.'

"'Okay.'

"'Pull it.'

"'Okay.'

"'Deep drive.'

"'Okay.' Those words made sense.

"But then he said, 'You've got a runner on. Move her over.'

"And I hit it, but I hit a line drive back up the middle. To me, I think, 'Awesome. That's my job.'

"He said, 'No, go the other way.'

"'Why? What do you mean, move her?' It didn't make sense. I didn't understand the terminology. It was like I was learning Japanese with no translator."

She made the Silver Bullets squad because her hitting was outstanding and the coaches were willing to work around the learning curve for her fielding. Still, it was not a happy season for her. She was playing Minor League ball, which is a rough world whether you're male or female. She was separated from Marc and her family in Southern California and traveling around the country on a barnstorming women's baseball team. They were a professional team and were expected to attract enough spectators to be profitable. They played night games against men's teams, so working people could attend the games. "It was a schedule of wake up at noon, go to the park at three, get home from the park at one or two in the morning and sleep till noon. That was not my culture. It was difficult. [. . .] I think I saw Marc two times that summer in four months. I told him, 'Don't ever let me do this again, never, ever, ever, ever.' But it wasn't because of the baseball. This was not the lifestyle I wanted to have. I knew that I was going to have to leave behind this game too."

She returned home to Marc after that summer season, even more uncertain about who she was. The couple was blessed with their first son in July of the following year. Marc accepted a position as the head strength and conditioning coach at the University of Kentucky in early 1999, and they moved to Lexington. Jenny was hired as an assistant coach with the University of Kentucky softball team but still struggled with the loss of competitive athletics. "It's like this lost love that there's no closer to. Where you don't say good-bye, you just leave. So I lost myself. But there is Superman in there somewhere. Superman is underneath all this and can't figure out where to go."

This was her life for more than a decade. Then, in 2010, she reconnected with her Silver Bullets teammate Kim Braatz, sister of her Arizona teammate Leah Braatz.[3] Kim invited Jenny to USA Baseball tryouts that summer. She was selected for the team, along with her former Arizona teammate, Laura Espinoza-Watson. In Venezuela they both shared the spot at first base, much as they had both played middle infield at Arizona more than fifteen years earlier. Jenny Dalton Hill was invited back to help coach the 2012 U.S. women's national baseball team. USA Baseball is enthusiastic about her ability be a liaison with softball. She has the cache of a celebrity and vast athletic experience. She can "speak softball" to the Division I softball players that USA Baseball is hoping to recruit and train. Jenny has found some peace bridging the gap between the worlds of softball and baseball.

PART 3

Softball and
Baseball Players

7

Tara Harbert

"They made softball for girls, and they're told what to do."

"The only time I'd ever touched a baseball is throwing in the backyard with my dad. I never touched a baseball to play until 2008, when I tried out for Team USA. But some of my first memories were sitting on my dad's lap and watching baseball on the TV. I grew up in Colorado, and we didn't have a baseball team until the Rockies came in '93. So I just remember my dad on Sunday afternoons watching baseball and sitting on his lap when I was four or five, just watching my dad and how much he loved the game and the passion he had for it. My dad is definitely the reason why I fell in love with the game. He would get me ready for school in the morning, and we would stand outside and wait for the bus, starting from when I was in kindergarten. And we would throw a baseball before the bus came."[1]

Tara is the fleet-footed, graceful center fielder on Team USA. She is the youngest of three sisters: Tanya is ten years older than Tara, and Tammy, seven years older. That age difference gave Tara plenty of time alone with her parents, Joanne and Roger. She was her daddy's girl: "My dad always called me the miracle child because I was born during the World Series, October 18, 1983." Roger Harbert was born in Australia, the son of a Colorado-born American serviceman stationed in the South Pacific during World War II. The soldier, Keith Harbert, fell in love with a girl he met, Doris Webb, and after his tour of duty, he married her and stayed in Australia to raise a family. Their son, Roger, grew up in Australia and played baseball from the time he was young. He played in the Australian professional league in the 1960s and still loves to regale his family, and especially his baseball-playing daughter Tara, with his stories.

After a stint as a pro ballplayer, Roger moved to the United States to attend college at Colorado State University (CSU). His father's ten siblings still lived in Colorado and made Roger feel at home so far from his parents. He earned a degree in veterinary medicine and married Joanne Perry, who was also a student at CSU. The couple settled down in the small town of Niwot, Colorado, just outside of Boulder, where Roger started his veterinary practice. All three of their daughters are athletes. Tanya was a gymnast who attended Denver University on a gymnastics scholarship; Tammy was a standout softball player throughout high school. Tara also excelled at gymnastics, but when people began comparing her to Tanya, she shifted her attention to softball. Seeking her own spotlight, and not that of either of her sisters, she avoided playing softball in the same league Tammy had.

Roger's first impulse for Tara was to try to sign her up for Little League when she was old enough. The two of them had a special bond and a shared love of baseball. But his attempt to give his daughter the opportunity to play the game he loved was quickly squelched. Their small-town league wouldn't allow it. Tara recalls, "I remember him trying to get me into Little League Baseball, and where I lived, they said girls were not allowed to play with boys. That was why they invented softball, they said. My dad tried to fight it, but he also didn't want to be 'that dad,' and he didn't want me to be 'that girl,' and so I guess he was protecting me a little. It wasn't like, 'Yes, sign her up!' and then you're the only one with all boys. He signed me up for softball instead."

Tara doesn't regret it and, in fact, is thankful that her father saved her from the pressure and discomfort of being "the only girl." Softball worked for her. "In a way, I thank him for that because the path that I did take was amazing. I wouldn't change it for anything." She loved it from the start because she was a natural at it and was always the best girl on the team. She believes she would have loved baseball just as much if she had played

FIG. 7. Tara Harbert, Colorado softball girl, age seven. Courtesy of Tara Harbert.

it from the start, and right now in her life, she prefers baseball to softball. "It's kind of fortunate that I didn't start out playing baseball because I would probably never have found that love for softball because . . . well . . . I know I would have loved baseball more. So it's almost a blessing that I never tasted baseball at that early age." Softball was the path that was open to her, and she embraced it. "I loved it because I was the star. I was the best one, so of course I loved it. My parents also put me in basketball, and I took dance lessons, and I remember I loved dancing. I remember trying soccer one year, and I went to kick the ball and missed it, and everyone laughed, so I never played soccer again." So softball it was. She was always the fastest on her team, played middle infield throughout her young playing years, was the shortstop at Niwot High, and then became a center fielder at the University of Hawai'i, where she played for most of her Division I NCAA career.

Since her two older sisters had successfully navigated high school and college sports, Tara's family had a store of experience from which to launch their youngest child on her path to the NCAA. She played competitive softball at the highest A-Ball level in her region for ten years, beginning when she made the ten and under team as an eight-year-old. She advanced to twelve, fourteen, and finally eighteen and under. At that stage Tara's A-Ball team qualified for the national elite league. The Colorado Stars, coached by Dan Burns, played at the most competitive level in the nation, the American Softball Association Gold League. "They have A-Ball, and then, when you get to eighteen under, they have what they call a Gold League. They're all tryout leagues. My dad, if he was going to have me do something, I was going to do it right. It was going to be competitive because high school softball isn't very competitive. Summer ball is where you get noticed and get scholarships." Roger found the leagues, but he was working full-time at his veterinary practice, so Joanne did the driving. "She drove me to practice every day and all summer long to these tournaments that were never local. I mean, we had one tournament in Boulder, which was ten minutes from us, but everywhere else was an hour to three hours, plus the tournaments that were out of state. She was there every single game, every single trip."

Tara would leave school early every Friday, or take off Fridays entirely, to travel to weekend tournaments that were often played until Monday. She made a serious commitment to her sport: she was playing for a college scholarship, and she knew it from a very early age. "That was why we played travel ball. That was why we went to out-of-state tournaments and put so much money into travel, and that was why I was doing it, was to get a scholarship one day. I mean, that wasn't the only reason I loved it, but I wanted to get to that next level and play."

Tara's efforts to attract the attention of college coaches shifted into high gear the summer before her junior year. The two coaches of the Colorado Stars, Dan Burns and Chuck Pringle, made videos of all their players. Tara's oldest sister, Tanya, joined her effort and accepted a job working for a company that sent out videos and résumés for athletes to every college in the country. Tara was not a wealthy kid whose family had thousands of dollars to spend each year on development in her sport. The whole family worked to advance her athletic career. "It was actually my sister, Tanya—my dad honestly had no idea about recruiting—it was Tanya who was working for this company and knew about it. I mean, she sent my résumé to every single school in the country. She had gone through the whole thing herself. But even though Tanya went through it in high school, my dad was never really a part of the recruiting process because he was so busy working. He just really didn't have the time. Someone had to pay for it, and my mom worked really hard too."

In spite of all the support, Tara did not receive the attention of Division I recruiters the family had hoped for. "I was approached by Division I schools during my junior year but never offered an official recruiting trip. I got a few Division II visits—Azuza Pacific and Towson University in Maryland." But she didn't accept the offers to visit either school. "At that point in my life, unfortunately, I was dating the wrong person, and it was leading me into a different area. And I also did not want to play Division II. I knew I was good enough to play Division I, and that's what I was going to do."

The boy she had been dating throughout high school didn't want Tara to pursue her athletic career and almost derailed it. Luckily, over the

Christmas holidays of 2001, Tara's senior year, the Harberts took a family vacation to Australia to visit grandparents Keith and Doris. On their way back to Colorado, they stopped in Honolulu to visit Pearl Harbor and honor the sixtieth anniversary of the bombing. Pearl Harbor loomed large in Harbert family history: it had marked the beginning of the war that had brought Tara's grandfather to the South Pacific and Australia. On that family pilgrimage during the winter of 2001, away from the influence of her controlling boyfriend, Tara fell in love with Hawai'i and its university. "We were actually at Pearl Harbor, and I remember telling my dad, 'This is where I'm going to play softball. This is where I'm going to go to school.'" She finally had a clear vision of what she wanted: a Division I softball program in paradise.

"That day, my dad said, 'Okay, we'll call the coach and set up a meeting,' and that's what we did. I called and went in and talked to Coach Coolen [Bob Coolen, Hawai'i head softball coach] and Coach Dee [Diedre Wiesneski, Hawai'i assistant softball coach]. And they were interested, and they took my video. We stayed in contact, and they didn't have any more scholarships to offer, but they offered me a preferred walk-on, which is where you don't get money as a scholarship, but you're on the team. You still have to try out, but you're not just a walk-on, and I feel that that's what made me the best player I could be. I didn't have a scholarship. I had to prove everything. I had to earn everything, and it was hard. I started at the bottom, and Coach Coolen made me the best player. He was the hardest coach I ever had but also the best coach I ever had because he pushed me, and he rewarded me for my success. My junior year, he gave me a full-ride scholarship."

But before that happened, the family returned to Colorado from their transpacific holiday journey. Tara's boyfriend hoped she would marry him. The two had been together for three years, since she was a fourteen-year-old high school freshman and he was a seventeen-year-old senior. He joined the navy when he graduated high school and did not want Tara to go away to college or pursue softball. He was persistent. She married him the week after she graduated high school and quickly realized it was a mistake. She had an offer to play softball at Hawai'i in hand, and he was pressuring her to turn it down. Luckily, she came to her senses in time. "I was very young, and he was in the navy, and I thought maybe I shouldn't go to Hawai'i after all. He came back after being gone for two weeks, and we were married, and he turned out to be a really, really . . . just a mean guy, and I was done with him and just wanted to leave, so I still went to Hawai'i. I'm very glad that I didn't stay with him. But it couldn't be annulled because I waited too long to file, and then it actually ended up taking almost two years to divorce him because he wouldn't sign the papers."

Tara thrived at Hawai'i. "I loved the girls. I loved it. I was lucky because there were a lot of local girls, and it's hard to go to Hawai'i on your own and not know anyone. It's just such a different culture. It is very spiritual, and it was nice to get to know the locals because I learned a lot about Hawai'i and its history. They celebrate their culture there. I think it was probably about 60 percent local, and the rest were mainlanders. I was lucky to be with the local girls. They embraced me and took me into their families, and once you're in, you're in. It was one of the most amazing times of my life."

While her teammates were embracing her, the coaches were giving her tough love. "Those first two years, Coach Coolen was really hard on me because I was a walk-on and I had to prove that I deserved to be on the team, and it was every single at bat, every single play, I was proving myself. He really made me into a competitive player because he never ever let up on me. My freshman year, I pretty much only pinch-ran, and then my sophomore year, I did a lot of pinch running, but then I did get some starting time at second base. And then they made me more of an outfielder."

Coach Coolen was honing Tara's fielding and running skills, while Coach John Nakamura worked on her batting skills, teaching her the art of strict slap hitting. "He was a slapping specialist, and he taught me power slapping, and I could actually hit home runs slapping. But that's where I got into that groove of moving my feet and being so, you know, hands oriented, rather than legs and hips." This is specialty softball hitting, and it is unlike anything in baseball. Indeed, a baseball swing requires nearly the opposite skills. Slap hitting in softball is running up on a pitch, using the momentum of that run-up and power in the wrists and hands to place the ball. A baseball swing requires the batter to keep her weight back and her back foot planted until she swings, generating power with her hips and legs. Little League Baseball coaches tell their youngsters to pretend they're squashing a bug with their back foot as they pivot firmly into the ground.

Coach Coolen moved Tara from second base to center field during her sophomore year because of her speed and because she was a natural at reading a fly ball off the bat. Then, at the end of her sophomore year, he offered her the ultimate reward for her hard work. "Our last tournament of the year we were on the road. We were playing Stanford, and he offered me a scholarship. It was amazing. That was one of the best feelings I've ever had because I knew I had earned that." Tara responded to the coach's faith in her during her junior year by playing with the confidence that comes from knowing your coach supports you. "My junior year was the best season I have ever played. I mean, I just came out. I hit, on the year, .423, and in conference it was .486, and I was a power slapper, as well as soft slapping and bunting, and so it was cool. I was in center field, and I got All-Conference, NFCA [National Fastpitch Coaches Association] All-West Region, and then Thirteen East, and All-American, which was really cool for me."[2] This was the year that vindicated more than a decade of effort Tara had poured into making herself an elite softball player. She was recognized as the dominant Division I athlete that she knew all along she could be. She was in a supportive environment with her coaches and teammates and was playing at the top of her game.

Tara did not return for her senior year at Hawai'i. The decision was difficult to make, and she now refers to it as "one of my biggest regrets." But she had had an upsetting experience with some friends the previous spring at Hawaii, and after having spent the summer at home in Colorado, she decided to stay there to finish college. Her decision baffled her coaches and teammates, but she kept her reasons to herself, seeking the emotional comfort of attending CSU, the school her parents had attended. She began studying veterinary medicine, like her father.

"When the coaches at Colorado State found out that I was coming there, they were excited. At first Coach Coolen was reluctant to give me a release. But the week before school started, he finally gave me a full

release, so Colorado State gave me a scholarship immediately, a full ride."
She was set to play center field at Colorado State when the regular second
basewoman left the team. Tara was the only outfielder on the team who
could also play infield, and she started at second all year. She would have
preferred to play center field but was happy to have landed on her feet
after her difficulty at Hawai'i. "I made All-Conference team because I hit
really well and my on-base percentage is always good. I ended up stealing twenty-eight of twenty-nine bases. I was top five in the nation at the
Division I level for a lot of the year, but that's what I do." She was naturally
fast, even in high school, but at Hawai'i she had been under the tutelage
of strength and speed coach Chris Kidawski, and "with his combination
of workouts and running, he made me so much faster."

Her dominance in base stealing tapered off a little toward the end of
the season, as the team faltered and the coach was more reluctant to send
her. "I kind of tailed off toward the end because we were not doing well
and all of a sudden my coach was scared to ever let me run, and in softball you do what you're told. You don't steal unless your coach gives you
the steal sign. In baseball some people are given the green light, and you
can go when you feel like it. In baseball, if the coach gives you the steal,
if you don't feel like you've got a good jump, you don't go. In softball, if
you don't go, you're in trouble."

In the summer of 2006, after her final year of softball at CSU, she was
recruited to play softball by Team Parma (Italy) in the European Professional Softball League. In the fall she returned to CSU to finish up her
remaining courses and earn her degree. When she graduated two years
later in 2008, "some people" she knew urged her to try out for the USA
Baseball Women's National Team. The people were none other than two
members of the Colorado Rockies organization with whom she was friends:
Walt Weiss and Mark Strittmatter, former Major Leaguers who were now
coaching the Rockies. Weiss and Strittmatter had become aware of the
Silver Bullets, and later Team USA, from a former teammate whose wife,
Kim Braatz, had played on the Bullets. Walt Weiss had been a first-round
draft pick in 1985 for the Oakland Athletics, Rookie of the Year in 1989, and
a star on the A's, Rockies, and Braves for fourteen years of Major League

ball. Now he was living in Colorado and coaching for the Rockies. He urged Tara to try out for Team USA, taught her baseball skills, and coached her in preparation for the 2008 tryouts. Once she began playing, she realized that she loved the mental aspects of baseball. "I think if I had started out playing baseball, Little League, I wouldn't have wanted to go to softball."

Baseball required major technical adjustments for Tara, especially in hitting, but she embraced the challenge. In spite of her Major League coach, Tara didn't have enough time to learn the intricacies of baseball before the 2008 Team USA tryouts. "I had only been playing since 2008, and I came in like a deer caught in the headlights. The only reason why I made the team is because of my speed and my defense. I couldn't hit. It was so different. It was an adjustment to the diamond because it was so much bigger. In softball [the pitcher is] twenty feet closer, and [the ball is] coming so fast. So you don't think. You just react. In baseball, especially with girls pitching, you have to sit there and wait and think, and you're like, 'Is it ever going to get here?' That was what was hard. I was so used to seeing a rise ball because in college softball it's mostly a rise. In baseball, the curve ball just froze me. I didn't even know what to do. In softball a curve ball actually curves. It doesn't drop. A baseball curve ball actually drops. It just goes twelve-six."

As a slap hitter at Hawai'i, she had been taught to run up on a pitch, and her coaches had encouraged her to hit left-handed only, rather than switch-hitting as she had always done before. That meant that as a left-handed hitter, softball curves would come in at her, giving her an advantage. To hit a baseball, however, she had to relearn how to swing a bat: weight back, legs and hips powered to give her a chance to hit curve balls that travel almost twenty feet farther than a softball pitch. It was really hard to change her swing. "Just from the muscle memory of always moving [running up on the pitch], swing after swing, rip after rip, thousands of times in my softball career. Then in baseball it was hard just to stand there, and not move my feet toward the ball to hit it. . . . Everyone in baseball has been trying to get me to just stand, but my whole life I've been told, 'Just touch and run. Touch and run. Touch and run.' And then I get in a baseball game, and I'm thinking, 'Stay back. Stay back. Stay back.' And

FIG. 8. Tara Harbert, Team USA 2010, Tournament Best Defensive Player. Courtesy of Brian Fleming.

then the pitch comes in, and all of a sudden my body just reacts, like it's saying, 'No . . . touch and run. Touch and run. Touch and run.' It's like I'm trying to stop and stay back, but my muscles are just going."

But Tara is such a gifted athlete, with such an instinct for playing ball, that she quickly learned enough to become the starting center fielder on Team USA, the fastest and most prolific base stealer on the team, and proficient enough with her softball style of hitting to become the lead-off hitter in the 2008 and 2010 World Cup tournaments. She earned the nickname "Ichiro" because of that softball style of hitting, as well as her speed on the base paths and in the outfield.[3] Baseball captured her heart as she became enchanted by its mental complexity. She came to respect the longer wait at the plate, and the freedom to steal bases at her discretion, with a green light from the coach.

"Baseball is a much more challenging game for me, and that's why I love it: because I still don't know all that I need to know about it. I mean, I'm never going to know everything about any sport, but I love baseball because

FIG. 9. Tara Harbert at bat, New England Women's Red Sox. Courtesy of Patricia Wagar.

I'm always learning something new and it's a much more difficult game. It actually requires more thinking and initiative than softball." Pausing a moment to reflect, she offers an insight that may explain America's puzzling insistence that softball is for girls and baseball exclusively for boys: "It's interesting. . . . In softball, you do what you're told. It's like how our culture is with girls. They made softball for girls, and they're told what to do. You don't do anything unless your coach tells you to. In baseball it's more, 'All right, we're going to give you guidelines, but you do what you think is right. We trust you.'"

That remarkable observation goes to the heart of the cultural distinction between softball and baseball better than any I've heard. Traditionally, men have been expected to act, and women have been expected to follow orders. Sure, the different dimensions of the fields in baseball and softball and the different size balls affect the way the game is played. But that doesn't explain *why* girls have been excluded from baseball in the United States or why the two sports are segregated. Tara's insight pinpoints the

FIG. 10. Harbert beats a throw back to first against Japan, 2010. Courtesy of Patricia Wagar.

underlying cultural reason for gendered segregation. Baseball requires that the *players* think and take responsibility for their actions, while softball leaves decision making and responsibility in the hands of the coaches. This is what Jenny Dalton Hill was referring to when she said *hated* the mental aspect of baseball because it required that she think. "Just tell me what to do, and I will do it," remarked Hill.[4] What Tara says she *loves* about baseball in comparison to softball is that she is *required* to think and take initiative. Women have the strength and skill to play baseball. Size isn't what keeps them out. From this perspective, the real threat women's baseball poses to American culture is not the dimensions of the field, but the independence of the athletes.

Still, Tara remembers enjoying the freedom that comes from just sitting back and taking orders from the coach in softball: "I like the freedom [of not having to think] sometimes. If you mess up, it's not your fault." But baseball is now the sport that engages her precisely because it is so intricate and difficult to master. She relishes the opportunity to learn and become a better player. "Well, I know I'm not going to have my speed forever, but I'd like to continue on the team. Obviously, I'm bringing speed to the team, and working on my hitting, and trying to learn what Coach Kevin [Marden] with the [New England Women's] Red Sox is trying to teach me, because he knows I can hit so he's always on me.[5] That's helping me try to make the adjustment. I know I can power hit, and I know I can be a good hitter, and I want to add that to my repertoire so, you know, when I do lose a little bit more speed, I'm still one of the top players in the nation. It almost kills me to think that in a few years when I don't have speed, I won't make the team, so I work really hard."

Playing several tournaments a year with Kevin Marden's New England Women's Red Sox and her teammates from Team USA and playing every two years with USA Baseball in the Women's World Cup is almost, but not quite, enough to satisfy Tara. What she would really like to see is women's baseball in the Olympics. "To go to the Olympics . . . I mean, I feel like we're so close. We can taste it. Even for softball now, what you dream about is the Olympics." But how to prepare to send a U.S. women's baseball team to the Olympics? "Gosh, this is so tough. I thought about that. Like, we need to start a girls' Little League. When I say that, a lot of people just look at me like, 'Are you stupid?' Because there's already a softball league and those baseball girls won't get scholarships. It's so hard to imagine any college women's baseball. We need to start with a girls' Little League. And I think that girls should play with boys until they're twelve because it makes them good, but only up to a certain point. Except for the few like Lilly and Marti, you just can't compete with boys because they are bigger and stronger. It's not any sexist thing. It's just the fact of life that, genetically, men are bigger and stronger and faster, and so I think at about twelve they just need to start a girls' baseball league where you can really hone your skills of baseball."

She doesn't see any conflict between women's athleticism and femininity. The majority of men she has met think it's fantastic when they meet an elite-level woman baseball player. "They hear that we play baseball, and they just think it's the coolest thing. I've played in front of [Major League Colorado] Rockies players, and they're just amazed at how I can play. I've never had a negative experience because I've never been trying to compete against the boys." Only occasionally when playing baseball in a men's adult baseball league did she encounter a few men who did not want her to be there. "Some of those guys were just complete assholes, and they would throw at me . . . I'd get into the box, and they would throw as hard as they could. I'm like, 'All right! I'm better at fastballs. Throw me a few fastballs. I'll see it, and I'm going to hit it.'" Then, with a laugh, she adds, "If you throw me a curve ball, I'm not going to hit it. But it's those egos of the guys that never made it professionally, so they're not going to let a girl show them up, and they think if they throw you a fastball you won't be able to hit it. The elite athletes respect us."[6]

Anybody watching Tara's speed and grace in the outfield and on the base paths can hardly do anything except enjoy the show. She would like to play baseball professionally, but no matter how good she is, there is no outlet for that. For the time being she competes in body-building competitions as a fitness figure competitor. At heart she really wants the opportunity to continue playing the sport that has been hers from that World Series day on which she was born. Baseball is still the game that makes her feel alive.

8

Veronica Alvarez

CATCHER

"The ball's coming. You should hit it!"

"The coach laughed. They looked at me and said, 'Huh? Tu?' They're like, 'You?'

"'Yes, I just really need to practice. I need some live action. Just let me know if you want me to catch a practice; I need to get some squatting time.'

"And he goes, 'No, but like, we have a guy that throws, like, ninety.'

"I say, 'Yes, I can catch anybody. Throw me whatever you want.'

"And he's like, 'Huh? Look at this girl,' and he turns to the other coach and says, 'Check this girl out. Check out what she just told me.'

"I go, 'Hey, I can catch anything. I just need to squat.'

"This was a high school coach I was talking to about practicing with his team so I could get ready for the USA tryouts."[1]

Veronica Alvarez, catcher for the USA Baseball Women's National Team, was talking about the difficulty of finding a team in her hometown of Miami, Florida, to practice with in preparation for the 2012 Women's National Team tryouts. She was begging one of the local high school coaches to allow her to catch bullpens (pitching practice) for his team of teenage boys and being laughed at in response. "It's bad, but I mean, I'm used to it. I don't know if it's because when I'm saying these things I'm in Spandex and have my pearl earrings on. I don't know. I don't get it, but they usually laugh at me. That's the reaction."

Veronica is not a ballplayer to be laughed at. She has been a baseball and softball catcher for twenty years, from Little League to college, with a scholarship on the NCAA Division I Villanova softball team. She is a dominating presence as the catcher for the women's national baseball team. Yet here she was, scouring the Miami area to find even a high school team to practice with for her third season with Team USA and being greeted with scorn.

"What was really ridiculous is that the coach had invited me to come to his high school practice after he saw me hitting at some local cages. He was the one who initiated the conversation with me when he saw me hit. He recognized my ability and joked about how he wanted me to show his high school players how it was done. He wanted me to come because he could see that my [hitting] mechanics were what he was trying to teach his team. I also think part of what he wanted to show his guys was that even a girl could do what he wanted them to do."[2] The coach seemed to think he could shame his ballplayers by bringing in a girl and also actually show them the mechanics of hitting a baseball. It was a conflicted message.

Veronica walked away from that disrespect. "I ended up practicing with another high school team. They treated me as one of their own, and without hesitation they assigned me to catch for one of their former players who was practicing for a Major League tryout. He threw ninety-plus miles an hour. You can't keep playing baseball at this level if you don't really want it because it takes so much effort. It's not something you do casually. Every year I've been lucky to find good guys to practice with daily. But it's because I'm very persistent, and I won't take no for an answer."[3]

Veronica is the daughter of Cuban immigrants, the younger of two children in an exceptionally close-knit family. Parents Julio and Ofelia Alvarez have always been baseball fans, but their children, Raul and Veronica, have both been players. Raul, three years older than his sister, stopped playing competitive ball during college, when he married and started a family, and Veronica is certain he could have gone far with baseball. "If my brother had my love and my passion for the game, he would be in the Major Leagues."

Now Raul's three-year-old son, Julian, is showing signs of the family passion for the game. The youngster takes "batting practice" for hours on end, with whatever is close at hand (a plastic sand shovel today) and whatever object is pitched to him (a little beach ball at the moment) by his adoring *abuelo*, *abuela*, *papi*, and Tia Veronica. The adults are no match for his endurance: they relieve each other as they pitch to the tireless Julian in the living room of their weekend home in Key Largo. Abuela Ofelia is careful to explain to me that Julian is *allowed* to hit the ball inside the house. She delights as his towering *jonrons* bounce off the dining room light fixture. Visitors had better have hands quick enough to catch his fly balls and foul tips or divert their drinks to safety. It soon becomes evident that Ofelia tolerates baseball indoors because she too enjoys her turn at bat. When she steps up to take a pitch from her son, Raul, she hits a searing line drive across the full length of the living room, over the kitchen counter, bouncing off the refrigerator door on the far side of the kitchen. This is a hit worthy of *The Natural*, the indoor equivalent of hitting a bomb off the center-field scoreboard. Raul's wife, Frances, holding their seven-month-old daughter, Francesca, laughs as her mother-in-law goes yard. With pearl earrings and flowered headband, Francesca will undoubtedly also soon want to take her turn at bat, but she'll need to learn to walk first. This is the environment in which Veronica Alvarez grew to become the best female baseball catcher in the United States.

But all the support at home hasn't made it easier for Veronica to find opportunities to prepare for the Team USA tryouts in 2008, 2010, and 2012. As one of the power hitters on the national team, she has moved beyond taking batting practice in her family's living room. So she battles to convince the Cuban men in her Miami community that she can actually catch their pitching.

It is remarkable that as a Cuban American girl growing up in Miami, Veronica was encouraged to play sports at all. "I praise my parents. They're my number-one fans, and because of them I was able to do what I did. They didn't fight me, and they supported me every step of the way, where the majority of Cuban parents wouldn't." People ask Veronica if her father or her brother played baseball, as it seems the only explanation for why she plays. She tells them her father didn't play. Her brother played from

Little League through college but didn't begin until he was eight years old. Veronica was five at the time, fell in love with baseball as soon as she saw it, and refused to be excluded. Even when she was too young to play Little League, she earned herself the job of bat girl on Raul's team.

It didn't take her brother or her father to help her fall in love with the game: "I loved this since day one. That's what I wanted to do." But that went against the cultural grain of the Miami Cuban community. "In Miami, when a boy is born, they give him a baseball, right? These Cuban men, they love their baseball, and they want their kids to play. If they have big legs, they're going to be a catcher, or if they're short, they're going to be a second baseman. That's how they see them in the hospital when they're born. He's going to be an amazing catcher because he had big legs when he was born. When a girl is born, you put them in ballet or give them a bow and some earrings and teach them how to shop." She quickly adds, "Don't get me wrong . . . I love to shop!"

By the time she was five, Veronica would have none of it, and her parents were responsive to her needs and desires. She emphatically refused the ballet lessons that were a cultural requirement of the daughters of the Cuban community and insisted that her parents sign her up for Little League instead. "My mom tells the story that they took me to ballet, that I was in the shopping center and I saw where we were going and I just hauled ass, slipped away. I started running, and I said, 'No!' And they're like, 'Come on, come on.' I said 'No! I want to play baseball!'" She had to wait a year until she was old enough for Little League, but she used her time well, continuing as bat girl and practicing with Raul's team.

At the tryouts for Little League the following year, she was one of only two girls. "We weren't even friends. We were on opposite teams. We were probably enemies at that point because we were each 'the other girl in the league.' I remember tryouts. We were all at third base, and they were hitting to us. There was an actual tryout with the potential coaches drafting their team. [Talk about a community that takes baseball seriously: a six-year-old draft!—JR] We were making throws from third to first, and only some of the other kids could reach. When they saw me, a girl, come up, the coach standing on first took a step closer to me. I threw the ball at

FIG. 11. Veronica Alvarez, five-year-old bat girl on brother Raul's Little League team. Ht: 3 ft. 1 in. Wt: 40 lbs. Bats: Right. Throws: Right. Courtesy of Ofelia Alvarez.

him, and everyone was like, 'What??' I was chosen for one of the teams and became their third baseman."

With an arm like that it wasn't long before she found her way to the catcher's position. "One day the coach said, 'We need somebody to catch today.' And in my head it was 'Yesss!!' and I immediately raised my hand. And my mom was standing there shaking her head going, 'Nuh-uh.' She was like, 'No!' I said, 'Come on!' And then I ended up catching." Ofelia was obviously no match for her daughter's will when it came to baseball. Veronica became the team's catcher and also pitcher. "There you are in the center of the field waiting for them to just make fun of you. They would laugh, and they would say, 'Oh, my God, a girl is pitching!' And then the typical story: you'd strike them out. They'd laugh, and then they'd cry. [. . .]

"My parents were friends with the mother of one of the other players, and she still tells the story of how her son came home crying, and his parents asked, 'Why are you crying?' He sobbed, 'Because a girl struck me out . . .' as if it were the worst thing possible. When I made the All-Star team, I went in to pitch for one inning, and the other team was making fun of me, and I struck them out. That's the typical story of a girl who grows up playing with the boys. I guess we fight and we're always fighting. We're fighting because we have to prove ourselves. The boys know to make fun of you. Or that's what they think they should do. And then another year I wasn't picked for the All-Star team because of the coach . . . that was an All-Star team that I should have been on, and I wasn't picked for it. But I think that coach is totally the guy that doesn't want his ego busted or his son's . . . so they didn't take me."

She played Little League for three years. There was a slow-pitch softball league for girls at the park where she played baseball, but she wasn't interested: "I said, 'No, I don't want to play. I want to play baseball. I like my league, and I like my guys.'" When she was ten and entering the fifth grade, her parents enrolled her in a parochial school, St. Thomas the Apostle, a coeducational Catholic school with a middle school softball team. Veronica's friend Angie Eguilior attended St. Thomas and wanted Veronica to sign up for softball with her. At first Veronica declined; she was happy playing baseball. But Angie's mother, Mina Eguilior, was active in bringing fast-pitch softball to the Miami area, and soon softball became a more attractive option for Veronica.

Mina Eguilior started a fast-pitch softball league for girls in the local park where Veronica played baseball. Eguilior recruited Hector Torres, who had been a star pitcher on the Cuban national softball team, to coach the girls. "Angie's mom started fast-pitch softball in Miami, and she brought this guy, Hector Torres, who was actually the USA Softball pitching coach a couple of years ago. He came in from Cuba, and she basically got him started here [in the United States] in this league. Now everyone in Miami knows who Hector Torres is. He throws, like, a hundred miles per hour underhand, something ridiculous."

Fast-pitch softball for girls quickly caught on in Miami. The park where Veronica played baseball now had a fast-pitch league, and at the end of the season, the league was putting together an All-Star team. "They wanted me to switch and play on their All-Star team. I finally gave in and said, 'Okay, I'll play on this All-Star team, but I'm still going to play baseball.'" She continued to play baseball with her guys and also played with her girls on the softball team, but the pressure to give up baseball was intense. "I played on the All-Star softball team, and then they convinced me that because I was going to be playing on this team for St. Thomas, I shouldn't be playing both softball and baseball because it was a different grip. 'You don't want to mess yourself up, you should just switch to softball,' they said to me. So I don't know if it was so much baseball pushing me out as softball pulling me in. Eventually, I think I would have probably been approached to stop playing baseball."

Veronica was ten years old when she quit Little League. If she had stayed until she was twelve, she undoubtedly would have faced the same pressure to leave baseball that all girls face. She was ahead of the curve in choosing to leave on her own. Veronica was also growing weary of being the only girl on her baseball team. She embraced the opportunity to play with girls and still believes it's important for girls to have the opportunity to compete on a high level with other girls. She has no deep regrets that baseball was unavailable to her during her teen and college years.

Playing softball with an eye to a college scholarship involves intense traveling tournament play every summer, from as early as possible in childhood. "In softball, most likely there are only three or four good players on a high school team. Not all nine players on the field are college quality. It's a waste of time for recruiters to go to a girls' high school game. So summer league and travel ball are very important in women's softball. And the sooner you start, the better. I started summer travel ball when I was ten years old. At first it was just in South Florida and a little less intense. But the next year I started on another team where Hector Torres was the coach. He started the Miami Wildcats, and we were the best of the best in Miami, and we ended up being the best of the best in the state. As twelve-year-olds we won the state championship. And we went to nationals. We got fourth. We were practicing every day of the summer, playing every weekend. So that's very important. As you grow, you get better and better, and the girls stay together, and the stronger players want to come to your team. The Miami Wildcats turned into the Miami Stingrays and became the dominant team in the whole area. Now any girl in Miami who wants to take softball to the next level wants to be a Stingray."

As we saw with Tara Harbert's story, preparing for college play requires that young athletes and their families devote time, effort, and money to their sport for many years. "Playing at that competitive level with the dream of playing at the next level is a lot of hard work, and there's a lot of time you put into it. There are all the showcase tournaments, the big ones where the scouts will go, and you learn what to do as you go along. You hear what you have to do with regard to making a recruiting video to send out. In the video you include hitting, a little bit of this, a little bit of that, and you send it out to whatever colleges you're interested in. On top of that, you're also getting seen by the college coaches at your tournaments. Then you get letters from the schools that are interested in you, and you get invited to visit them."

It worked out well for Veronica. She was recruited by Villanova, Cornell, and the University of Florida. The Florida coach who was interested in her moved to another school, and the Ivy Leagues don't offer athletic scholarships. But Villanova was the school she preferred anyway. "That was my favorite. I always wanted to go to the northeast, so it was perfect. Finding the right school was something that we kind of figured out as we went along."

A softball scholarship to Division I Villanova was her well-earned reward for the years of dedication and sacrifice, and Veronica has no regrets about switching from baseball to softball. "For me softball was great, and I will always promote it to everyone because it allowed me to play in college. I played in Spain. I played in a Euro Cup in Italy, so I was able to do all these things that allowed me to continue playing, to get better and experience a world of things. So I would never have anything against it because there is that opportunity in softball. Unfortunately, there wasn't that opportunity [in baseball], so I had to take advantage of the opportunity that I was given."

The two games are different, she says, but not so incompatible that the experience of playing with other girls isn't worth the price of switching. "In softball you're with girls growing up, and you get to develop that aspect of your friendships." She thinks that if she had continued to play baseball with all-boys teams, she would not have developed the confidence she needed to succeed as an athlete. "A girl playing on a high school boys' team, it's hard for them to develop certain aspects of their personalities . . . or just speak up, because you're always that outcast, always that person that shouldn't be there. That's why I promote girls going to softball . . . so that they develop their personalities. They're all female, and they're given that opportunity to develop their personalities, speak up, say what they want."

It's difficult to imagine outspoken, charismatic, hilarious Veronica being intimidated by boys, but she credits the all-girl environment at her high school, Carrollton School of the Sacred Heart, as well as her parents, with nurturing the leadership skills she needed as a catcher. "For me as a catcher on the field, you're telling people what to do. You're the leader. You see everything. You have to be able to speak and have confidence. If I played catcher on a boys' team, I wouldn't have been able to develop into the personality that I am. It's almost like you're being held back, right? You're not really allowed to speak because you're a girl, and these are boys, and this is baseball, and you're not supposed to be here. You're good, yeah, but you're still a girl." As a catcher on Team USA, Veronica leads from the dugout as well as from behind the plate. She directs defensive play on the field and rallies her teammates at bat and on the base paths with encouragement and wisecracks that draw laughs from players and spectators alike, even in tense moments.

In spite of her appreciation of softball, she admits that she has never witnessed the same level of passion among softball players that she has experienced with women who play baseball. She believes the social resistance faced by women who play baseball causes them to care even more about the game. "Playing softball, I've never experienced somebody having that much passion. In softball we don't sit around and talk about it, where in baseball I've met so many people who are so passionate about it. Since we have to fight for it, people show their passion. For instance, if Donna Mills is talking about it, you just sit there with Donna Mills for hours and hours and hours because she's so passionate about it, right? Malaika will talk about it forever, and Sarah Gascon, Lilly . . . everyone. In softball you don't have to fight for it. There doesn't need to be that much passion."

She describes the pressure to stop playing baseball as "in your face"—a constant presence even in the most subtle ways. "The other day I was talking about buying myself some new cleats, and my roommate's boyfriend was like, 'This girl plays five games a year, and she's always buying new cleats!' That is not even a thought in my mind. Those five games are the most important five games of my life, and that's what matters. If I have to buy a pair of one-hundred-dollar cleats, I will. I need the best gear, and I need to be as good as possible those five days. Whether it only happens every two years or not."

Even though the games with Team USA feel like the most important of her life, they're an absurd challenge to train for. "I was giving a softball lesson the other day to a little girl, and she asked me, 'So how often do you guys practice?' I said, 'Well, what do you mean? With my baseball team?' And she said, 'Yeah.' I said, 'We don't practice at all. I have to practice on my own and then just be ready for when it comes time for tryouts and for actual practice.' And she said, 'What? You have that much discipline that you go out here by yourself?'"

This was a thirteen-year-old girl, taking private softball lessons with Veronica to prepare to try out for the team at Veronica's old high school, Carrollton. She persisted: How could Veronica possibly have the discipline to practice on her own? Veronica responded, "Well, I find people to help me practice, or I throw with my dad." In retrospect that conversation seemed ridiculous to her. "It's like, 'Man . . . !' But it's true. Being twenty-nine years old, with a job . . . I live in Miami where there's always something to do and always someone wanting to do something. . . . It takes a lot to say, 'I have to hit first.' And my friends are like, 'What? Why?' 'Because I've got to.' And it's not even a burden on me. 'Yeah, I've got to go hit.' That's what matters. That's my number-one priority. Me with a tee and a bucket of balls. While I'm in training, it's hard to be around people who don't have that passion for it and don't understand it. I think it scares them."

It's a lonely business. Throughout her life Veronica's local access to baseball has been largely through her Miami Cuban community. The cultural prejudices that have kept her from being taken seriously are tiresome. When she arrived in Pennsylvania as a freshman at Villanova, she was surprised to see how much support other women athletes had enjoyed throughout their lives. "These girls were strong. I mean white Americans.

I feel like the parents put them to play soccer. Those legs were so strong. It's different. I feel like up north, if they see it [female athleticism], they'll believe it and support it, where here [in Miami], it takes a lot more."

If playing softball throughout her adolescence helped her to develop confidence, playing baseball with Team USA has opened her eyes to the cultural resistance female athletes face. "Playing baseball has made me an even bigger feminist than I was. There is a need to spread the word . . . it's made me very passionate about describing the capabilities of women. I see the issue more than I did before I played baseball [for Team USA]. You say you play baseball, and people can't even handle it. They have to say, 'No, you mean softball.' 'No, I said baseball, and I meant baseball. I think I know the difference. If I played softball, I would say softball.' It's like they want to fight you on it."

Her awareness of the issues faced by female athletes emerged after she had graduated from Villanova. She was shocked at her athletic career's brutally sudden ending after her senior year and realized that something was wrong with forcing an athlete to quit in her prime. "After college you're done. In every women's sport. You've played and practiced hard for your entire life. Your friends are going out, and you're practicing, not because it's a burden. It's because you want to, and now you're twenty-two years old, twenty-three years old, and that's it. You're done. Imagine a male at twenty-two years old. He's not developed. He's still in the Minor League system, learning and developing as a player. It takes years of practice and being in control of your body and learning your body. I learned how to use my legs properly really when I began training for USA Baseball. If I knew how to use my legs in college or in high school, it would have been out of control! Those young girls that I coach, it's hard for them to use their legs . . . they're not even fully developed. We [women collegiate athletes] are not even at our peak before we have to quit. You grow into your body just as boys do."

A college athletic career is a launching pad to the pros for the best male athletes. But after college, women are usually done, no matter how good they are, and it comes as a rude awakening. "When I got to my senior year, I couldn't believe that that was it. I put all my time and effort into softball because I loved it. If I knew then what I know now, or if I developed my body as much as I have now, it would have been incredible. We're kind of cut off at our prime."

Veronica graduated Villanova with a degree in communications, returned home to Miami, got a job at the local Channel 4 news station, and an unpaid internship at MTV. She would have preferred to play professional ball, but she had to support herself, even though her parents were happy to have her move back home for a while. "There are a couple of professional softball teams, but they're paying you $10,000, and you can't live off that. Society's telling you, you're twenty, it's time to get a job. You graduated college. You're a female. You've got to start a family, all these things that are part of being a grown-up, I guess. So it's tough. I worked from three in the morning till one in the afternoon at the news station, and then, from one thirty to seven thirty, I worked at MTV. I did both things because I needed the internship but I also needed the job. I would get home, eat dinner, talk to my parents for two seconds, and by the time I went to sleep, it was ten o'clock, and I would have to wake up at two thirty in the morning again."

Veronica maintained that schedule for the entire year. When her friend and Villanova teammate pitcher Shannon Williams suggested they look for a European softball team to play on the following summer, she was ready. The girls sent out emails and got immediate responses from several European teams. The women's softball team in Valencia, Spain, recruited them persuasively, offering them free housing, meals, a stipend, and plane tickets to Spain for the following week. Before they could catch their breath, Veronica and Shannon were playing softball in Europe. They traveled throughout the continent, played ball, ate great food, and went to beautiful beaches after their games. Veronica's fluent Spanish made the path easy. "They flew us out there, put us up in an apartment; they would give us a stipend and take us grocery shopping. It wasn't that we were making money, but we were playing and living for free." But it wasn't real life, or a real professional softball career, and they were far from their families. After one glorious romp of summer ball, they returned home.

"Your goal is to go to college and play softball, and that's the end of your career. Which is horrible. So let's compare it to baseball. The boys have their Minor League teams, where they're making maybe nothing or close to nothing, right? They're traveling all day, but at the end of the tunnel, there's that option or that possibility, where if you work hard, you may make the Major Leagues. They dream and work hard, and there's something to go for. In softball, you go and play in these professional leagues, and that's it. Basically, it's like the men's Minor League, but there is no goal. I don't want to say it isn't worth it, because you love it and that's why we continue to play. But it almost doesn't make sense to play in those leagues when it's taking up all your time. If you can't make a living from it, and it impedes your advancement in another career by taking up all your time when you should be gaining experience . . . I don't know. I don't know . . ." With sadness and a little anger, she says quietly, "I didn't quit softball; softball quit me."

She returned to Miami after that summer in Spain and took on adult responsibilities: a good job with regular hours, working for the Miami-Dade public school system. It wasn't long before she could buy a car and put a down payment on a condo on Biscayne Bay. Veronica Alvarez is a successful young adult: a homeowner, a jobholder, with plenty of friends and family in a city she loves and regards as home. But the need to play ball wouldn't let go of her, and it wasn't long before she was once again trolling the Internet for a team to play on. "So I get back, and I got the job in the school system, and I'm sitting in my office and I'm thinking, 'I need to play. I need to figure this out. Somehow I need to find somewhere to play.'"

At first she looked for professional softball teams in the United States, but she knew that she would have to wait another year for a new season and then have to uproot her life once again for an inadequate salary. So she redirected her search to local amateur teams. "I was Googling things. I Googled the Silver Bullets. Because as a young child I would watch them, and I loved them. So I went from one place to another, and I found USA Baseball. I'm a Google master! I saw the website about the 2006 World Cup. Then I found Jim Glennie and the American Women's Baseball Federation website. So I wrote him an email, and I laid it all out. I said, 'I'm Veronica Alvarez. I played softball at Villanova. I started playing baseball when I was a child,' this and that. 'I'm a catcher. Just seeing what opportunities you had or if you knew of anything in Miami.'"

Jim Glennie called Veronica and told her she had just missed the 2006 Women's Baseball World Cup Tour. But he promised to contact her the next time there was an opportunity to play baseball. She doubted he would call back and put the conversation out of her mind. But she was beginning to take control of her own athletic life for the first time since she had been away from the discipline of college softball. "It just so happens that around this time, I became a completely different person. I was overweight, all this stuff, and I completely changed my life. I started running marathons. I started working out like a maniac, taking care of myself. As much as I'm active, for me, it's hard to keep my weight down. If I didn't play softball, I would have been obese. I was so active, and it was still hard for me to maintain my competitive weight." She pauses for a moment, then smiles cheerfully, and adds, "I like to eat."

The discipline paid off. A year and a half later, Jim Glennie got back to her. She had forgotten about Jim's promise to call her back and was surprised when he contacted her in 2008 and asked if she was interested in attending the preliminary national team tryouts in Kenosha, Wisconsin, over the July Fourth weekend. "July Fourth we're [the Alvarez family] usually in the Keys, and you know, I even considered not going to Kenosha. Then I thought, 'Why not? If anything, it'll be like *A League of Their Own*, where they're all in the field and having this tryout, and it's an experience, and we'll go on from there. I'm in the best shape of my life. Let's do this. So I went and got my catcher's gear and went up to Kenosha. My parents went with me." When she arrived at the Wisconsin ballpark, it was as though she had entered a field of dreams: "And then I walked into this world where . . . I watched, and I'm like, 'Oh my God! Look at all these women. They've never switched to softball! It was amazing. I was super excited to be invited back for the final tryout."

Then she got serious. "I had one month to switch back to baseball. My boss was very supportive. I told her, and she was super excited for me. I would go in to work early, and by two o'clock she would say, 'Go practice baseball.' So I would leave, and I would go practice. I was really lucky that

Kim Braatz Voisard lived in Miami and was willing to practice with me. I had only one month to train, and she spent every second she had with me. It was a month solid practicing every single day for four hours a day. I loved it, every second of it. In the middle of Miami heat with my catcher's gear, I would just sweat buckets . . . it was intense."

She had no difficulty switching back to baseball, and she believes her years as an elite softball player actually helped. The shorter distance from pitcher to batter and the high speed of Division I softball pitching was more challenging than the pitching Veronica faced at that preliminary USA tryout in Kenosha. She had to train herself to keep her weight back and wait on the baseball pitches, which were coming slower and from nearly twenty feet farther away than what she was used to in softball. "I'm not taking any credit away from the baseball pitchers or anything like that, but in softball, it's different. We're at a closer distance, and these girls [college softball players] have been groomed to pitch faster and faster as the years go by. Not that the baseball players aren't putting in the time; it's just their opportunities are limited. I faced Monica Abbott in college, and she threw seventy miles per hour. She's six foot something. By the time she takes her step and lets go of the ball, she's forty some feet away, so that ball's moving fast, and you have a small reaction time. [. . .]

"In softball, you tend to be up in front [your weight is on your front leg]. You have a limited reaction time. They are all up in front because of the shorter distance between the pitcher and batter in softball. Their weight is on their front foot but you don't even notice it because of the small reaction time. So for baseball I was learning to wait and keep my weight back. Baseball in general is slower. The pitcher takes more time. In softball, the moment the pitcher starts, you should be ready to go for it."

But since Veronica began playing baseball as a child, she has always had a "baseball swing." She never changed her swing specifically for softball, and she doesn't teach her young softball students to swing any differently than she does in baseball. "I think a baseball swing should be the only swing. I don't think you should alter a swing. That's the swing. The ball's coming. You should hit it! That's what I teach my students."

Baseball's slower pace requires more thinking, and more time for

FIG. 12. (*top left*) Veronica Alvarez in charge, Team USA 2010. Courtesy of USA Baseball.

FIG. 13. (*top right*) Veronica Alvarez, Standard Bearer, Team USA 2012. Courtesy of Veronica Alvarez.

FIG. 14. (*left*) The Alvarez family: Julio and Ofelia standing behind their daughter as always. Courtesy of Veronica Alvarez.

thinking requires more mental discipline. It also may provide the temptation to overthink, to doubt and second-guess yourself. The cure for that is more time on a baseball diamond than most women ballplayers can get. Lack of regular access to baseball simply amplifies the stress level in games as well as in tryouts.

"All you can do is play your best game. All you can worry about is training, being ready and coming in and playing your game, because all that outside worry will kill you. I mean, baseball's such a mental game. You can't go to bat thinking, 'If I don't get a hit here, I'm not going to play.' Hitting is the most mental thing in the world. Imagine having a clear mind and knowing that you're confident. But if you have that negative thought in your mind, it's too much to do both [hit and doubt yourself]."

The stress and mental pressure women carry into the batter's box in baseball is even more intense than it is in softball because women baseball players have to prove they belong in the game at all. As one member of Team USA has remarked several times, "Every time I get up to bat, it feels like the future of women's baseball is on my shoulders."[4] Alvarez agrees. "Right. Everybody's judging you. When you're hitting, you have the thought in your mind that people are judging women's baseball based on you right now. If people see one woman playing who is not so skilled, they're going to judge everybody on it. In a sport like, let's say, men's soccer, if people see one kid who's not playing right, they're able to say, 'He's not that good'; it doesn't put a negative light on men's soccer. But in women's baseball, if they see one girl who's not good at baseball, they instantly judge the sport. They don't judge that person; they group it with everyone who plays women's baseball and assume that's the level of our sport."

Adding another stressful dimension that male athletes rarely have to confront is the inevitable issue of the sexuality of women athletes. As adolescent girls develop into collegiate athletes, they face social pressure to prove that they are sufficiently feminine "in spite of" being athletes. Veronica was aware of the pressure but not focused on the sexual preferences of her teammates at Villanova. "There were eight of us in my senior class at Villanova. When we step back and we look at all eight of us, we're completely different people. We're spread out over this whole spectrum of one type of person to another and everyone in between. Softball brought us all together and made us love each other and be great friends. We all got along, and we played the game, and that's what mattered. So if there's a person who isn't straight on the team or is, you know, whatever, that's not even an issue. I don't see it as an issue.

"But it is an ongoing stereotype, and it shouldn't be: 'Oh, she plays softball—is she a lesbian or . . . ?' Whenever you say something about softball, people relate it directly to being a lesbian, and it's like, well, this doesn't even make sense. Why does it even matter? It doesn't matter to me. People assume all women in power are lesbians. Or if you're a feminist, they immediately think, 'You're a lesbian.' I honestly think every woman should be a feminist. If they're not, I mean, what are they doing?"

Veronica simply wants the opportunity to continue to improve as a baseball player. For that, there must be coaches who are worthy of the elite athletes who play on Team USA. "We are all willing to work our asses off, willing to commit the time to becoming the best baseball players possible. We need coaches that can handle our desire and passion to learn and win." When Veronica and her USA teammates are on the field, they are ballplayers plain and simple, not "female ballplayers."

"When I put on my gear, I'm a beast. I don't care. There's no thought even. I'm in gear. I'm playing my game. Not that I'm playing like a man, but I'm intense, and I'm going to be aggressive, and I'm going to be all these things that probably wouldn't be categorized as a female characteristics. Those characteristics aren't qualities that a female is supposed to have in society." Perhaps it's time for that to change. Team USA's rollicking, charismatic powerhouse of a catcher, Veronica Alvarez, will undoubtedly give women's baseball a nudge in the right direction.

9

Sarah Gascon

SHORTSTOP

"I always felt I was born to be an athlete."

"One of the earliest memories I have was in kindergarten when the teacher asked us to write what you want to be when you grow up. I remember putting 'athlete.' I remember putting that, and my teacher said, 'You can't be an athlete, Sarah.' She was a nun. I went to Catholic school. I remember her telling me that, and I was so disappointed. I said, 'But why not?' And she said, 'Girls aren't athletes, Sarah. Only boys are athletes.'"[1]

It seems incredible that a teacher in 1988 could tell any child that they could not be an athlete, but thirty-year-old Sarah Gascon knows what she heard: "Yes. I remember it. And I remember changing my answer to 'nurse.' I looked at all the other girls to see what their answers were, and the majority of them said nurse. It was either teacher or nurse, so I put 'nurse.' And I'm like, 'I don't want to be a nurse. I just want to be an athlete.' I always felt that I was born to be an athlete."

Sarah had been aware of that feeling since 1984, when she was two years old and watching the Los Angeles Olympic Games on television. "I remember sitting down watching TV, watching the Olympic Games, and knowing that I wanted to do that. I wanted to be an athlete." This is not as far-fetched a toddler memory as it may seem to be. Sarah's father, Dave Gascon, was an officer with the Los Angeles Police Department. In 1984 he was assigned to work the Olympics at the Los Angeles Coliseum. Sarah, the third of four children and particularly close to her father, was always excited when he came home from work. She watched the games on TV and knew her dad was there. "Two years old, yes. That's my very first memory. I remember watching the one-hundred-meter sprint, actually. My next memory was hitting a baseball in my backyard off a tee and playing 'pickle' with my siblings.[2] It was my favorite game. I loved that game. I played it all the time, and then we would hit. There's a picture of me, and I have a bat in my hand, and there's a tee, and I'm two years old, and I'm hitting. So those are my first memories of actual sport . . . and the Olympics on TV."

Sarah learned to love sports by playing with her siblings. "I think I owe my competitiveness and my desire to my siblings and my parents, because they put us in sports, but we were always playing with each other in the backyard or in the front." She was closest in age and temperament to her brother, David, two years older. "We'd go to the park right down the street from our house, and we played roller hockey, or street hockey. My brother was the goaltender, and I was just a sister following him around." David was predictably resistant to his little sister's constant presence, but both parents were supportive of their daughter's athleticism and liked their children to play with each other. "My dad tells this story that my brother said to him, 'Dad, I don't want Sarah to come. All the boys are going to make fun of me.' Dad goes, 'David, is Sarah as good as the boys?' 'Well, yeah, she is.' He goes, 'Then she has a right to play.'"

But it wasn't easy keeping up with David and his friends: "You couldn't cry." Even when she fell and broke her wrist while playing roller hockey with the boys, all she could think was, "'Oh my gosh, Sarah! You can't cry in front of the boys! You can't do that!' So I pulled it together. I was like eight years old, maybe nine." She had been getting a drink of water when she took a spill coming back to join the game. She picked herself up, quieted her tears, rollerbladed back down the hill to her father, and calmly reported, "I think I broke my wrist." He took her to the emergency room, where the diagnosis was confirmed and Sarah's wrist was put in a cast. This was the first of many athletic injuries Sarah has endured throughout her life, and her youthful stoicism set the tone for her response to all of them.

In spite of both parents' encouragement, Sarah was continually embattled with the sex-segregated culture of her school. To her parents it seemed natural for the four siblings to play sports with each other. "It's not like they raised us saying, 'Okay, Sarah, you, Stephanie and Samantha can only play together, and then Dave plays by himself.' No. We were all playing at home. But the teachers, even at preschool . . . I always got in trouble because I always played with the boys." It's no surprise that Sarah was a natural athlete. Her mother and aunt, Suzanne and Sandra, are twin sisters who were both standout athletes as girls, setting records at the same high school that Sarah would eventually attend. She was aware that her mother and aunt played softball and baseball but didn't realize quite how good they were until she attended that high school and heard stories of their exploits. Sarah was not "groomed" in any calculated sense to be an athlete. Both her parents worked full-time—Dave as a policeman and Suzanne as a teacher—and encouraging their children took the form of an open invitation to play whatever they were drawn to, rather than a prescribed program aimed at future goals.

In spite of her mother's status as a high school softball legend, Sarah was not drawn to the sport. Her parents signed her up for softball in a T-ball league when she was six, but she didn't take to it.[3] The experience made such a faint impression on her that it takes some effort to recall it: "I don't remember softball leagues. . . . Ho, you know what? I do. T-ball. T-ball is what I first played for softball, and I remember that I thought it was the most boring sport. And I know softball people are going to hate me for saying that. I remember just hating it, and I told my parents, 'I don't like it. This is not fun for me.'"

Sarah's parents insisted that she finish out that first season, teaching her, "You don't quit. You finish. You finish this, and then next year we'll figure out something else." Sarah agreed, but proclaimed, "I want to play baseball. Sign me up for East View boy's baseball." The following year she tried out for a baseball team in the East View Little League. When she finally got on that baseball field for the first time, she thought, "This is it. This is what I want."

She was known at school and around the neighborhood as "the girl who plays with the boys." She paid it no mind: "Obviously, you're labeled as a

FIG. 15. Sarah Gascon, Eastview Little League, age ten. Courtesy of Sarah Gascon.

tomboy right away, which is fine. But I didn't know it. It's like a racehorse, like I just had blinders on. I just knew exactly what I was doing and knew where I was, and I didn't really pay attention to anything else around me. If there was harassment going on, I didn't know, because I don't remember it. I don't ever remember having a bad experience."

And then she thinks about it again: "The only bad experience I had playing baseball was the year that I thought I should have made the All-Star team, but I don't know if maybe I thought I was better than I was and I really wasn't that good." That was when she was twelve years old, in her last season in the Little League "Minors" before moving up to the teenage division, "Majors." She believed she had had an exceptionally good season, and when she was passed up for All-Stars, it hurt. Recalling that moment, Sarah still doubts herself, instead of doubting the politics of youth baseball. She went on to become a multisport star in high school and college and a representative of her country on two different women's national teams, baseball and handball.[4] But she still struggles with the message from Little League Baseball that her performance wasn't good enough to warrant playing with twelve-year-old "All-Stars." "Looking back on it now, I don't know if I was as good as I thought, and it's funny because . . . not that I need accolades. But I knew what accomplishments were, and I wanted that to be one of my accomplishments, and that's what it came down to. You set a goal as an athlete, unintentionally."

The selection process for Little League All-Stars is not SABR metrics. The coaches' sons and a few others are selected. But Sarah took the rejection to heart; she feared, and still struggles with, the sense that she wasn't as good as she thought. In one sense she was correct to suspect there was something bigger at stake than being named to the All-Star team. Being selected is more than a symbolic honor: it is an invitation to competitive tournament play all summer long, a road to local recognition, and one of the few opportunities to play summer ball for youngsters who do not have the resources to play private travel ball.

All-Star selection might have validated Sarah's self-confidence and helped her to avoid some of the self-doubt that plagued her for the next two years. But it became apparent that being passed up for summer play was a prelude to a series of setbacks in baseball that led her to withdraw from the sport entirely. The second discouraging moment came right on the heels of that first rejection. She was told she would not be allowed to move up to the "Majors," the age division for twelve- to fifteen-year-olds because she was a girl. "Not only did I not make the All-Star team, but they also weren't going to move me up to the Majors. They were going to keep me in Minors because I was a girl, so I wasn't going to be able to play with the guys that were the same age as me. I was going to play with the guys that were younger because I was a female."

The third rejection that finally pushed her out entirely was her coach's refusal to let her learn to play catcher. The catcher's position carries more risk of injury through contact than any other in baseball, but Sarah was given no choice about taking that risk. Nor were her parents consulted about their willingness to let her learn the position. With their history of encouraging Sarah and not being excessively worried about her getting injured, it seems likely that they would have allowed her to play whatever position she wanted. But "the coach wouldn't let me be a catcher. I played pitcher, first base, outfielder. Then I said I wanted to start learning how to be a catcher, and he said, 'No, you can't catch.' He didn't give me any reason why I couldn't catch. I was like, 'Okay. This is enough.' That was the final straw for me."

Sarah was being pushed out of baseball. She was told that her outstanding performance was not outstanding enough for the All-Stars; she was informed that she would be held back with younger boys, separated from the friends and teammates with whom she had played all her life; and she was denied the opportunity to learn a new position. At twelve years old she was given the message that she wasn't good enough to continue in the sport she loved most. It was the beginning of two difficult years for her. Sarah was losing a part of her life that anchored her and allowed her to feel at home with herself, just as she was entering adolescence.

She still played sports with boys at school, ignoring her teachers' disapproval. But when her girlfriends began to question her choice of companions at recess, she found it difficult to persist. She was also facing criticism from the girls for continuing with baseball. "Some of the girls were saying, 'You know, you're not going to play baseball in high school. You need to play softball.' I was thinking, 'I don't know . . .' I didn't necessarily have the most confidence. I had confidence when it came to being an athlete, but not socially. It was like I didn't know how to interact with people. I knew how to interact with boys and play sports, but I didn't know how to interact with the girls. I was the only girl playing with the boys during lunchtime or recess.

So when you have that additional pressure and you're not really confident and feel socially awkward, you think, 'Okay. Yeah, maybe they're right.'"

She signed up for softball when she entered middle school, but it only added to her struggles with self-confidence. "I was terrible because I was hitting like a baseball player and I had to get used to the field. It was just awkward for me." She was allowed to play catcher at last and was also a talented middle infielder. But because she was a newcomer to softball at age thirteen, there were dues to pay before she was accepted. "I heard the coaches, parents, and players saying that I was kind of an outcast because I was a baseball player coming into the softball world." She hadn't come up the same path as the others, and in youth sports these days, thirteen is old.

Sarah quickly got past the learning curve and excelled on her softball team. She believed her performance was worthy of selection to the All-Star team, but once again she was denied that honor. This time Sarah had no doubt that the reason for her exclusion was political rather than athletic. She refused to second-guess her ability as she had done with baseball. "So they didn't put me on the All-Star team when I was . . . I'm not going to say I was the best player on the team. I was one of the better players on the team, and our team was very good. We had a great pitcher. She made the All-Star team, and I think one other person made the All-Star team from our team, which was fine. So I just said to myself, 'Okay. I'm tired of not making the All-Star team. I'm making the All-Star team next year.' Sure enough, I did. But I still had people that didn't really want me to be on the team. They had to put me on the team because I was good enough, but they didn't have to play me, and so that's what happened." After two years in softball, she could no longer be denied athletically, but the softball community still resisted her presence.

During that second season, she earned a spot in the starting lineup, overcoming the resistance to her presence. But it was not the goodwill of her coaches that got her in the lineup. "We were getting smoked, and they said, 'Okay, Sarah, you can go in,' and I played second base. It was two outs and we could not get the third out, so that's when they put me in. Sure enough, what happens? Of course when you go into the game, you get the ball hit right to you. The ball was hit up the middle, and I'm laid out for it, caught it, a line drive, caught it, third out.[5] Then after that it was like, 'Oh, Sarah can play softball.' So I have to laugh at that."

Those two middle school years were unsettling for Sarah. Separated from the boys with whom she had played all her life, she was now also marginalized by the girls she was trying to join. She was willing to accommodate social expectations by playing softball, but that only seemed to cause more difficulties, caught as she was between two worlds. "Those two years, I think that's when I started to develop more of a chip on my shoulder. People always said that I wasn't big enough because I wasn't. I was short. The girls were a lot taller than me. I grew five inches going into my freshman year in high school. So I was just a little later than everybody else." Both the boys' and the girls' teams to which she had looked for a sense of belonging had failed her. She felt like an outsider, doubted her abilities and desires, and also doubted that she was justified in feeling so alienated. "Nobody could really say that you're wrong. It's just how I viewed it, what I felt internally. I'm thirty years old, and this is the first time I'm expressing my experience. I've never expressed it because I just felt that it was a part of my life and it was great regardless of whether it was positive or negative. It helped me to grow into the person I am today. [. . .]

"As insecure as I was growing up, I wanted people to like me, and I wanted to be in with the 'in' crowd. Popular. Even though I knew I was different. I mean, you know you're different . . . I don't know if I'm an old soul. I don't know what's wrong with me." But Sarah's inner strength would not allow her to relinquish the athleticism that was so central to her identity. Finally, in high school, at a time when so many athletic girls feel there's no place for them at all, Sarah came into her own as a multisport athlete.

"So the difference came. My freshman year in high school I made varsity volleyball, made varsity basketball, made varsity softball after only two years of playing softball. Not only did I make the varsity teams, I started on every team, and I made All-League on every team. So it was different because there's a whole new crowd now. You're in high school. I don't have to be hoping that I'm popular because I already am because of sports. That and credit to my siblings, because my sister was a senior in high school, my brother was a junior in high school. I would walk through, and people would be like, 'Oh, you're Gascon. You're the super athlete, aren't you?' I was like, 'Yeah, yeah, I am.' So I started holding my head up a little bit higher." She also inherited the legacy of her mother and aunt, "the Sena twins." The school welcomed Sarah as her family's heir apparent, and she felt at home with herself.

She developed a close relationship with her high school softball coach, Jesse Espinosa. "Jesse Espinosa was probably one of my favorite coaches of all time." But Sarah never learned to love softball with the same passion as her other sports. "To be honest with you, I'd never really felt like softball was my sport. People always said that I was a great softball player, and I just never felt like I had the same love and passion as I did with volleyball and basketball. Or baseball. Once Jesse asked me how much I loved softball. I said, 'I don't. I don't really love softball. It just never got to the heart of me.' He was so heartbroken by my answer. He's like, 'I can't believe you would say that!'

"I'm just being honest, because it's a different feel. As much as I loved playing for him and I loved playing softball with my teammates, I know the difference between loving a sport—dreaming and thinking about it all the time—compared to playing it because you do enjoy it and you want to win the championship. I know that difference. I enjoyed playing softball. I just didn't love it. I love baseball, and I knew it."

Sarah's sense of well-being as a high school athlete was reinforced when she was recruited by colleges in all three sports. Many young athletes, especially those with the means to hire private coaches and join expensive travel teams, are urged to specialize in one sport only. Childhood is consumed with precollegiate and preprofessional preparation. But coming from a working family that didn't have time to make their children's athletic careers the center of life, Sarah hadn't been involved in "the recruiting game" and later realized that her college choices were somewhat circumscribed by that. The Gascons' encouragement to their children—"Play whatever you want!"—was out of step with the current, calculated, single-minded pursuit of future athletic success.

"I was so late to the recruiting game, I didn't understand it. My parents didn't understand it." She had played some travel softball but really preferred basketball and volleyball. "The passion and love was just more toward basketball and volleyball than softball. So I did play travel volleyball, and that was what helped me to earn a scholarship." Although she had always dreamed of being a collegiate athlete, she hadn't followed the prescribed route to achieve it.

Her first experience with the high stakes of collegiate sports came when she was playing for South Bay Volleyball Club at a major showcase tournament in Las Vegas. With college coaches in attendance wearing their "UCLA or USC [University of Southern California] or Berkeley gear," it became suddenly real. "I was never really nervous, but before the tournament I was thinking, 'Oh my gosh, this is a big deal. This is your career!'" She didn't know where she wanted to go and didn't get enough offers from volleyball. She attracted partial scholarships from Towson University (near Baltimore), Northern Iowa University, and a few smaller schools in California. She had wanted to attend the University of San Diego, where brother David was a student. When Southeastern Louisiana University in Hammond, Louisiana, offered Sarah a full ride in volleyball and a chance to start her first year, she responded with interest. But she wanted to be a two-sport athlete in college and asked whether she would be able to play softball as well. When the coach gave her an affirmative answer, Sarah accepted the volleyball scholarship from Southeastern Louisiana, intending to try out for the softball team after volleyball season ended. It was a long way from Los Angeles. But she took the risk because it seemed to be her best chance of fulfilling her athletic dreams: she could be a two-sport collegiate athlete and possibly a future Olympian.

Sarah recounts key moments in her life when, after she had been told that she could not do something by teachers, coaches, and peers, she turned right around and did it. That rebellious streak is not her most obvious personality trait. Sarah is a devoted team player whose impulse is to be supportive and loyal, whether to family, school, team, or country. She is politically conservative, is fiercely patriotic, and wanted to be an Olympic athlete in part for the honor of representing the nation. Sarah is no "radical" in any sense. Yet, paradoxically, being an athletic woman in the United States means on some level being a rebel—being willing to resist norms to stay true to self. Participating in the national pastime becomes an act of rebellion for an American woman.

Sarah's rebelliousness was engaged when she chose her college. "People" at her high school had been telling her that volleyball was the weakest of her three sports. She should go with softball, "they" said. She was enjoying softball in high school, but "I knew I wanted to play volleyball in college because people told me I couldn't play. 'You can't play volleyball in college, Sarah. You're too short, and you're not good enough. You can't play with the boys because you're a girl. You can't play baseball because you have to play softball because that's what girls do. You can't play multiple sports in high school because you're only going to play one sport in college.' Don't tell me I can't do something. Because I'm going to do it, and then I'm going to throw it back in your face."

Sure enough, when Sarah arrived at Southeastern Louisiana, the coach, previously agreeable about her playing a second sport, discouraged her from trying out for softball. The volleyball team was terrible. It was the first time she had ever been on a losing team in any sport. She knew they were pretty poor before she accepted their scholarship offer. She had seen them play on her recruiting trip to Louisiana and had responded with cockiness, thinking, "I can definitely start, and I can make a difference, and I could put them on the map." Now she laughs when she thinks about it: "What a punk! Who was that punk eighteen-year-old kid?"

She gave it the old college try and was the only player to play in every game that season, 115 games her freshman year. Even armed with eighteen-year-old cockiness, Sarah alone couldn't turn the team into winners in a single season. During her meeting with the coaches after the season, she told them again that she intended to try out for the softball team. The volleyball coaches cautioned her that she would never become the volleyball player she could be if she played softball but told her to go ahead and try out if she must. They reminded her that she would have to make the softball team first, anyway.

She did. She had played shortstop in high school; her arm strength and lateral agility made her a natural in the position. But the Southeastern Louisiana Lady Lions already had an excellent shortstop, and Sarah was only a walk-on, or as she put it, "just this volleyball girl." The coach told her, "You're on the team, but you're playing third base." She managed to get the job as the starting third basewoman during freshman year, although she credits that turn of events to luck. "From nobody even knowing who I was in Louisiana to being a starting third baseman . . . it was all luck, because the third baseman at the time was a three-time All–Southland Conference third baseman, but she messed up her knee. They needed a third baseman just as I walked through the door."[6]

Sarah left her mark on Southeastern Louisiana Athletics. She finally began to love softball, in part because her team was excellent, but also because she enjoyed the culture of softball players, which she finds similar to that of baseball players. "I had a great team. They were crazy. They were typical softball/baseball type of teammates. Not that I didn't enjoy my volleyball teammates; it's just they were different. If anybody knows softball and baseball players, I think they know how unique their type of culture is." Sarah is referring here to the "dugout culture" of both sports. In a sport in which even the starters spend half of each game sitting on a bench with their teammates waiting for their turn to bat, there is plenty of time for high jinks, practical joking, teasing of both opponents and teammates. These are not activities associated with volleyball or basketball benches. But dugout shenanigans are actually welcomed in baseball and softball as indications of team chemistry.

Sarah silenced any remaining critics at Southeastern Louisiana by excelling in both sports. She was named to the All–Southland Conference team in softball four times and in volleyball twice. After her junior year she was ranked the number-one volleyball player in the country, and her school was also ranked number one. She accomplished her goal of helping to turn that team around, although it took several years. Sarah was named the Southland Conference's Defensive Player of the Week in volleyball a record thirteen times, including a period of nine consecutive weeks in 2003, and named Southeastern Female Student-Athlete of the Year for 2002–3. Most impressive, however, is something she doesn't even mention to me: she was inducted into the Southeastern Louisiana Athletics Hall of Fame in 2010.

Her senior year at Southeastern Louisiana ended on a disappointing note. Neither the volleyball nor the softball team made the playoffs, and although she had done well personally, it left her with a sense of incompleteness. "I didn't feel like I ended my career the way I wanted to. I didn't know what I wanted to do. I was about to be a college graduate. You go through this weird—I don't want to say I was depressed. It's just a weird type of uncertain feeling."

Sarah received offers to play volleyball in Europe, but that was not what she wanted to do: "I was brave enough to leave California and go to Louisiana, but I don't know if I was brave enough to go to an entire different part of the world. . . . I did receive offers to play professionally in Europe, and at that time I was scared . . . I didn't have the confidence that I had with everything else, to be away from my family and be in an unknown place and not know anything. Yes, that scared me." She had tried out for the U.S. Olympic volleyball team in 2002 and 2003 but didn't make it. "I was trying for Athens, but I was not good enough. I mean, there's some fabulous volleyball players in the country."

In the midst of Sarah's confusion about what to do after college, baseball reappeared. "Then I received this email from USA Baseball. 'All right! I'm going to the Chicago tryout.'" It was a godsend in the summer of 2004, giving her a focus for her athletic energy. Sarah was facing the same problem expressed by Jenny Dalton Hill and Veronica Alvarez: leaving college felt like being pushed off a cliff; there was nowhere to go with a lifetime of passion and training. USA Baseball solved that problem, albeit temporarily, for Sarah. "I was living in Louisiana still, and I started training for baseball. I got my assistant softball coach to help me with baseball because he was an old baseball player, played in college, and trained. My dad and I drove up to Chicago and tried out at Northwestern. I remember it was pouring rain there. It was in June. We were supposed to be out in the field. But we can't be out in the field. I walk in there, and there's tons of females in baseball uniforms, and I totally was a softball player, had a softball outfit on. I did have my pants on, but I had, like, a visor. I did not look like a baseball player. Are you kidding me?? So I walk in, and I look around. I remember the Silver Bullets because all I wanted to be growing up was a Silver Bullet. That was in the nineties, and I remember watching them play and thinking, 'I'm going to be a Silver Bullet one day. I'm going to play baseball and be a Silver Bullet.' And I walk into the USA tryouts, and I see Bridget and Laura and Kim.[7] They're all standing next to each other. Then I look around, and there are the All-American Girls. I'm thinking, 'Oh my gosh! This is heaven!'"

The young women who arrive at tryouts for the national team are usually seeing other women playing baseball for the first time in their lives and are moved to think of heaven. But being at a national tryout doesn't allow much time to dwell on the miracle of it all. Sarah quickly found that she needed to make an adjustment *back* to baseball after so many years away. She had played eight years of high school and collegiate softball and had become unaccustomed to the longer distances in baseball. "We have this tryout, and I'm at shortstop. I'm thinking, 'I'm a great fielder.' My dad was telling me, 'Listen, Sarah, it's 120 feet.' [. . .]

"There's a group of shortstops. Of course, everybody always measures everybody up, right? I'm looking at all the other shortstops. It's my turn, and I go to throw. Everybody's bouncing the ball, these shortstops are bouncing the ball to first. It's taking four hops, five hops to first! We're on turf. We're on the football facility [at Northwestern University in Evanston, Illinois]. Of course I go up there thinking, 'I'm going to hose it to first.' But no . . . I bounce the ball to first base! I'm like, 'Are you kidding me right now? What's going on?' It's so much farther away than I thought. So the next ground ball comes, and I'm, 'Okay, Sarah, come on. Throw the ball to first.' Same thing happens, and I'm thinking, 'You've got to be kidding me!' So then the third ground ball comes, and I'm like, 'Let me just run through it so I at least look good when I'm doing it.' So I field it. I'm running through the ball, I field it, throw it on the run, get it to first base. Only one out of three makes it to first. That's terrible!"

A few other terrible things happened too. They were practicing turning double plays, and a ball was hit up the middle, between the shortstop and second base positions. That's the shortstop's ball, and Sarah went to field it and then try to make the double play at first base. "Even if it was right next to the bag, I'm not going to field the ground ball and toss to a second baseman. I'm going to touch the bag (second base) and throw it to first.

FIG. 16. (*left*) Sarah Gascon, Team USA. Courtesy of Sarah Gascon.

FIG. 17. (*below*) Sarah Gascon hard-charging at shortstop, Team USA 2010. Courtesy of Dave Gascon.

I mean, that's Baseball 101, Softball 101. But the second baseman, who was a kid . . . probably a teenager . . . runs to second base and steps on it. But I'm also running to second from shortstop to step on the bag and throw to first. I knock her down because she's maybe a hundred pounds, and I'm like, 'Sorry!'"

To complete the comedy of errors at her first USA tryout, Sarah hit one of the coaches in the head with an errant throw. "At batting practice, the Silver Bullets are behind the cage, and they're catching the balls for people. I'm acting like I'm hustling and being out there so the coaches could see me. Twenty-two years old, and I'm still a punk kid. I get a ball, and I go to toss it to Laura Purser. She goes to catch it, but I toss it away. I just threw it away from her. I don't even know how I threw the ball, but I toss it away. Bridget [Veenema] is standing right next to her, but Bridget's not paying attention. The ball hits Bridget in the temple, and I'm thinking, 'Oh my gosh! I just hit a Silver Bullet in the head!' I was so embarrassed. The manager grabbed Bridget around the shoulder and gave me the dirtiest look. I was thinking, 'Oh my God, what do I do? Should I go run up to her? Well, no. I need to say sorry, but I can't act like a fool.' Bridget's all pissed off; they get her a cold wet cloth to put on her head. She's looks at me like, 'What's wrong with you??' My dad goes up with a cold Coke can, 'Here you go,' because nobody had ice. She's like, 'Who's this clown? Who's this guy giving me a Coke can for my head?' It was a two-day tryout. We finished, and I went up to her and said, 'I'm really sorry.' She said, 'That's fine. Just don't let it happen again. Pay attention to what you're doing. You're a baseball player. You have to be aware of certain things.' So I wind up making that first cut, and I thought I had a terrible tryout. I was so embarrassed after that tryout. But I got the invite list that was on the Internet, and I'm one of the thirty-four that were invited to the final tryout."

In spite of the awkward reentry after ten years away from baseball, Sarah was in love with the sport again. "I don't think I ever fell out of love. I think I always loved baseball. At that tryout, I knew, '*This* sport—*this* is what it is. *This* is how it's supposed to feel when you get on a ball field. Because it was either that or play professional softball, and I thought, 'No way. I'm playing baseball.'"

10

Jenna Marston

SHORTSTOP/PITCHER

"Of course I wanted to play in the Majors. Who wouldn't?"

Jenna Marston is a St. Louis native who has had a stellar collegiate softball career at the University of Missouri.[1] She grew up playing baseball and was able to play both baseball and softball in high school. Jenna attended Principia High School, a small Christian school where her father was the baseball coach and math teacher and where softball was a fall sport. When Jenna entered as a freshman, her older brother, Christopher, was the senior star pitcher and shortstop. She played baseball on the same team as her brother, coached by their father. She is truly "bilingual" in the worlds of softball and baseball, equally comfortable playing both sports. She pitched and played shortstop on the 2010 USA Baseball Women's National Team and won recognition for her standout play on both offense and defense. She has been a softball starter at Missouri since she was a freshman, playing catcher, shortstop, and outfield. No complaints from Jenna: she has been blessed with exceptional athletic talent, a loving and supportive family, and appropriate recognition of her abilities. She is at home in the world and with herself and exemplifies the ability to adapt to the athletic road open to a girl and succeed brilliantly.

Baseball was her childhood game and first love in sports, and like the majority of her USA Baseball teammates, she came to it naturally, as a matter of course, early in life. The youngest child and only daughter in a close-knit family of four, Jenna played baseball because her father and brother played. Bill Marston was a catcher when he attended Principia College. He held his teaching and coaching position at Principia High School for twenty-five years, including the years when his two children attended. He retired from coaching after Jenna graduated to have time to follow her softball games at Mizzou. Cindy Marston, Bill's wife and Christopher and Jenna's mother, is the academic technology coordinator at Principia High. Baseball is a family affair. "My dad was a coach and just a huge baseball guy, just loves the game, and his dad loved the game. Christopher is my brother, and he started playing, and that's what I wanted to do too. I wanted to be like my brother, and I wanted to do anything he could do. So I played baseball." Cindy is a happy spectator at her family's games and will watch a St. Louis Cardinals game with her family, but she herself doesn't play ball.

At five years old Jenna first played organized baseball on an all-girls baseball team, although she was so young that she can't remember whether it was T-ball, or if the coaches pitched, or even if it was baseball or softball. The following year, she joined an all-boys team, and her memory of that is somewhat clearer: "It was in the Manchester Athletic Association or something. The coach's daughter was the only other girl on the team. So it was the two of us. Then she switched over to softball at maybe sixth grade or so."[2] Her teammate switched to softball at the age when most girls do, but Jenna never gave it a thought: "That wasn't even a thought in my mind, really. I was going to play baseball. There wasn't a question in my mind, and I never really considered switching. Nobody ever gave me any trouble, and everybody was always supportive. I didn't even think it was that weird that I played because nobody said anything to me."

Jenna experienced none of the usual pressure to do the "smart thing" and switch to softball for a college scholarship. She recalls nothing but encouragement. "It was always, 'Do you want to play?' 'Of course I do.' That's just how my parents have always been with all my activities. They've never really forced me to do something. I just always wanted to play as much as possible." She was a multisport athlete right through high school, but baseball was her first love. "I played other sports, but baseball was

FIG. 18. Jenna Marston, an early at bat. Courtesy of Cindy Marston.

always my main sport. I played soccer through eighth grade. I played basketball through high school and played a little tennis at some point. But it was always baseball first. I think that that was because my dad and brother just loved it so much, they passed it on to me. We'd sit and watch Cardinal games. We're huge Cardinal fans. I think it was just that. It was an easy connection with them."

The year before she entered high school, Jenna played on a travel baseball team with the St. Louis Amateur Baseball Association (SLABA). "I wasn't the best player, but I always hung with the guys just fine. When you're little, there's really not a whole lot of difference between guys and girls, and so that wasn't an issue at all. I guess it was the year before going into my [high school] freshman year that some of the guys were starting to develop. Guys change so much through high school. Even there I hung with them pretty well, but definitely not the best. They were starting to get a lot bigger, faster, and stronger."

Jenna knew she could play both softball and baseball in high school. Because the school was small and her father was the coach, she was assured a spot on the baseball team if she wanted it. She also knew that she would not receive any special treatment. (Indeed, her father felt obliged to be more demanding on his own two children than on his other players.) So Jenna did not face the usual pressures that girls playing high school baseball in the United States usually confront. However, if she wanted a college scholarship, she needed to make a decision about whether to play baseball or softball during summers. "I had to decide what to do going into sophomore year. So I tried out for the fifteen-and-under boys' baseball team, and I didn't make it, but my dad was thinking about coaching it. If he coached, obviously I would be on the team, but that was the point I knew that I wouldn't play as much because obviously I wasn't as good. I had to decide whether I wanted to do that or play softball in the summer. It was kind of a hard decision for me because I really didn't want to have to go play softball, but I think I knew that was where I was going to play. I knew I wasn't going to get as much playing time in baseball as I would in softball."

So Jenna made the rational decision. Although she preferred baseball, she knew she would be a standout on a softball team in a way she could not be if she continued to play baseball on a boys' team. "I decided to go to softball, and I'm extremely happy with that decision. I would not change that at all. I've thought about it a lot, and if I had made that fifteen-and-under team outright, without my dad having coached, my guess is I would have chosen that over softball. But I'm glad I didn't. I think the fact that I knew I could play baseball at high school made it easier. It wasn't like I was just completely giving baseball up. In my mind, I was still going to get to play. I knew I would have three more years of playing baseball, and I guess that was enough for me."

She played tournament softball in the summers before her sophomore and junior years and learned to like the game. "My dad used to describe softball as a kind of watered-down baseball, but playing that first summer showed us both it really isn't. It's not that at all. Realizing that, I didn't really feel like I was giving up much at all." On the baseball team she was a utility player, or as she calls it, a "tenth man": "I went to a small high school, and whoever was pitching, I would play where they usually played. If an outfielder had to come pitch, I would play the outfield. If an infielder had to come pitch, I'd go play somewhere on the infield. I played third and second and pitched and outfield. My senior year I played some shortstop, but for the most part it was outfield, second, and then a little bit of third, and then pitching. . . . We actually didn't even have enough to have a full varsity and JV. I was like a swing player, so I would play for both JV and varsity my freshman year. There were quite a few kids that played on both because we didn't have enough kids."

The real thrill for her was playing on the same team as her brother. "In baseball, I would say all of freshman year of high school, just getting to play with my brother, that was an awesome experience, because I grew up watching him play. I watched his high school games for the three years previous, and so to finally get to play with him. . . . We're pretty close, and my whole life I've always looked up to him in everything. So getting to actually play with him was really cool." Christopher played pitcher and shortstop.

With characteristic modesty, Jenna dismisses the fact that playing high school baseball was anything exceptional. She believes her road was easier than most. "I'm sure my experience was different [from most girls who play baseball] because the high school I went to was a private school. My dad has worked there forever, and I went there through the elementary school all the way up. It's really a comfortable place for me. Just going to high school really wasn't a huge change or anything, and it wasn't a whole bunch of new people or anything like that." Jenna observes that if you find the right niche, anybody can succeed: "A lot of it is just picking the right level to play for wherever you're at." She was friendly with her teammates and didn't notice that she faced any particular challenges as the only girl. "I was friends with all the guys. I think I had enough respect. I never heard any issues from them. Who knows what they said in the locker room, but they never gave me any trouble. I was just another teammate to them."

Like most young ballplayers, whether male or female, she had Major League dreams and had to give them up when the unlikelihood of making the pros became apparent: "Of course I wanted to play in the Majors. Who wouldn't? That's what anybody wants to do who plays baseball growing up. I remember my family and I went to a game at ASU, a college baseball game, and that was the first real college game I'd been to, and I thought that was really cool. So for a little while after that, I wanted to play baseball at ASU. I don't really remember when I realized that none of that's going to happen. I don't feel like I've ever had a hard time letting go of it."

She also sailed right through the college recruiting process and, as usual, downplays her own ability, crediting her success to good luck and good coaches: "My story of getting into college softball is kind of different from the normal [softball player] because I'd played baseball. But really the way it worked out for me is I didn't do a whole lot to get recruited. I kind of got lucky and got recruited. I didn't really think much about playing in college and stuff like that before I started getting recruited. It wasn't ever a huge goal of mine because I hadn't played softball. If you talk to any of my [Missouri] teammates, I'll bet they'll all tell you, 'Oh yeah, I've been dreaming about playing college softball since I was a little girl.' But that wasn't my dream because I didn't play [softball] before high school. I've always known that I just want to play sports as long as I can in whatever way. So when I switched to softball, it was like, 'Okay, yeah I want to play,' but that was going into my sophomore year, and I didn't realize that you start getting recruited then. To me, I had plenty of time, and it wasn't a big deal."

Marston's soft-spoken modesty is genuine. Things have come easily to her, and she doesn't think it has involved any exceptional talent or effort on her part. In spite of that self-effacing attitude, she obviously had what it took to attract the attention of Division I softball coaches. But she deflects attention away from herself. "The way it works with softball is they'll have these big tournaments. They call them college exposure tournaments. They'll bring in a whole bunch of coaches at all levels, from top-twenty-five Division I programs to community college coaches. It's just whoever wants can come watch. The college coaches hear from people [about prospective college athletes] or have gotten emails or whatever, and so they have people they want to watch. So that's how I got recruited, just playing in those." Her summer softball coach made the phone calls and wrote the emails. Jenna was unperturbed. She just played her usual game. "Everything just kind of worked out for me, and a lot of that is because my summer coach is a really friendly guy and made a lot of the phone calls and [wrote] emails without me knowing."

Her parents undoubtedly knew about the coach's outreach, but Jenna was blessedly oblivious. She didn't even experience the nerves described by some softball players at showcase tournaments, when they are aware that their future college career is on the line: "When I was first getting watched, I wasn't even realizing that I was being watched because I wasn't thinking about it. The first time was freshman year or sophomore year that fall, I think. But it didn't mean much to me because I really wasn't thinking about it. Going into junior year, I was aware that we were being watched sometimes. There would be times when I was kind of nervous. You just want to make sure you do well, but when you're playing five to seven games a weekend, you just forget about it. It goes back to just playing."

She was invited on three Division I recruiting trips, but her recollection of the process is subdued in comparison to the usual anxiety experienced by many NCAA-bound athletes. "With all the NCAA rules, they couldn't contact me directly, so I had to email them first. So they would tell my coach, and he would tell me. I went on three visits. I visited Mizzou, Northwestern, and Mississippi State. There were other smaller programs that showed interest, but those were the three I narrowed it down to pretty quickly." Northwestern had the best softball program and also the highest academic ranking, but Jenna was reticent about going so far from home: "I didn't want to go north to play." Mississippi State was in the South, which felt more culturally familiar to Jenna than Chicago, but it was even farther away from St. Louis than Northwestern. Jenna is a serious student and regarded all three schools as acceptable choices for academics as well as softball. "None of them were slacker schools or anything. I didn't feel there was anything that another school could offer me that one of those three didn't."

It was easy to select Missouri because of its proximity to home and because, while Northwestern had a winning softball program and had already been to the Women's College World Series, Missouri was on the rise. Jenna hoped to be a part of the team's ascent. The full ride offered by Missouri was also attractive. She doesn't remember exactly, but she thinks Northwestern offered her "a full ride the last three years and something like 50 percent my freshman year or something like that. So pretty substantial offers from all of them." She committed to Mizzou spring of her junior year of high school and continued to play softball, baseball, and basketball until she graduated Principia. "That was a big deal to me. I didn't want to have to focus just on softball and give those up."

Was there a point in her life when she began to identify more with softball than baseball? "It's a good question. I'm trying to think of how to answer it. If you talk to other softball players, I bet they would say that I'm a baseball player at heart, because there's a difference in a lot of the little stuff, something as silly as the cheering.[3] So I guess if you talked to them, they would say I've got much more of a baseball approach than a lot of girls. But I would say, at this point, I'm a softball player."

Women softball players cheer each other on from the dugout, often with orchestrated cheers. Baseball players would never engage in boisterous dugout cheering: a manly high five and "good job" is how a baseball teammate is greeted in the dugout after an outstanding play, except at the end of an important game. Then piling on each other in victory is allowable. Jenna is quiet and thinks she behaves more like a baseball player in that regard—no cheerleading from the sidelines. Still, "I don't know that it's necessarily a baseball-softball thing. I think it's a male-female thing. If there were as many women's baseball teams as there are softball teams, I'm sure women's baseball would have the same sort of cheering culture that softball does. I really think it's a male-female thing as opposed to a baseball-softball thing."

Softball players also overtly communicate the location of a pitch to their teammate at bat, by audibly announcing where the catcher is setting up. The unspoken rules of baseball forbid signaling the batter from the dugout. "In baseball, if you're giving a location based on where the catcher is setting up and the other team figures it out, somebody is going to get hit and going to get hurt. That [sort of payback] doesn't happen in softball. The dugout [in softball] will watch the catcher, see where they set up, and tell the batter where the pitch is going to be. In baseball they do it too but much more subtly. I'll say it that way. If players in baseball did it as blatantly as softball does it, somebody would be thrown at. There's that sort of difference."

There are also differences between the fundamentals of the two games, but Jenna has had no difficulty moving from one to the other. Her swing has been a "baseball swing" since childhood. "Yes, there are definitely differences [between the two games], but as far as my swing, I didn't change my swing. I don't have a different swing when I play baseball. It's the same. I think, for the most part, that's true of softball players. A lot of softball players like to bring up that Jenny Finch [the great collegiate softball pitcher from the University of Arizona] has struck out Major League Baseball players from forty-three feet away [the distance from the pitcher to home plate in collegiate softball]. But if you put a softball player up against a Major League Baseball pitcher, I bet they'd strike out too. The pitch just looks different. If you give a good athlete enough time, they'll figure it out and make adjustments. So the swing really isn't different. If you can hit one, you can hit the other. It's just figuring it out. [. . .]

"My dad, obviously, was my coach growing up. I didn't take hitting lessons or anything like that. He was my coach. And here [at Missouri] our head coach played baseball, and he also played men's fast-pitch softball. So he knows they're essentially the same swing. We use different bats. Other than that, when we watch film here, we watch a lot of Major League hitters and try to have the same swing as them. Also, our volunteer assistant coach was a Major League ballplayer. He never played fast-pitch. Everything he knows is from baseball, but it works the same."

The biggest difference Jenna notes between the games is fielding. "Softball, because the bases are so much closer, is a much quicker game. It's less of a power game and more quickness. You have to field everything cleanly the first time and get rid of it quick. In baseball, if you stay in front of it, you have time to throw the runner out still. So I was getting used to that [in college softball], and because I came from baseball, I had a long throwing motion. I was shortening that up, and just little things like that, nothing difficult to change, but it was just little things that you have to get used to."

Jenna strives for calm and consistency as an athlete, a goal that is completely compatible with her personality. "I've always tried to be a calm, composed player, not get too high, not get too low. I figure that's better than having a five-for-five day and then an oh-for-five day. I'd rather be three for five every day, but that's hard . . . that would be unbelievable! Of course you're going to have ups and downs in the season, but if you can minimize it, I think that's better." Control and consistency are keys to excellence in any sport, but they are particularly important in baseball, where perfection is statistically impossible. It is an old adage that baseball is "a game of failure" in which even the best hitters succeed only one-third of the time and pitching a "perfect game" is a rare event. But from the standpoint of an elite athlete, failure is not acceptable, even when you know it is bound to happen. "I'd say I'm kind of a perfectionist, and I don't like messing up. Everybody calls baseball a game of failure, and that seems kind of strange. It bothers me when I make a stupid mistake. I understand that mistakes will happen, but I get frustrated if I can't figure something out. I've always been the type of person that if a coach tells me to change something, I can usually get it pretty quickly."

FIG. 19. (*above*) Jenna Marston, a later at bat, Team USA 2010. Courtesy of USA Baseball.

FIG. 20. (*left*) Jenna Marston, Team USA 2010, USA Baseball Sportswoman of the Year. Courtesy of Brian Fleming.

Although she is remarkably even-keeled and tries to keep herself that way, she admits to a few highs and lows. One great moment in softball came when, as a freshman at Missouri, she hit a walk-off home run against rival Kansas (KU). "KU is our school rival, and we just don't want to lose to them. So getting that one was pretty cool. The other one was last year when we won the Big 12 championship at home. Knowing that we would at least be tied for a championship, that was a pretty exciting moment too."

Her favorite baseball memories are playing with her brother when she was a freshman and he was a senior in high school. Only one baseball moment in her life was particularly disappointing: in her final at bat in the first game against Venezuela at the 2010 Women's World Cup, she struck out, swinging on a pitch that was over her head. But she recalls even that with a balanced perspective: "I don't know if I would say I was nervous, but it was definitely a different feeling than I've felt before. When I can play calm, that's when I'm the most comfortable. So when you're playing in front of that [Venezuelan] crowd, and they have the Battle of the Bands going on in the stadium, it was kind of hard to stay calm and everything. My last at bat, when I struck out on a pitch over my head, I would say it was because of the crowd. I wasn't focused in enough, and I remember that specifically. It wasn't even close. Who knows why I was swinging at it, except that the crowd was affecting me. It was kind of that anxious feeling, I guess."

The WCWS is the biggest event in women's college softball, but when Mizzou plays in that stellar venue, Jenna is able to tune out the noise of the crowd. She found the WCWS crowd less unnerving than that at the 2010 Women's World Cup because the college softball crowd is less partisan and less noisy. "We're always really excited to go, but once you start playing, you don't really notice that it's any different. You kind of zone in. The crowd there isn't really biased or anything. Yes, one team will have their section of fans, and the other will have theirs, but then the rest of the people are really just softball fans or little girls that just want to come watch you play. So they just cheer for everybody or nobody. It's different."

It was Jenna's play as a freshman during Missouri's regular season game against Texas A&M that brought her to the attention of the USA Baseball

Women's National Team. Team USA director Ashley Bratcher's mother had been watching Mizzou play Texas A&M on television, and when she heard from the announcer that Jenna Marston had played baseball in high school, she called Ashley. "Ashley emailed my coach and asked if any of the seniors would want to come to the tryouts, and also me since I've played baseball before. So my coach forwarded me the email. I read it and couldn't decide. He told me to do whatever I liked."

Jenna had planned to play a light summer softball schedule in 2010 to rest for her coming sophomore year at Missouri. She very nearly didn't even show up for the USA tryouts. At the last minute she went to the preliminary tryouts in Chicago over the July Fourth weekend, was invited to finals in Cary, made the team, and dominated the Venezuela tournament. She was a starting pitcher and shortstop, made the All-Tournament team at shortstop, and was named Sportswoman of the Year by USA Baseball. She hit .593, the second highest in the tournament, and led all tournament competitors with sixteen hits and eight doubles. She finished with twelve runs scored, seven runs batted in, and was three for three on stolen bases.[4] Yet when I asked her where to find her tournament stats from Venezuela, she replied, modestly, "I have absolutely no idea where to find the stats or anything."[5]

In January 2011 Jenna received the prestigious John E. Wray Award for Achievement in Sports Other than Professional Baseball at the St. Louis Baseball Writers' Dinner. As she was called up to receive the award, she was asked if she wanted to say a few words. Shy and understated as always, she managed, "Thank you. Go Cards!" and then smiled and stepped down. Indeed, when our interview was finished, she remarked to me, "I'm usually not very good at talking, so this is impressive." I was not shy about accepting that as high praise.

Jenna Marston now loves both baseball and softball. I asked how she would go about building women's baseball in the United States, and she was quick to respond that softball is the most efficient way to go. "I'd definitely start by going through softball. I'm sure there are other girls who started out playing baseball on other teams. There are some really good athletes at this level. Even if they hadn't played baseball before, they're going to pick it up really quickly because they're so similar. So I would say try to get the best athletes, and then even if they haven't really played baseball, they'll learn, because if they can play softball that well, they can play baseball that well. I would say in the long run obviously that's not your ideal situation. But I think it would kind of trickle backward. Then the interest will grow."

The only question that brings the unflappable Jenna Marston a visible moment of anxiety is, "What do you want to do when you graduate?" A cloud flickers across her face, and she responds, "That's a scary question right now. My teammates and I talk about it a lot, as upperclassmen nearing the end of our careers. We're always saying, 'I wish we could just stay here.' We always say, 'Well, I would just stay here and play forever. That would just be so much fun.' I think that's really how I feel at this point, is that I just want to stay in college and have this experience for longer. I'm sure I'll reach an age where I do not want to be in college anymore. But at this point that's not where I am, and so I do look at the Major Leagues and go, 'Oh, I really would like to get there,' if they had that for softball. Part of me goes, 'Yeah,' but then another part of me thinks there's something about playing for the college that's different than being a professional athlete, and I have loved my experience so much, I just don't want this to end."

When I interviewed Jenna in Columbia, Missouri, she graciously showed me through the inner sanctum of Missouri Athletics as she had a minor injury attended to by the team trainer. She was treated with solicitous affection by everybody in the varsity athletics center. She gave me a tour of the trainers' facility and locker room and proudly walked me over to the softball field and into the dugout and clubhouse. It was my first exposure to the privilege accorded NCAA Division I athletes. As I walked with Jenna, I found myself thinking about how difficult it would be for anyone good enough to earn an invitation into this aristocracy of sport *not* to choose to play among the best college athletes in the nation. Why would any girl *not* be eager to play softball, if this is the reward at the end of the road?

Collegiate softball players reap the rewards of being the best at what our culture approves of for girl athletes. But only for a little while. Our most accomplished women athletes are expected to end their careers after college. It seems a ridiculous waste of talent, both for the players who have devoted their lives to becoming the best in their sport, only to be turned out to pasture at age twenty-one, and for American sports in general. If anybody can handle the stress of the athletic sacrifice that we expect of our women, it is Jenna Marston. For now, her ability to live in the present seems like another wise choice for her.

PART 4

Baseball Girls

11

Malaika Underwood

SECOND BASE

"Baseball always finds me."

Few eighth grade girls think of querying local high school baseball coaches to determine whether they are amenable to having a girl on the team.[1] But Malaika Underwood has never been a conventional person. She insists that baseball simply found her when she was five years old, and she responded with instant love. By middle school she also knew she would have to take extraordinary measures to continue to advance in the sport and was determined to find a high school that would give her a chance to maintain the relationship. She sent a letter to five high school coaches in her district:

Dear Coach,

My name is Malaika Underwood. I am interested in attending your school. I am in the 8th grade and am presently attending O'Farrell Community School: Center for Advanced Academic Studies. I am in the process of choosing what high school I would like to attend.

I am a young lady 14 years of age. I am interested in playing baseball, not softball! Last year I played on the Chollas Lake Senior Minor Team for 13 and 14 year olds. I am a pitcher and second basewoman. Last year I batted third in the order, hitting .557. We played a total of 25 games, I had 61 at bats and 34 hits. I made no errors at second and had an ERA of 1.85 as a pitcher. I presently play for the Chollas Lake Senior Major team for 14 and 15 year olds. We are currently playing games. We will start the Tournament of Champions in about a week. After the Tournament, I will begin games for all-stars.

Now that you know a little about me, I would like to let you know that I don't expect some special placement or treatment, but I do expect a fair chance.

I would like to know if you have anything against women playing on your high school team? Has any girl tried out for your high school football and/or baseball team? Has any girl ever made the team?

I would appreciate if you would write me with the answers to these questions and anything you would like to tell me about the school, yourself, the athletic program at your school, or your team.

Thanks for taking the time to read and reply to my letter.

Thanks.
Malaika Underwood

Perhaps her family background nurtured that courage and confidence. Malaika's mother, Lynn Sharpe-Underwood, the daughter of a preacher from North Carolina, is African American, was educated at New York University (NYU), and is currently working with youth gangs in San Diego to help prevent violence and care for the families who are its victims. Malaika's father, Thom Underwood, is European American, was born in New York in 1949 into a family of four boys, and was educated in North Carolina. When he was in his twenties, like so many young people of his generation, Thom drove across country, intending to spend time in San Francisco. He arrived in San Diego during the night and slept in his car, planning to drive to San Francisco the next day. When he opened his eyes at daylight, he saw the Pacific Ocean stretched before him and thought, "It's not going to get any better than this." He never made that right turn north. Forty years later, he is still a Southern Californian who kayaks every morning, roasts his own coffee beans, and cooks gourmet food with his wife. Thom is an accredited jewelry appraiser, who got his start in the industry thirty-five years ago as a goldsmith and jewelry manufacturer.

Along the way he developed computer software, which he sells to other appraisers in the industry. Malaika describes him as "an underrated athlete, and someone who, when he gets into something, he does it until he's an expert."[2]

Thom was introduced to Lynn Sharpe by one of his brothers while on a return visit to his family in New York. Lynn had graduated NYU and was working as a journalist. That in itself took some independence of mind, since Lynn was of the generation of women who was told that their career options were teaching, and teaching. She did not want to leave New York. Thom had vowed never to leave San Diego. Lynn finally gave in and agreed to try living in Southern California. Her daughter wryly notes, "That's probably the only time my mom has given in to anything!" They married soon afterward. Malaika is the middle of Thom and Lynn's three children, and she clearly carries the double genetic endowment of independence. Her younger brother, Nicky, was adopted as a newborn when Malaika was four, and their sister, Edith, nine years older than Malaika, was a foster child who lived near the Underwoods and babysat for Malaika and Nicky. She was adopted into the family when she was fifteen years old and Malaika was six. The entire family is mixed race. Malaika is the biological child of her parents, Nicky's biological father was Moroccan, and Edith is half Japanese, half Mexican. Malaika observes, "It's a very diverse family, and it certainly affects the way I think of family—much less in a traditional sense than if we had all just been the same."

Malaika doesn't know exactly where her competitive athleticism came from. Both parents are active, outdoor people, but neither is a team sport athlete. "Sports really just found me, and I found myself in sports, and I felt comfortable there, where I probably didn't feel as comfortable outside of sports, because I was the tomboy. My earliest memories are playing sports on the baseball field."

The Underwoods lived in a neighborhood with other mixed-race families, and Malaika never thought it was anything but ordinary. "My mom is black and my dad is white, and we grew up in a neighborhood where all of my close friends were mixed race as well. There were two families we were very close to, who lived in the neighborhood and they were both mixed race, black and white. So to us, it was normal to be mixed race. And we all looked the same. It's funny because we would go out and it could be three or four kids from different families with a parent, maybe coming back from a Little League game, and people would think that we were all brothers and sisters." To anybody seeing Malaika and her mother today, there is no mistaking the family relationship, so closely do the two women resemble each other.

Growing up in San Diego, with its eternally perfect weather, Malaika was outdoors playing with the neighborhood kids all year round. "That's just what we did in the neighborhood. We played outside. We rode bikes. We were just active kids, and so sports were just always a part of my life. It's just what I did. I remember breaking my arm riding a bike at a very early age. But my real concrete memories start to come when I actually was playing baseball. I remember going up to the school that was only a couple of blocks from my house and practicing."

She played in the Chollas Lake Little League. Her first team was a T-ball team, the Brown Bears. She so cherished that brown baseball hat with the "CL" logo on it that she took it to school with her every day. The team of five-year-old T-ballers wore those hats, brown team T-shirts, jeans, and tennis shoes. They would graduate to baseball pants and cleats the following year.

During her second year of Little League, when teams moved from hitting off tees to using a pitching machine, Malaika was playing outfield and wanted to try second base. Her father told her, if she didn't speak up, she would stay in the outfield. "At some point I got up the courage to go up to my coach and say, 'I really want to play second base. Can I try?'" The coach gave her a chance, and she knew immediately, "That was my position. It's where I felt at home." Twenty-five years later, it is still her position. In 2008 for Team USA she was asked to try playing third base. "I remember going over there and standing in position and thinking, 'This is like a foreign language to me.' The game just looked so different from that side of the field, the way the ball came off the bat . . . I just felt so uncomfortable over there."[3]

Even early in her Little League career, Malaika wasted no time assuming

FIG. 21. Malaika Underwood, Chollas Lake Little League. Courtesy of Malaika Underwood.

a leadership position on the field. There was another girl on the Brown Bears, playing outfield. "I remember there being a pop fly to this girl, and she caught it, and her first reaction was, 'I caught the ball! I caught the ball! I caught the ball!' And I turned around to her from the infield and said, 'Throw it in! Don't hold it!' Of course, that's me, you know: She's just out there having a grand old time, and she caught the ball for the first time in her life, and here I am ruining the moment telling her to get the ball in!" Her teammates on Team USA would have no trouble recognizing that take-charge six-year-old.

Baseball was the place where Malaika felt most comfortable with herself. Little League was "the beginning of my love of sports and being able to identify who I felt I was. I really found myself on the field." She regards that comfort as a gift; she never went looking for it. "I really do think baseball found me. Maybe my parents have different memories of this, but I don't remember walking up to my parents and saying, 'I want to play baseball.' They just got me involved in what was available in the neighborhood, which happened to be baseball, and I fell in love with it."

When there wasn't a Little League game scheduled, Malaika and the neighborhood boys devised pickup games. "You never see this anymore, but we'd play two-on-two baseball. We'd cut off right field, and you could only hit to left field. You would pitch to your own teammate, and the other team would play shortstop and left field, and they would try and get the ball in to the shortstop before you got to first base. Or we'd do a home run derby. If we were playing up at the school, we would play with hard balls. But if we were playing in someone's front yard, we used tennis balls or Wiffle balls. Once we did play in someone's front yard with a real baseball, and we broke a window, so we figured, 'Maybe we should stick with something that's not going to break a window and get us in trouble!'"

The softball leagues in her community were at separate parks from the Little League fields. She never saw girls playing softball, and she was never tempted to switch games. "By the time I was nine or ten, I was playing real Little League Baseball, and by that time there weren't other girls in the league. So I was the Lone Ranger at that point. But I never really thought about it all that much. It's not like I saw all these girls over there playing on their softball teams, which might have made me think, 'Hey, maybe I am different because I'm playing baseball and all the other girls are playing softball.' That didn't happen to me. I just played, and all my friends were playing. Baseball was just what we did."

The baseball fields were closer to her house, and the boys who played there had become her closest friends, so baseball felt natural. There may also have been racial or socioeconomic differences that unconsciously discouraged Malaika from seeking out softball farther from the racially diverse neighborhood where she felt at home. She doesn't recall the details but simply remembers that she was happy playing baseball and saw no reason to change anything. And like so many athletically gifted girls, she felt more comfortable playing with boys. "In my neighborhood, I felt comfortable because I was among friends, and they didn't care. Malaika was just Malaika. But in school, I wasn't girly enough. I had crushes on boys, but the boys liked the pretty girls and the girly girls and not me, because I was the tomboy. So I felt more comfortable on the field; I felt good about myself, and I felt like I belonged there. Once you get past all of the politics and parents, when the game starts if you can hold your own, it doesn't matter whether you're a girl or a boy. I just felt comfortable out on the field, and it didn't matter to me that I was the only girl out there because I wasn't really thinking about it. I was thinking about the next play and focusing on the game."

Beyond baseball's appeal as a refuge from expectations about gender and race, Malaika loved the game because it suited her personality and temperament. She is thoughtful and deliberate, not given to impulsive decisions. Even at the youth level, she found baseball to be a sport that requires thinking. "It was also, quite honestly, a game that was at my pace. You have a chance to think about what to do and then the opportunity to make the play and then reset. I was really drawn to that. I like to think about things before I do them and before I talk, and baseball is the type of sport where I get to do that. I get to think, 'Okay, there's a runner on first. If the ball is hit to this side, I'm going to do this. If it's hit over there, I'm going to do that. And then when it happens, I'm prepared. All those things combined to make baseball a real good fit for me. I did play other sports, and I did enjoy being on the court and playing basketball, and I eventually did take up volleyball, but I always felt like baseball was meant for me, or I was meant for baseball."

When Malaika turned twelve, she faced a decision that her best friends and teammates did not. That's the age when Little Leaguers move from a small to a regulation-size baseball diamond. The game becomes more serious and competitive. American Legion ball and private traveling and tournament teams are the way the more serious players prepare for the next level. Nearly all girls who have not already left baseball switch to softball at that point.[4] Malaika stayed with her friends and moved up to the big diamond.

Malaika's Little League coach, Tim Neff, is also the father of her best friend and longtime teammate, Jasiah Neff. Tim was planning to continue coaching Jasiah's team, and he leveled with Malaika. He told her that she would face pressure to switch to softball for the rest of her playing days. "He said, 'Look, I will support you in whatever you choose, but just know that there are going to be a lot of parents who want you to switch to softball, and you will have a lot of opportunity if you do switch to softball, because you will be able to play in high school. You'll get college scholarship offers. There'll be a lot of things that open up for you. If you want to play baseball, that's fine, but I want you to decide at this point what you want to do, and then commit to it."

There wasn't a moment's hesitation as twelve-year-old Malaika responded, "Well, I want to play baseball. I've always played baseball. That's what I do."

Coach Neff replied, "If this is what you want to do, that's great. We'll support you, but just know there's this door here that you can take, and no one would fault you for it. Everybody would support you, and you'd have a great future playing softball." Malaika answered again, "No, I want to play baseball."

Nor did she relinquish the belief that she could play high school baseball after middle school. The San Diego public school system provided Malaika with the option to attend the modest high school for which she was zoned or a partner school in a wealthier school district. She had been attending a magnet school (O'Farrell Middle School) for its instrumental music program and its nontraditional academic structure, which her parents preferred for her. Choosing a high school for baseball didn't require a major departure from the educationally independent path Malaika was already on.

Thom had told her all along she could quit playing whenever she felt it was too difficult to swim upstream. Lynn supported Malaika's independence but found it stressful to watch her daughter out there alone with all the boys. Still, both parents supported Malaika's decision to attend a school that would allow her to play baseball if that's what she wanted. Lynn hoped to make things a little easier by alerting the coaches to her daughter's presence before she got to high school. "[My mom] was the one who thought of writing the letter and said to me, 'Let's figure out which coaches are going to be supportive.'" Lynn was hoping she could lure a high school coach out to see Malaika play before she made a decision about which school to go to.

"Once I made the decision to play [baseball] in high school, we sent those letters to five different high schools, which were the high schools that I could go to. In San Diego at the time you could go to your neighborhood school, and then your neighborhood school had a partner school. Generally, south of Interstate 8 is lower-middle-class neighborhoods and above I-8 is upper-middle class. So they partnered schools above and below to try and integrate schools a little more, both racially and socioeconomically. But since I went to a magnet school for middle school, that opened up a few other high schools."

Malaika wrote to the coaches at schools she could attend. Two responded positively: Crawford High, for which she was zoned, and its partner school, La Jolla High. Two more directed her to the softball team. The fifth school didn't answer at all. Malaika was on an academic track and wanted the advantages of the better-endowed La Jolla High. Varsity baseball coach Robert Allen took the time to answer her letter, assuring Malaika, "If you're good enough to play, you'll make the team." She took him at his word: "That was all I asked."[5] In addition to an open-minded baseball coach, La Jolla High School had all the benefits of being in one of the wealthiest communities in the nation, at the doorstep of the University of California, San Diego. Malaika was delighted when her best friend, Jasiah, decided to attend as well.

But she still had to make the team. "To keep myself from getting bored before baseball season rolled around, I tried out for the volleyball team in the fall and the basketball team in the winter. My focus was on baseball as I counted down the days until tryouts." Malaika was nervous as they approached but took comfort in the fact that Jasiah was also trying out. "It was a constant reminder that I had played the game all my life, with friends like him, and this was no different—the bases were still ninety feet away, the mound was still sixty feet six inches from the plate, and I had taken thousands of ground balls at second." After practice one afternoon, senior third baseman, Jeff Rizzo, who was headed to Stanford on a baseball scholarship, took the time to compliment Malaika with "Nice work out there." Malaika glowed.

She made the junior varsity team but did not let herself relax. "Making the team was only the first step in my mind; I wanted to prove without a doubt that I belonged. Unfortunately, the pressure I put on myself never ceased, and looking back, I wish I had let myself enjoy the experience more."

She continually faced adults' "well-meaning" advice to quit baseball so she could earn a college softball scholarship. She felt as though she had to justify her presence on the baseball field to her new teammates and to the entire La Jolla community, which was new to her. College scholarships were not yet on her radar; she was playing baseball because she loved it, not because she was making a long-term decision about her college career. "I didn't necessarily think that I wanted to go to college and play baseball. I felt that when I ended up going to college, there were going to be plenty of options for me, and it turned out there were. I got scholarship offers for basketball and volleyball, so it all worked out."

"So I played baseball. My freshman year, I played volleyball, basketball, and then I made the JV baseball team. I didn't play much that season, but I got a chance to get into some games, and there were some sophomores who had been on the JV team the previous year. I honestly felt my entire career at La Jolla that I was treated with absolute fairness. I played two years of JV and two years of varsity. I started on JV my sophomore year, and I started on varsity my senior year. So there were two years when I wasn't the starting second baseman, but I didn't feel like I was being wronged in any way. I was earning my spot just like other kids on the team were earning their spot."

As a rising high school junior, Malaika needed to move up to varsity or give up baseball. She was making a name for herself on the volleyball and basketball teams but refused to relinquish her favorite sport. "Despite the success I was experiencing on the court, my focus was on baseball. I needed to make varsity. To add to the pressure, basketball playoffs ran right through baseball tryouts, and I was forced to earn my spot on the [baseball] team during a preseason game. I was thrown into the late innings of our game against Carlsbad High School to sink or swim." She swam: "On the field I was in the middle of a 6-4-3 double play.[6] In my only at bat, I hit a double down the right-field line. I was standing on second trying not to smile, and the guys on my team were cheering from the dugout and calling out my name, and I finally broke a smile. Somebody hit a grounder to right center field, I made it to third, and Coach looked at me and said, 'Congratulations on making the team.' I remember distinctly hitting that ball down the right-field line and just motoring around to second thinking, 'This is awesome.' It was the best double I ever hit!"

When Malaika made the varsity team, some boy did not. She has no memory of resistance or objections, but she also had a knack for blocking things like that out. "You know, there probably was some resistance or resentment, but I really—and I kind of still do this, and it's probably something I learned just playing sports—I just don't pay attention to all that shit. There's a lot of stuff going on, there's parents and there's politics and there's coaching personalities, and you just can't control any of that. There may have been parents who were upset or who questioned why I was on the team. You make it worse if you pay attention to those issues or if you respond to it because it creates an environment that's not positive. By essentially focusing on playing and getting better as a player and fitting in with my teammates, I never felt like my teammates were bitter toward

FIG. 22. Malaika Underwood, La Jolla High School Vikings. Courtesy of Malaika Underwood.

me. They were my teammates. And they quickly learned that I could joke around with the best of them, knew baseball just as well as they did, and I respected the game. They accepted me pretty quickly once that happened."

She doesn't recall difficulties with her social life because she played baseball, although she admits that might also reflect her talent for selective memory. "I wasn't like everybody else [at high school], but at the same time—and again, maybe it's just me putting those blinders on—but I was friends or acquaintances with most of the kids at school. I was the girl who played baseball, but it wasn't like I was shunned or stood out because of it. That was just me. That's who I was. I don't know . . . I probably wasn't as observant, and maybe it was on purpose because I didn't want to know if people were talking about me in a negative way. I just kept chugging along."

She suspects that being in the dugout and locker room with her teammates had some impact on her social life, because she sought friendship first with boys, and romantic relationships only later. She doesn't think that was a bad way to do things. In fact, it was the way she and her partner, Chris Bellamy, first got together. But in high school it was unusual for a girl to be looking for a practice partner rather than a date. "I found myself looking for a boyfriend who could play baseball with me—a friend first and a boyfriend second—probably because I was around boys and they can be good friends. I had friends who dated boys in high school, and their experience always seemed so different to me." She had girlfriends too, especially from the volleyball and basketball teams, and some of them appreciated her access to the boys on the baseball team. "Sometimes my friends used me to get close to the boys they liked on the team. It was like, 'Man, she's got the "in" to all these guys. Let's hang out with her.'"

During her junior year Malaika made a decision that eliminated any time for a social life: she realized that she really did want to go to a Division I college as an athlete. Few athletes who attract the attention of Division I coaches start as late as their junior year of high school. Her parents did not have the means to pay for her college education but expected her to go. They told her she would have to bankroll it herself. They were willing to help her try to get an athletic scholarship, if that was what she wanted, but she was already a sophomore, and they would really have to hustle to learn that game. "If I wanted to go to a smaller school, I probably could have pursued baseball at some level. But I had shifted my goals, and a big Division I experience was what I was shooting for." Her parents asked the parents of other athletes and learned what it took to get noticed by college coaches: "I needed to play club ball, to travel to tournaments where hundreds of teams are playing. College coaches go to those tournaments because it's a good way for them to see thousands of players at one time."

Baseball was still her favorite of the three varsity sports she played, and she refused to relinquish it, even though she knew she wouldn't be playing in college. So she just buckled down and did it all: attracting the attention of college recruiters in basketball and volleyball, while she was attempting to be the first girl ever to make the varsity baseball team at her high school. "My junior year, I played three high school sports and two club sports. By the spring of my junior year, I was practicing baseball after school from two thirty to five thirty. I would go get myself dinner somewhere in La Jolla. I would drive to basketball club practice from six thirty to eight thirty. And then our club volleyball practice was late, from nine to eleven. I would drive to club volleyball practice, practice for two hours, and then get home around eleven thirty, do my homework, go to sleep, and drive back to school the next day. I was doing that three or four days a week and then on the weekends playing in tournaments, whether it was a basketball tournament or a volleyball tournament." In addition to the rigors of her sports and studies, Malaika's commute from San Diego to La Jolla meant that she put in many more solitary hours on the freeways than her wealthier teammates who lived in La Jolla.

"It was a huge commitment, and I did that for one year, my junior year. And then the summer of my junior year, I realized that I was getting more interest from volleyball coaches, and I started to take some recruiting visits. In the spring of my junior year, I was playing all of these club sports and traveling around like a crazy woman. I did the same thing through the summer, and then I started to get letters and plan official school visits. It wasn't easy, but I had to do all of that if I wanted college coaches to consider me."

The summer before her senior year, she was offered a scholarship to the University of North Carolina (UNC), the University of San Diego, Boise State, and the University of Rhode Island. "There was a basketball-volleyball dual offer from the University of San Diego. But UNC was the ultimate opportunity to me because it was a big Division I school. It had such a fantastic basketball history, and I was a basketball fan." She accepted the Tar Heels' offer of a full ride for volleyball. Remembering her parents' requirement that she pay for her own college, she notes with satisfaction, "So I paid for it myself. And I don't have any outstanding loans!"

Spring of her senior year seemed like a romp by comparison to the previous year. "I was just playing club volleyball, to get ready for college, and playing baseball because that's what I wanted to do."

As she prepared to graduate high school, her baseball career seemed to be over. But she was so busy anticipating college athletics that she was not aware of sadness at the loss. She had been her high school's starting second baseman and achieved what she wanted: to be treated as just another ballplayer on the team. "I was getting ready to move across country and play volleyball at a Division I school. I was excited to wear Carolina blue. There was so much to look ahead to that I didn't really dwell on the fact that, for all I knew, I was not going to be playing baseball anymore."

To commemorate her career and to honor the fact that she had been the first and only girl to play baseball at La Jolla High, she received an award at the end-of-season team banquet: the Golden Jock Award, a gold-painted jock strap mounted on a plaque. Malaika recalls, "I cherished the team award I received at the end of my high school baseball career—the Golden Jock Award. It was the final acknowledgment that I belonged on the team. At the time it seemed I had come to the end of my baseball story."[7] She was named Female Athlete of the Year in San Diego County her senior year of high school.

When Malaika arrived at North Carolina, she experienced the initial shock of attending a Division I school where all the other players were equally accustomed to being stars in their sport. "You go from being athlete of the year to being one among many all-stars who had very similar accolades in their own cities. So it's an adjustment." She learned that being a Division I athlete is a full-time job and chose to stay in Chapel Hill during the summers as well to take advantage of the training facilities. "You just don't have the option to not be there on campus training every day, even in the off-season. Summer comes around, and you're allowed to do whatever you want to do, but when you come back, the first day is test day, and if you're not in shape, you are in trouble."

Malaika was a substitute her freshman year, played more her sophomore year, and was a starter during her junior and senior years. "I played well, I had my moments, and I do have a few awards. I have an ACC [Atlantic Coast Conference] Tournament Most Valuable Player Award from my junior year. But there were a lot of stars on our team. We made it to the Sweet Sixteen my senior year. I was happy with how I played and with my experience overall."

When asked which sport she prefers above all, she is as unhesitating as she was when Coach Neff asked her if she wanted to play baseball or softball after Little League: "I love baseball. I love being an athlete, and I've tried a number of different sports. I like competing. But I love baseball. Volleyball provided me the opportunity to get the college experience I wanted. But it was not my favorite sport. Probably out of the three I played in high school, it was my least favorite, to be quite honest. It was baseball, then basketball, then volleyball."

After graduation she was accepted into the graduate degree program in sports administration at Chapel Hill, where she stayed for two years to earn her master's degree. Then baseball came to call again. She was twenty-four at the time. Actually, baseball had refused to go away after high school. It began quietly knocking at her door almost as soon as she arrived at Carolina as a freshman. "That's when I got into coaching Little League. I actually coached in Chapel Hill for six years, but there was still something missing. So I started to look around for a team to play on after I finished grad school. I was looking for an over-thirty or maybe even over-forty men's team. I was looking for anything."

She stumbled upon Jim Glennie's American Women's Baseball Federation website, announcing open tryouts for the 2006 Women's National

Team. "I thought, 'Holy shit, I didn't even know there was a women's baseball team that was funded by USA Baseball. Maybe I should give it a shot.' And that's how I got back into it. I made that team, and I haven't stopped since, because on that team, I was roommates with Donna [Mills] throughout that tournament, and she said, 'Hey, if you want to play in the off-season, we've got this team the New England Red Sox based out of Boston. We play in tournaments all over the place, and we're about to play in the Roy Hobbs Tournament in Florida.' And so I joined her. I had no idea there were other girls who played baseball through Little League and high school. It was so eye-opening!"

Thinking about how serendipitous her discovery of Team USA was, she remarks: "You know what, though? I think it's very much like the way I started in the sport. Baseball finds me. It is the game that I love, but it found me when I was five, and it found me when I was twenty-five. The fact that I found open tryouts for the 2006 USA Women's National Team and I happened to have enough time to get back into the game is astounding. It just found me, and it always has."

Malaika credits USA Baseball with bringing baseball back into her life. But as an elite athlete she also knows what's missing for American women ballplayers. Even the most committed become discouraged by the difficulty of finding opportunities to play. Her preparation for those first USA tryouts provokes a laugh: "God . . . ! I basically had the guy I was dating at the time hit me groundballs until I felt comfortable again. Then I found a cage in the local area, and I went and hit and just tried to get as many swings as possible. It's hard." This training regimen for world-class competition would be a joke in any other sport.

Malaika knows that lack of access to training opportunities undermines the team's competitiveness. "We are the best athletes in that tournament, in the World Cup, every year. But we have not been the best team. We always go with really, really good athletes, but we aren't the best team because the other countries have invested in trying to create a good *baseball* team. They are putting together teams that have been playing together for a much longer time, and there are things about baseball that you can't do just because you're an athlete. There's a rhythm as a team that you can't

FIG. 23. (*top left*) Malaika Underwood, Team USA 2010, All-Tournament Second Basewoman (2008). Courtesy of USA Baseball.

FIG. 24. (*top right*) Underwood goes airborne to make an out at first, Team USA 2012. Courtesy of Veronica Alvarez.

FIG. 25. (*left*) Malaika Underwood, Team USA 2012. Courtesy of Malaika Underwood.

make up in a week. You have to be training together and understanding each other, talking to each other, laughing, having a good time together, in order to develop that rhythm. That's when you become good, and that's when you become, instead of the best athletes in the tournament, the best team in the tournament."

Malaika is not one who thinks that relying on Division I softball players is an effective way of building a championship baseball team. "It's two totally different games. Softball is right in your face. It's coming from a different angle. It's a totally different swing. You don't have the same rhythm when you're at bat. I mean, it's a different game, just different. I respect what [Team USA] is trying to accomplish by recruiting softball players, because at this point the best way to find athletes who are at least familiar with baseball, even though maybe they don't play it, is through softball. But until we have a youth system that supports girls playing baseball, you're just not going to have the pool to build a world-class baseball team. I've actually thought that ideally we should have Little League Baseball, where boys and girls could play together until a certain age and then, instead of having high school baseball and high school softball, have high school boys' baseball and high school girls' baseball, just like we have boys' basketball and girls' basketball. It's the same sport. Soccer is the same way. Tennis is the same way. So why not baseball? I mean, ask anybody . . . baseball is America's pastime, right? So why can't girls play it?"

Malaika has a rewarding job in sports marketing. She and partner Chris Bellamy have recently bought a house together in the lovely Virginia Highlands neighborhood in Atlanta. They plan to stay. She still wants to play baseball and wants to win another gold medal on Team USA. (Malaika was on the 2006 gold medal team.) She is aware of the difficulties of preparing for world-class baseball competition while living an adult life and has made some peace with those frustrations. "At this point I'm living the life I want to live. I have the opportunity to still play at an elite level with elite female athletes and have a great experience playing internationally. It is difficult to train without having a team to play on, without having access to facilities, without being close to my teammates, but we just have to find a way. Staying in athletic shape is not difficult. It's being in baseball shape and getting the reps, the hitting and fielding reps. The difficult part is the baseball part, not the fitness part."

Malaika hopes that the current generation of women athletes will teach their daughters about sports, the way many fathers teach their sons. But it will take several generations to normalize female athleticism. "Women have only had the opportunity a fraction of the time men have. And even within that fraction of time, you've seen an evolution of athletes. There has to be the physical part of being exposed to opportunities, and also the cultural part: having your mom be an athlete, and now you are and your daughters and your grandkids will be."

She is bothered by the cultural assumption that being an athletic woman signifies anything about sexuality. "What's frustrating to me is that I want people to see me as an athlete, period. But once people learn that you're an athlete the next question is often, although not always vocalized, 'I wonder if she's gay or not?' Why can't it just be: You're an athlete. You're strong. You're athletic. Period. That's it."

She hesitates to bring the subject up. It's important, but she doesn't want to feed stereotypes about the sexuality of women athletes. "You know, it's my one hesitation when you talk about female athletes and start to address the question of sexuality. It almost becomes like, 'Oh, of course you're talking about lesbians and sports.' And the focus should not be on that. Let's talk about the fact that there are some fantastic athletes who are female. Period." She regrets that she sometimes capitulates to the impulse to be "proactively heterosexual": "When I tell people I play baseball, sometimes, unfortunately, at some point very early in the conversation I figure out a way to talk about Chris and say, 'Hey, my boyfriend does this . . . he plays soccer,' or something to establish that I'm not gay without them questioning it. And I don't feel like I should have do that . . . let's get over that stereotype and support all female athletes no matter what, just like we should support male athletes, gay or straight."

She has never regarded herself as an activist for women's sports, but she is increasingly aware that she is a role model in spite of everything. At the time of this interview, she was coaching a team of seven-year-old softball players and knows that her presence has an impact on the girls.

She will be coaching a baseball team in the same league next season and is aware of the impact she will have on the boys too. "My entire life has been a relatively selfish focus on playing because that's what I love to do. It hasn't been about setting examples, but I realize now that if you don't talk about it, you're doing a disservice to hundreds of kids who can be inspired by your story. If you don't tell it, nobody hears it."

Malaika Underwood brings her even-keeled sense of calm to the USA dugout, along with her sense of humor and passion for the game. She is a leader, deeply respected for her toughness and athleticism. Baseball has persistently tracked her down all her life, and she will undoubtedly find ways to direct the game to the next generation of girls who are looking for it.

12

Marti Sementelli

PITCHER

"Baseball is who I am."

Martina Sementelli has no memory of life before baseball.[1] She was raised to be a baseball star and has been in the public eye as "that little girl who pitches" since she was a toddler. An online search for Marti Sementelli yields archives of stories from the *New York Times*, the *Los Angeles Times*, and *USA Today* and scores of video clips from CBS, NBC, and ESPN. She was interviewed by Jimmy Kimmel when she was ten years old. Her father, Gary, knows how to get the media to pay attention, but she has earned her recognition by being an exceptionally good baseball pitcher. A girl striking out boys is a story the media finds irresistible. Marti never played softball, and she has paid a steep price for turning her back on that recommended route.

Marti was born in Boston, November 17, 1992, the first child of Rosa and Gary Sementelli. Her sister, Allie, is five years younger. Gary introduced Marti to baseball at age two, taught her the fundamentals and fine points of pitching, and practiced with her every day of her life until she left in 2011 for Montreat College in North Carolina on a baseball scholarship. He coached every team she played on until high school. Marti recalls, "In the beginning baseball was just something to do in the house. It was kind of like a hobby that my dad got me into. My dad grew up playing baseball all through high school and taught me everything that I knew—really wanted me to just be a pitcher. I don't know what his reasoning behind that was. He taught me the windup, and that's something that I liked to do."

When she was three, the family moved to Southern California, and baseball moved outdoors. "In Boston, everything was pretty much indoors because of the weather. Then we moved to Sherman Oaks when I was three, and we were directly across from the Sherman Oaks Recreation Park, so we played every day. My dad would just throw the ball really high up in the air for pop flies, and people would see this two-foot-something little girl running around, catching fly balls, and it kind of caused a scene."

When she was five, Gary enrolled Marti in coach-pitch baseball at the Sherman Oaks Recreation Park baseball league. By the time she was seven, she was old enough for Little League. "My dad knew a guy at the Sherman Oaks Little League that had a team going. When I turned seven, that windup that my dad taught me, we used it in the games and pitched against batters. My first year, I struck out a hundred batters. My dad kept a count, and when I reached my hundredth strikeout, it was on the local news. When I was eight, we moved to Triple-A, and every year after that, I kind of got a hundred strikeouts, and then a hundred strikeouts after that, so it just kind of led up to five hundred strikeouts." Gary kept track of his daughter's stats and notified the local news stations at each benchmark. The only trouble occurred when he called the local television station before the game in which Marti was on track to throw her five hundredth Little League strikeout. The news station was willing to send a crew, but when parents on the opposing team learned that one of their sons would be the televised victim of Marti's five hundredth strikeout, they asked the coach not to put the team on the field with a television crew present. The game proceeded without the media, and Marti got her five hundredth strikeout without being on the evening news.

These statistics are not officially maintained by Little League Baseball. Gary was the team's coach, and he kept the stats. There is no reason to doubt his math: if Marti struck out five or six batters per game in a Little League season, she certainly could have struck out a hundred batters each season during the five years that she played Little League. Her name is posted on a plaque at the Sherman Oaks Little League Fields, along with those of other players who were standouts during their years at that Little League park. She notes matter-of-factly, "My name's all over the place. I got my name on the banners because the teams that I was on won championships, and I was on the All-Star team every year. My dad coached all of my teams, so yeah, he did help. The only team he didn't coach was when I went to high school."

Marti is nonchalant about the stats and the attendant publicity, and she's not sure why her dad kept count and kept calling the media: "I didn't keep track of any numbers. My dad did all that. I don't know why. That's just the way he did it. I don't know . . . thinking now, if I had a kid, I wouldn't count how many strikeouts they had. Like, that's crazy, but he did, and every time I was close to getting that hundredth strikeout of the season, he would contact the news. They wanted to do a story on it because I was the only girl in Little League striking out all these boys, and they thought it was a great story. So I had news crews after me my whole life."

Poise in front of the camera didn't come easily. "When I was little, I was the shiest kid ever. I didn't want to talk to anybody. My dad's like, 'Okay, the TV people are coming. Just answer the questions and try to say more than yes and no.' When I was little, I didn't have the best interviews. I would just say a sentence here and there, but as I've gotten on [television] so many times, I got friggin' professional at it. So now I'm just like a chatterbox . . . it's like I'm talking to my mom or somebody. You know, it's just easy to do, camera work and all that stuff."

Although she didn't know who Jimmy Kimmel was, appearing on his show was an exciting moment for her: "The Jimmy Kimmel show . . . that was one of the best days ever . . . late-night talk show. My dad's like, 'You're going to be on Jimmy Kimmel's show.' I'm like, 'Who's that?' My dad just thought it was an amazing thing what I was doing [playing baseball with boys]. I guess he wanted people to know about it and feature it."

Baseball and her dad defined Marti's life during her young years. Her parents divorced when she was eleven. Marti and Allie stayed with their mother, and then, two years later, Marti moved in with Gary. She doesn't dwell on whatever emotional impact the upheaval might have had on her, but she recalls that she was quiet and withdrawn when she was young.

"When I was little, I didn't talk to anybody besides my dad, pretty much. I just kind of hid behind him and didn't really talk to anybody, and when I was forced to talk to people, it was camera people. Around the park all these people would want to talk to me. I didn't really say a word to them. I went to day camps at the park and was at my dad's side the whole time.[2] When I was in high school, I started to talk a lot more. I just have to get to know somebody to talk to them."

Marti's childhood friends were her Little League teammates. "I only had guy friends when I was little. At my birthday parties, there were twenty boys. I didn't know any girls because I didn't play with them. Even at school when you would play kickball or handball or team sports, they didn't want the girl that sucked. They wanted the girl that knew how to play, so I was always with them."

There was no thought of switching sports after Little League. Her best friends were her teammates, she was a standout on the team, and she felt at home on a baseball diamond. Why would she give that up? In addition, even if the argument is made that baseball skills transfer easily into softball skills, Marti is a pitcher, and the pitcher's position is unique. There is no overhand pitching in softball. If she had switched to softball, she would have had to abandon her lifetime of training and find another position to play. That didn't stop people from badgering her about when she was going to give up baseball. "When I was thirteen and fourteen, I played at this juniors' league. It was public, so same kids, same thing, but then people were starting to ask me, 'So are you going to switch to softball?' And I said, 'Well, does it look like I play softball? I've never played softball before.' There weren't any softball leagues around me. It was a prime baseball community, nothing around softball. I'd never seen a softball game until I went to high school. I mean, I heard of the game. I'm not dumb, but I just never saw it. Sherman Oaks was surrounded by baseball, baseball, baseball, baseball."

She faced the usual skepticism about her ability to play on the bigger diamond. "That was the big thing: 'Oh, you can pitch in Little League, you know. That's only forty-six feet. But you can't pitch sixty feet six inches. You can't reach the plate.' Or, 'You're going to get injured out there.' But

FIG. 26. Marti Sementelli ready to start, Sherman Oaks Little League All-Stars. Courtesy of Marti Sementelli.

I didn't even think about it like that. Like, I'm just going to throw the ball. My dad was like, 'Okay, well, we're going to stretch it out a little bit. We started practicing.'"

Of course, the boys also had to learn to deal with the bigger diamond, with its ninety-foot baselines and three-hundred-foot outfield fences. But the impact of the longer distance is most dramatic on the pitcher, whose every pitch is affected. Fastballs have to stay fast for another fifteen feet. Breaking balls have to break at the right place. Marti is not a big person now, and when she was thirteen, she was tiny. So she and Gary went to work, practicing the longer distance. "At first, it was, 'Man, I can't even see your signals. You're so far away!' But you get used to the dimension. For me, the big question was, 'How's my curve ball going to break?' But it actually helped it because you get so much time for it to break. It's harder to throw in a shorter distance. There's not much time for it to break and move, stuff like that. My pitches started getting more effective when I started moving it out. It actually played to my advantage."

The boys were getting bigger, which added to the challenge. "You know, they hit that stage where they start growing, like fourteen, fifteen years old, and it never stops. By college, everyone is big, and there aren't any weaknesses in the [batting] order anymore." But she never gave a thought to quitting. "I don't really see where I would be without baseball in my life. It's a huge part of who I am and what I'm doing. I'm going to college for it. I'm playing for USA. I don't know what I would do without it. It's always going to be with me. And I think that's how it is when, you know, the Major League players, they play baseball all their life, and what would they do without it? That's what they do for a living, and that's probably what I want to do for the rest of my life, but in a different kind of way, because there's not many opportunities for it. But as long as I'm playing all the time, it's fine with me. So, yeah, baseball is who I am."

Now that she has friends who are collegiate softball players, she understands how much more difficult it was for her to stay with baseball. "If you play softball, you get so much more. Things are given to you, and you have more opportunity, and it's like a glamorous kind of thing, so most people go for that. I'm not saying that I don't like baseball, but it's harder to do." She means not that baseball is the more difficult sport, but that it's more difficult for a girl to persevere with baseball. The battle to stay in the game is discouraging, and continual noise about when you'll quit is a tedious distraction. "I don't hate softball. I used to kind of dislike it a little when I was younger. I used to think of it as selling your soul because people want you to switch from something that you love to something that you'll settle for. You don't really have much choice, because you want to keep playing the game, but baseball won't give you that opportunity. But I've realized that I don't dislike the game of softball. I just don't like what it has done to us, baseball players, to make us switch."

She rejects the idea that the sports are interchangeable for girls. "There are so many differences. People look at it like it's the same concept: you hit a ball, you run the bases, you throw a ball, you get outs. But there's so much more to it than that. It's like saying ping pong and tennis are the same. Yeah, it's the same idea: you're hitting the ball over the net; you have paddles. But look at the dimensions of the field or the court. I mean the courts even look the same: they have four little things [the quadrants on a tennis court or ping pong table]. Maybe if I started playing softball at a really young age and kept with it, it would have been the sport that I loved. But you always love what you grew up with. Well, baseball is what I grew up doing, so that's why I like it so much."

High school was a crucible of sorts for Marti. At Burbank High she played on her first team that was not coached by her dad. She liked the school and her friends there, but she wasn't having an easy time with the baseball coach. Gary watched the team practices from a respectable distance, disagreed with the coach's training regimen, and came to believe the coach wasn't open to Marti's presence on the team. She wasn't getting much playing time and was experiencing a lack of confidence on the baseball diamond for the first time in her life. Reluctantly, she agreed to consider Gary's suggestion that she transfer to a school where she might have more success with baseball. "I started at Burbank, and the school's great. I loved all my teammates. But I wasn't in the best year for baseball, meaning I was going to be a sophomore and there were so many more people ahead of me." (That is, so many pitchers were a year or two older than her that she wouldn't have a chance to see much action.)

She decided to transfer to Birmingham High before the start of her junior year, even though it was an emotionally wrenching move. Besides leaving her friends behind, she and Gary would have to move to Birmingham's school district, farther away from her mother's house. She struggled with the decision, and it took a while before she agreed with Gary that the opportunity was worth the price of switching schools. "We contacted the coach [Matt Mowry of Birmingham High] and visited the school. Transferring schools was a huge thing for me. I was just like, 'Oh, God . . .' I was in the middle of high school. I was in a really confusing stage for a while, just trying to figure out if I wanted to do it. It took a lot of time for me to [make up my mind], and then I finally just said, 'I'll just do it.' I knew a couple of people at Birmingham, but I didn't know anybody on the baseball team, so that was hard for me to adjust. But you know, I got used to my teammates, and it ended up being fine." The fact that the media finds Marti a good story and regularly showed up to watch her at Birmingham didn't seem to affect team chemistry. "I'm not that hard to get along with. I don't have that side. I'm not a mean person. So long as you give me the same respect as anybody else, I'll be fine with it. I don't fight with people. So high school was good."

Coach Mowry gave Marti the respect she needed and a chance to pitch in relief. She learned and became a better ballplayer. "In high school everyone's bigger, and you have to get smart as a pitcher. You can't just throw the ball over the plate now and expect them to strike out. It's going to be location, because if you miss your spot, they can really smack the ball, especially in the division that we were at. We were in Division 1 high school ball. It's the biggest schools, and it was really good competition, and we had one of the hardest conferences in all of Southern California. I couldn't really be in a better position than I was in, competition-wise. When the college coaches looked at what league I was playing in, it was really positive."

She finished her senior season with a winning record, two wins and one loss in twenty-two innings, against strong competition. She also pitched a complete game in the first game she started that season: that stunning 102-pitch exhibition game against San Marcos High School of Santa Barbara, led by her USA teammate Ghazaleh Sailors.

Three years before that matchup, during the summer of 2008, Jim Glennie, in his capacity as player development coordinator for USA Baseball, emailed Gary, who convinced Marti to attend the preliminary tryouts for the Women's National Team in Kenosha, Wisconsin, over the July Fourth weekend. Marti was reluctant; she didn't know of any girls who played baseball and couldn't imagine that they would be worthy competition. But the first glimpse of the girls on the field changed her life. "I remember Kenosha. I've never seen so many girls try out. There was one tryout in the whole United States that year,[3] so there were, like, a hundred girls there, and I was just going, 'Wow! This is amazing! This is so cool! Look how many of us grew up playing baseball. I've never seen it. I thought I was the only one. Wow . . . this is crazy.'" Marti was invited to the final tryouts in Compton, California, and then selected to travel with Team USA to Japan. At fifteen she was the youngest player on the team and pitched so well that she was honored with selection to the All-Tournament team as the best right-handed pitcher.

Two years later, in 2010, Marti was about to enter her senior year in high school and was seeking both to make Team USA for the second time and to play college baseball. When she traveled to Cary, North Carolina, for the 2010 USA tryouts, it all came together in her mind: she loved North Carolina and wanted to attend college there.

When she returned to California in the fall, she considered several small colleges in North Carolina that seemed positive about her chances of playing baseball. She settled on Montreat College, a small Christian-based liberal arts college located in the Blue Ridge Mountains near Asheville, North Carolina. Coach Michael Bender invited her to visit the campus. She worked out with the team for four hours, enjoyed dinner arranged by some of the players, and left feeling positive. Bender and Montreat were able to put together a combination of athletic and academic scholarships that made it possible for her to attend. Marti was profoundly relieved to know that she would be able to continue to play baseball after high school. At the press conference her parents held when she signed her letter of intent, she was identified as only the third woman to receive a collegiate baseball scholarship.[4]

Nobody becomes a path breaker of that caliber without paying a price. Sure enough, Coach Bender's willingness to accept Marti ignited a controversy. Because Marti is an excellent student, Montreat was able to offer her an academic scholarship to supplement the athletic scholarship. It

FIG. 27. Marti Sementelli, Team USA 2010, All-Tournament Right-Handed Pitcher (2008). Courtesy of Brian Fleming.

FIG. 28. Sementelli warming up, Team USA 2012. Courtesy of USA Baseball.

is nothing like an NCAA full ride in softball. She was making a financial sacrifice to play college baseball. Montreat isn't even an NCAA school. The amount of the baseball scholarship was not disclosed, but Bender referred to it as "chump change" in comparison the full cost of attending Montreat, which at $33,000 per year for tuition, room, and board, is comparable to other small liberal arts colleges.

Nonetheless, the very idea of a woman getting a baseball scholarship provoked some ugly responses. Local rumors circulated that some of the players planned to transfer if she were allowed on the team. It was a shock for Marti to learn of the negative reaction, and it didn't jibe with the hospitality she had enjoyed during her recruiting visit. In an interview with Jill Painter of the *Los Angeles Daily News*, Marti noted, "I never had this kind of attention in this kind of way, with some negativity. There's a lot of heat toward the coach. I feel really bad about that. I'm bringing this on him. But he's totally backing me up every way possible. . . . I haven't heard anything about people transferring, but that would be their choice. There's nothing I can do. I'm going to be there, and the people who want to be there will be there too."

Coach Bender stood by his recruit: "I'm going to stand tall. I'm going to do it. I was raised by a woman. I was raised not to think in this prejudicial fashion that women can't play baseball. Baseball is all she knows. She knows how to pitch. She's not just a girl. She's a baseball player." Marti didn't understand the hostility. "What's the big deal of a girl playing college baseball? That's such a horrible thing to happen? I don't understand why it's a negative thing. Shouldn't that be a positive thing? I don't understand why this coach is looked down upon. He should be praised. This is a coach that is giving a girl an opportunity."[5]

Once at Montreat Marti buckled down in her classes and endured the rigors of the fall baseball training regimen. When baseball season arrived, she knew she was stronger and able to throw the ball harder than she could in high school. The coach planned to use her as a relief pitcher. Marti doesn't know how hard she throws. She says the coaches at Montreat haven't clocked her pitches, and she doesn't care. She regards the continual questions about pitching velocity as one-dimensional, a way of distracting attention away from her effectiveness. "I've had that question asked more than what's my name: 'How fast do you throw?' I always say, 'I don't know. I don't know. I don't know. I think this is the range. I don't know.' But that question is haunting me. I don't necessarily have to have a ninety-four-mile-an-hour fastball if I can come in and just get hitters off balance. As a relief pitcher, my thing is just having that movement of the ball and *not* coming the same velocity as anybody else."

In February and March the Blue Ridge Mountain campus of Montreat College is wet and cold and not ready for baseball. The Cavaliers play the first part of their season on the road. Marti got her first college strikeout on the road. But when Montreat played at home during the second half of their 2012 season, Marti finally had a chance to pitch in front of her friends. She was well known at the tiny liberal arts school, especially since her arrival had been so highly publicized. The whole campus was eager to see her in action. Her roommate, Dakota Icard, a softball pitcher at Montreat, had become her close friend and helped her to manage her nerves. As a relief pitcher, Marti not only carried the pressure of being the only girl on the team, but felt obliged to warn friends that she never knew if or when she would be called in to pitch.

"All my friends were excited about the game and said, 'Oh, finally, we get to see Marti play!' I was like, 'Oh, gosh. I can't do bad!' Sometimes I don't want anybody at the games because then if I do bad they'll think, 'She's on the team, but she's not really good,' and you've always got to be proving yourself. I think, 'Please, just let me have a good outing,' and then I can have a great night.'" The first time I went out there, I thought I was going to die. I was a mess I was so nervous. What if I let up a double and single there? That could have been the game, and who knows the next time I'd pitch. I was like, 'Oh, please. I need to do good.' I pray a lot before the games or before I'm in there." With a smile, she adds, "Hell yeah, I pray! I mean, it *is* a Christian school."

When the moment finally came for her to step onto the mound, it was before the biggest hometown crowd of the season. "I came in there, and I struck the first guy out. He was this big right-hander. He was their number-four hitter.[6] It [the count] was, like, 0-1, 0-2, he fouled the third one off, and then on the next one I got him with a combo, and the crowd . . . like the second it caught the [catcher's] glove, the fans went nuts. I tried not to smile, but it was hard not to crack a smile a little bit. Then the next batter hit into a double play, so I got out of a huge jam, and then I went out the next inning, and I got one, two, three outs, and then I was done. It was a great outing, and I was feeling, 'Oh, my God. That's all I wanted. I was just like, 'Oh my gosh!'"

She feels good about her freshman year at Montreat. "I learned how to pitch the college game. Everything is more precise. Now it's got to be hitting the corner and to the knees and lower . . . you've got to be perfect to where nothing is hittable. Because these guys are huge, and they'll hit any mistake, and they can hit the ball far."

Marti believes in her own talent. She has made big sacrifices to stay in the sport she has loved since she was a baby. The public attention foisted on her from a young age undoubtedly added to the pressure. Being in the public eye, on the Internet, on television, and in the national print media provokes negative as well as positive commentary, even if Marti tries to ignore the bad stuff. Her hometown press is the Los Angeles media: hardly an intimate and supportive local environment. The constant exposure and the posting of occasionally vulgar commentary directed at an adolescent Marti must have added pressure to everything she did.

To continue to play baseball, Marti has had to place herself in the lonely position of being the exceptional woman on a college campus far from home. For most college students, being far from home is a mixed blessing—liberating as well as lonely. Marti misses Gary at her games, but being on her own has also enabled her to separate her baseball identity from his. "Before I came to Montreat, my dad never missed a game in my life. This was a lot different. At first, I liked it a lot because I just wanted to do my own thing and get away from a lot of people. I went far away, and so no one knew me, and it was cool. It would have been nice just to have, like one visit [from her dad], maybe toward the end of the season or something. It was planned that he was going to come, but he never did. But I guess he will, like, next year or something. You know, a lot of the families would come make the trips every weekend because they're not that far. Some moments I was thinking, 'Oh, that'd be nice if someone would come to watch,' but I'm fine. It's what I wanted, so it really doesn't bother me."

In some ways the pressure she feels as a college baseball player is no different from that felt by any other college athlete. In other ways the uniqueness of her situation amplifies her sense of responsibility. She feels that she represents the future of all women in baseball and worries that both parents, and particularly her father, are so heavily invested in her success as a woman baseball player that she simply must succeed. She is burdened by the sense that she cannot quit—although she doesn't want to. If she did, however, it would be harder on her dad than on her mom. "It wouldn't be a big adjustment for my mom. It wouldn't really change who I am or whatever. But she really loves that I do play. It's like, 'This is my daughter. She's playing baseball in college.' She loves saying it, you know?"

With Marti's father, however, the baseball connection is much deeper, and baseball is central to their relationship. "My dad, I think that's kind of what his whole life is based on, so if I didn't play, I don't know what he would really do, because he always says, 'That's the only good thing that I ever did in my life was to teach you how to play baseball.' There are so many family things that have gotten . . . ridiculous. [My playing baseball] really is the only thing that's keeping him going or that he kind of did pretty much right. So I think it's just a major part of his life through me, in a way. It's not like he won't love me anymore. It's just a part of him. I just can't even imagine what I would be doing without it."

Looking closely at the words Marti chooses to express these powerful emotions, it appears that she and her father are so closely intertwined, she's not sure who would be more at a loss were she to quit baseball. It's a major part of *his* life, but she can't imagine what *she* would be doing without it. Occasionally, Gary will try to assure his daughter that she is free to do whatever she wants. She can quit playing if she is tired of the pressure. But when he says this, she doesn't buy it and feels even more strongly that quitting is not an option. "Yeah, he always says to me, 'You don't have to do it if you don't want to.' But then I get mad at him when he says that. 'Why do you say that? What are you talking about? I'm not even talking about quitting. Everything that I did, and then quit now? Are you kidding me?' It makes me mad. He says, 'I'm just trying to be like . . .' And I say, 'No, don't tell me that.' If something tragic happens, then you can tell me that, but not randomly out of the blue. Don't tell me, 'Everything's going to be okay if you quit.' It's going to mess you up too, if I quit. You know, it's not going to be okay.' I think he says that because he knows I'm not going to quit. I can't. And it's true."

She can't quit, but her future in baseball is severely constrained. "I'm just taking it year by year, season by season, just knowing the next three years I'm going to have the opportunity to play, and then after that, who knows what's going to happen?[7] Maybe I can play on some independent team somewhere in the United States. Maybe you're not getting paid big bucks, but you're getting paid to play, and it's a salary. I don't know, playing overseas somewhere, I don't know if that could happen. In the future maybe coach somewhere, like, be a pitching coach. And I'll always be affiliated with USA Baseball up until I physically can't do it anymore. I want to go to every country and keep doing it every two years and see how far I can go, because there's still the girls on the team that are, like, mid-thirties, almost forty, playing, and I'm only nineteen. I can get a lot more World Cups in. So I can always count on that, you know, to keep playing baseball. Things just pop up randomly out of the blue. There could be a new league somewhere or something. I don't know."

Marti's story is a brave one. She has maintained her belief in her talent, in her sense that baseball *is* who she is and wants to be, and has worked tirelessly to be the best female pitcher in the United States. From that perspective, she has grown into and appropriated the sport that she inherited from her father.

13

Lilly Jacobson

RIGHT FIELD

"It still is my sport."

Lilly Jacobson is a pure baseball player.[1] She has never played softball, and she has, with the exception of three years in high school, chosen not to be a pitcher. She's a left-handed hitter and an outfielder, and she likes to play every day. When she was eight, she was described by her Little League coach as the "best pure hitter in the league." Staying in the game she believes she was born to play has required that she go head to head with boys, and later with men, hitting the ball hard enough, throwing the ball far enough, and running fast enough both in the outfield and around the base paths. Being left-handed and not as tall as a first baseman is expected to be has meant that the positions open to her to are pitcher and outfielder. There has been no place for her to hide.

Lilly is the younger daughter of two political science professors, both lifelong baseball fans. Her father, Norman Jacobson, grew up in the Bronx, a Giants fan who stayed loyal to the team as they moved to San Francisco and he moved to Berkeley as a young professor. I grew up in Los Angeles, my father a Dodger fan from Brooklyn and my mother a Yankee fan from the Bronx. I favored my father's "Bums" in Los Angeles. When I moved to Berkeley to study political science and later married Norman, we had two children, and the Oakland A's were the team of least resistance in a family divided between the Dodgers and the Giants. The A's are beloved by both Lilly and her sister, Johanna (JoJo).

Lilly's childhood baseball journey resembles those of many of her teammates on Team USA. She, like them, was born with natural athletic ability and became focused on baseball at a very young age. Unlike many of her teammates, instead of following an older brother around the neighborhood or catching baseball fever from her father, Lilly, at age three, inserted herself into a game of catch I was having with her seven-year-old sister JoJo on the front lawn. JoJo was humoring me: she was not interested in the game, but she didn't appreciate her little sister butting in. After trying to chase Lilly away, an exasperated Johanna threw the ball at Lilly and walked away herself, seeking an activity more to her liking. Lilly seized the moment and never looked back. Norman watched the family drama with bemusement from the sidelines, and after Johanna left, he retired indoors to the family room to watch a Giants game on television. Lilly wasn't deterred: she and I played catch until JoJo and Norman came out and reminded us that we needed to get ready to join some friends for dinner.

That scene is Lilly's first memory of the game. "I think my first memory is trying to play catch. You were trying to get JoJo to play catch. JoJo is my sister, who is not so much an athlete . . . never really had an interest in playing baseball, though she put up with a lot of our craziness about it. And I remember saying that I wanted to play and jumping in the middle. I think I was probably two, or three maybe. You were saying, 'You're too little. Maybe in a couple of years.'"

Telling Lilly that she can't do something because she is too little may have launched her on a lifelong path of insisting on doing whatever she believed she was big enough to do, which became a prominent theme in her baseball journey. When I asked what first moved her to want to join Little League, she remembers, "You and dad. I mean I have two baseball player parents. I knew that I liked baseball more than anything else I was doing, but it didn't feel special. It didn't feel odd to me that I was playing baseball, because why should it? I was a six-year-old kid playing a sport. But yeah, I guess I do remember knowing that I was good and people describing my swing as looking like Will Clark's."

FIG. 29. Lilly Jacobson, Reno National Little League, age ten. Courtesy of Jennifer Ring.

When she was six, Lilly joined the Little League in Albany, California, the same Little League and the same municipal diamond as her future teammate, Tamara Holmes, had played on fifteen years earlier. The next year, we moved to Reno, Nevada, where she played in the Reno National Little League and continued through Babe Ruth youth league and high school baseball. Like her teammate Malaika Underwood, Lilly insists that she didn't find baseball; baseball found her. "Baseball chose me. I never decided to play baseball. I started playing it, and I loved it. I think I was born a baseball player. I don't think twice about that."

She had such a natural swing that she enjoyed admiration from the time she first picked up a bat. Before her six-year-old Little League team had played its first game, a father watching batting practice remarked, "She looks like Will Clark!" During key moments in games, parents would cheerfully exclaim, "The bases are loaded, and here comes Little Miss

RBI!" So she learned to identify herself as a hitter. Her earliest memories of Little League, like those of most of her USA teammates, reveal the joy of playing baseball and little awareness of gender difference.

At age eleven, she suddenly found herself the only girl in her Little League. The one other girl, a year older, who had always been in her league on another team, switched to softball when it was time to move on to middle school. "There was one girl who was older than me, who I looked up to, who played in Little League with me, and she was really, really good. I hoped that she would keep playing baseball, and make my path easier, and that I could follow in her footsteps. But she decided to switch, and I was really disappointed by that. I also knew that it wasn't going to affect my decision: I was going to keep playing baseball."[2] At the time Lilly did not identify the moment with gender: "As an eleven-year-old kid I don't think you really think about these things in terms of gender and equality. You think about them in terms of what you want to do. At that point, I knew it was different that I played baseball, that I was good enough to keep up with the guys, and that I wasn't switching to softball. But I don't think it was ever a conscious decision. It was never a statement about gender or equality. It's really just about saying that as a human being I should be able to play what I want. And do something that I love."

She was passed up for the Little League All-Stars when she was eleven and twelve. The first year it didn't bother her. By the following year, when she was playing her final year in Little League, the omission was glaring enough that a coach from one of the other teams tried to nominate her for the All-Star team. He was told by the president of the league that he could not nominate a player from a team not his own. In response he tried to draft Lilly for the second-seed All-Star team that he was slotted to coach. Again he was rebuffed. Lilly's coach had not nominated her for the All-Stars, even though he had played her every inning of every game. The league president was his wife, and she was the final appeal on her husband's decision. Lilly had been double-teamed and knew, for the first time, that something was not right.

"I think anybody knows when they are good at something. I mean, I was a good hitter, and I loved hitting. It's still my favorite thing to do in the world. I can take batting practice until my hands bleed. I played well and got playing time because I played well. That's the first time that it started to become apparent that there were going to be obstacles in my way. Until that point I had just been playing with a bunch of kids, and I was good, so I was playing, and I hadn't really thought about it, even though people were telling me that I should switch to softball. But it's All-Stars . . . who cares? It's not like anybody was telling me I couldn't keep playing baseball. It meant that I was unjustly not chosen for a team that I should have been on, but I knew I would play the next year, and it didn't really matter. And honestly, it may not even have had to do with gender discrimination. It's not like my coach didn't give me playing time. It just, I think, had to do with the number of coaches and coach's sons that were on the team. Which is kind of an issue with youth sports in general."

When she did not switch to softball after Little League, resistance to her presence in youth baseball intensified. It was never a problem for the boys who were her teammates: they knew she could play, and they liked her. But the coaches all had their own sons on their teams and believed they were preparing them for high school baseball and beyond. The boys also played on private travel ball teams, which Lilly had not been invited to join. She was told by adults that she was wasting her time playing baseball.

"After that business with the All-Stars, I started playing Babe Ruth [twelve- to fifteen-year-old public youth league], which was not all that pleasant an experience. Babe Ruth is when you move up to the big diamond. And I still hit great. They wouldn't put me at first base anymore because the boys were getting bigger than me and you typically use tall people at first base. They put me in the outfield, and I didn't feel very confident in the outfield at that point in my career because I hadn't played it at all. I don't think anybody does when they're twelve. I mean I guess maybe there are some people that are born outfielders, but in my mind I think outfielding takes a lot of work in order to learn how to read a fly ball. It just takes practice and repetition and seeing the ball off the bat. So I didn't feel very confident in the outfield, but I could hit."

"But there was the coaches' sons issue again: having multiple coaches, four coaches on a Babe Ruth team. You've got the coaches' sons that get all the playing time, and then the coaches' sons' friends who get all the remaining playing time. And that's when parents also start taking things really seriously, thinking that somehow Babe Ruth is going to translate into college baseball, and so they freak out and think that since I have no quote-unquote future in baseball, there's no point in giving me playing time. I've had this experience a lot where coaches don't play you, and they don't put their confidence in you, and it's really hard to play with that. You can't. I mean if the coach doesn't show his confidence in you, there's no way that you can really power through without losing some confidence in yourself. Especially if you're not getting the opportunity to prove yourself and boost your own confidence. If you're just sitting on the bench, then how do you know that you're good enough to play? So in Babe Ruth I probably started to lose a little bit of confidence in myself, though not significantly. I was more frustrated at that point. I played in that league for two years and left halfway through my third year." She left because the coach was playing her only the minimum required by the league rules.

She would enter high school the following September and try out for the JV baseball team at Reno High School with the boys she had always played with. She hoped the high school coach would be fair-minded. She was aware that many parents objected to a girl playing high school baseball. "One dad came up to my dad at a Babe Ruth game and said, 'She won't play high school baseball in this town, not so long as I'm around.' Dad said something smart in response, but I can't remember what it was. Some parents were fine, but there were definitely some people that didn't want me to play. It was obviously because of sexism, but the rationale was that I would just be taking a spot away from a boy who could have a future. That is just the most ridiculous argument in the world because, if I'm good enough to beat them out, then they are not going to have a future anyway. If they are not good enough to make a high school baseball team, then they are not good enough to make a high school baseball team; you can't say that I'm taking a spot from anyone. I'm taking my own spot. [. . .]

"I went through Reno High's four months of preseason training. It was really intense, and I was keeping up, and I was doing fine. But I got cut because they said I wasn't big enough, fast enough, or strong enough. Keep in mind that we're talking about freshmen: fourteen-year-old boys, who are not exactly big, fast, or strong. One of them was overweight and had asthma and couldn't even finish the running drills. He made the JV team, but they cut me. And they also cut the only Asian and the only Hispanic kid on the team. I mean, it was pretty apparent that I was never going to get a chance at that school to play baseball.

"I don't even think I went to school the next two days because I was so depressed. I really thought my baseball career was over at the ripe old age of fourteen. I thought that somebody could tell me that I couldn't play anymore and that was it. I definitely lost confidence in myself at that point. It started in Babe Ruth, and then this was a big one, and I thought maybe I can't play high school baseball. Maybe I've reached the limit. Maybe people were right when they told me to switch to softball. At that point I was not willing to switch to softball because that would mean defeat. It wouldn't be defeat because softball is an 'inferior sport.' It would be defeat because somebody told me I couldn't do something that I wanted to do, and I said okay and switched to what they wanted me to play."

She had been taking lessons with the assistant coach at Reno High for almost two years. He was a young guy with a new teaching degree who had been very enthusiastic about Lilly's baseball ability when she was twelve and was introduced to him by a Little League teammate's father. During the Reno High fall preseason, however, he suddenly told Lilly it would be a "conflict of interest" to continue to coach her privately when she was about to try out for the team. He was not conflicted about continuing to give private lessons to several boys who were about to try out for the same team.

To enable her to prepare for high school tryouts and to continue to grow as a ballplayer, Lilly needed a batting coach. The University of Nevada had recently hired a new assistant coach, Jay Uhlman, who several years earlier had been a star shortstop at Nevada. I called him to ask if he would be willing to coach a girl who wanted to play high school baseball. When I brought Lilly to the Nevada batting cages so she could meet Jay and show him her swing, he was impressed and enthusiastic about giving her lessons. He became an important mentor and friend.

"Jay Uhlman is one of my favorite human beings in the world and is one of the people who really enabled me to regain my confidence by remaining confident in me. I remember going to hitting lessons with Jay during our preseason at Reno High. There was one time where I was just hitting line drive after line drive, and he said, 'I've got nothing to say. I can't even . . . there's nothing. This is perfect right now; there's nothing for me to say.' He asked a UNR player who was hitting in the cage next to me what he thought, and he watched me for a while and was like, 'You're just a line drive machine over there.' And then I didn't make the Reno High team, and Jay was shocked. He said it wasn't right that I got cut and told me to transfer schools.

"So I started thinking about it, and obviously, all my friends were at Reno High, but there was really nothing else there for me. I mean it is a good school academically, and I was in the choir and stuff, but I thought, 'If I don't have baseball, what am I doing here? I'm cutting out a huge chunk of who I am.' Wooster [High School] has an International Baccalaureate program, which is an academic magnet program that would enable me to transfer there. We visited Wooster and met the JV coach, Coach [Bryant] Wambolt, and he said, 'If you're good enough to play, I don't see why you shouldn't be able to play.' He seemed like an honest guy. And I also just fell in love with the school. It was so much more real than Reno High."

Reno High School is wealthy, suburban, and predominantly white. Wooster High is working class and predominantly Latino. Students at Reno High refer to Wooster as a "ghetto school." But Lilly found comfort at Wooster and thrived academically. Perhaps she associated the gender discrimination she had experienced at Reno with the racial and socioeconomic discrimination her classmates at Wooster were dealing with. The school and its athletic teams are perennial underdogs in Reno, which suited Lilly fine.

"So I tried out for the Wooster JV team my sophomore year, and I was so nervous. Every practice, every preseason practice I was nervous as hell. And I was so quiet, even after I made the JV team. When I got my jersey and pants for the JV team, and it said 'Wooster' on it, and it was a button-down jersey, I was so excited (I never had a button-down jersey before). Throughout that whole season I was pretty quiet. Initially, I was like, 'You need to prove yourself, be quiet, show that you're not trying to make any statement, show that you're just a ballplayer. I was so excited when I made the team, and there was relief. But I also thought, 'Okay, that was one step, and now you've got to prove that you belong here.' This was also a new group of guys. And a group of working-class Reno guys, not exactly the most liberal and open people. But they were fine. They were totally fine. I mean, they ended up being like my brothers, but that first season I just felt like I just needed to shut up and play."

Lilly got plenty of playing time, the Wooster coaches were attentive, and she was learning a lot about baseball. The coaches' confidence helped her to rebuild her self-esteem as a ballplayer. A moment of vindication came quickly, early in that first season when the Wooster JV team played the Reno JV team. "I was getting my confidence back. I hit like .340 that season. Yeah, I hit really well. I remember I hit a double off the opposing pitcher's head when we played against the Reno High JV team. I was just standing on second base and waiting while the coaches helped him get up." These were the same Reno High coaches who had cut Lilly from the team the previous year. Now they were attending to their pitcher whom she had knocked down with a line drive right back at him.

"And another thing about Wooster: I never really pitched before in my life because nobody had said, 'You should try pitching.' But I'm left-handed, and one of the coaches saw me playing catch with Ty Beardon in the outfield, and he said, 'Have you ever thought about pitching?' And I said, 'No, that's so scary, are you kidding me? Just let me hit. I don't want to do that.' And he said, 'All right. I want you to throw it at Ty's left shoulder.' So I threw it, and it went right to his left shoulder. He said, 'Okay, I want you to throw it to Ty's right hip.' And I threw it there, and he said, 'I think you can pitch.' And I was like, 'Okay.' Just having a coach who has the confidence in you and sees your ability and says, 'I think you can do this,' is huge. I mean, that's huge. He taught me a curve ball, and that was my pitch through high school. So yeah, having coaches that were supportive and gave me playing time was really great. JV was great because I could really keep up with those guys. I didn't have any trouble, so I got a lot of playing time, hit well, and learned how to pitch. And by the end of the season, the guys were totally fine with me. I mean, I didn't feel like I had to just be quiet and play anymore.

"Then my junior year, I tried out for varsity, and I was so nervous for that too. But I did really well in tryouts and most of the guys on the team were my year [at school], and I was pretty close with them at that point because I played with them all sophomore year. The older guys I hadn't played with, but they knew me because I'd done preseason with them, and they saw that I could play. Most of them were pretty supportive in a brotherly kind of way, encouraging me from the vantage point of someone that is older and has played varsity already.

"But there was one kid who hated me: Chris. Not only because I was a girl, but because I'm Jewish. I heard him say to Frankie, 'Did you know Lilly's Jewish?' in this disgusted voice. Chris also thought that I just made the team because I was a girl. That's clearly how easy it is. So let's see, I faced Chris when I was pitching during tryouts, and we were doing an intra-squad scrimmage. I pitched against Chris, and I struck him out. And he was furious. Then he was pitching, and I came up to bat. And I hit a line drive into left field and everybody was laughing . . . they would come up to me and be like, 'Do you have any idea how furious Chris is right now?' And I think after that scrimmage, I felt pretty confident that I had a good shot at making varsity. [. . .]

"I remember sweeping up the dugout after tryouts when they were going to make the cuts, and Pete Lazzari was talking to me, and he said, 'I think you should make it. Look at how you played.' And I was like, 'Yeah, maybe you're right.' Well, actually, then Coach [Ron] Malcolm came up to me before they made the official cuts, and he asked me, 'Would you rather play on varsity and not get a whole lot of playing time your junior year or play on JV and get a lot of playing time?' And I said I wanted to play varsity because you always want to play at the highest level you can. He said, 'Okay,' and I could tell that was the answer he was hoping for. He also clearly knew I was going to choose varsity because, twenty minutes later when he told me I made the team, they already had my nameplate with 'Jacobson' inscribed on it for the varsity locker room. [. . .]

"There were a couple of juniors that got cut from varsity. One of them was Tom Beardon and one was Nick Eppert, and they were still my buddies, and they weren't resentful at all that I made varsity over them. Because most kids know their ability, and they knew they weren't that great. Tom Beardon didn't make it, but his twin brother, Ty, made it, but he knew that Ty was the better ballplayer and Tommy just played because he liked it. And Eppert was our football quarterback, but he didn't do very well at baseball. [. . .]

"It was so exciting when I made varsity. They already had a little article in the newspaper [the *Reno Gazette Journal*] about me when I was on JV. But now I was the first girl in Nevada history to play varsity 4A [the largest high schools] baseball. And making it as a junior meant that I was good."

Lilly recalls a dramatic moment during her first season when she was called in to relieve the team's starter, who got in trouble in the first inning against one of the best teams in Northern Nevada: "Actually, my junior year was when I had that game against Douglas [High School]. One of our ace pitchers, Jeremy Joustra, who threw like eighty-eight and went Division I, started that game and just couldn't get an out. I remember being in the bullpen with Hunter Smit, who is this big, tall senior, and I was a junior, and we were warming up in the bullpen, and I thought, 'Oh, of course they are going to throw Hunter if Jeremy can't get out of this.' I just assumed that they would put Hunter in. And then Coach Malcolm comes out calling for the lefty, and I was like, 'Wait, Hunter is right-handed.' And I was like, 'What??'And my heart rate went from . . . from thinking that you're not going to play, that you're just warming up in the bullpen, to realizing that you're going in to face the best hitting team in the league . . . my heart jumped probably from 60 to 120. My heart was pounding. I kept saying, 'Are you sure? Hunter, did they just call me?' He just smiled and was like, 'Yeah. Go for it.' I went out there, and I don't really even remember what happened, but I had a great game: pitched about five innings, had a couple of strikeouts, and gave up two runs I think. We won. Jeremy wasn't my hugest fan either, until that point. And actually, apparently at some point later on, he made some comment about me being on the team only because I'm a girl, and somebody said to him,

'Are you forgetting when she got you out of that mess against Douglas?'
And he was like, 'Oh, yeah. Right.' He 'friended' me on Facebook a few
years ago, so it must be good."

"I heard that the next day one of the Douglas coaches who was throwing batting practice came out in a wig and a dress. One of the kids that I
struck out that game—I think it was a change-up, and it was a called third
strike—he was just furious, he was so angry. It probably didn't help that
Pat Kealy, my best friend, was up on the fence in the bleachers yelling,
'Excuse me, sir. You just got struck out by a girl! Excuse me!' I actually
faced this kid again in regionals, and he wanted revenge or whatever, and
he asked to pinch hit, just so he could face me. So he came in, and I struck
him out swinging this time. And so he was even more upset, and his mom
came up to me in the parking lot as we were getting on the bus. She said,
'You struck out my son!' All my teammates were laughing, and I didn't
know what to say so I said, 'I'm sorry!' My teammates were like, 'Don't say
you're sorry!' I didn't know what to say to that either, so I just got on the
bus. To make it even worse for him, the local news station was videotaping
the game and kept showing footage of this poor kid that I struck out. It
was on the local news shows all weekend. He's probably still in therapy."

Lilly's coaches didn't treat her with kid gloves, and that also boosted
her confidence, letting her know she was a regular member of the team,
like the guys were.

"Coach Malcolm and Coach [Nick] Custer and all of them also had
confidence to call me out if I screwed up. It's not like they toned it down
because I was a girl. They weren't afraid to yell at me. I remember at one
practice where I couldn't do anything . . . I was just screwing everything
up, I screwed up every bunt defense, I was throwing the ball all over the
place, and Malcolm screamed at me and was like, 'Get your head out of
your ass! What are you doing?' I think he came up afterward and gave me
a hug and told me to go get some pizza or ice cream or something, but
still. I really was a part of that team. I wouldn't say that I wasn't treated
differently, but the way I thought about it then, was that we all had stuff
that we would make fun of each other for, and mine just happened to
be that I was a girl. Like you know, we'd make fun of Jeremy for being a

FIG. 30. Lilly Jacobson pitching for Wooster High School, 2006. Courtesy of Jennifer Ring.

giant human being who shook the ground when he ran. Everybody had something that they would get ragged on for. And mine was just that I was a girl, so that was my thing. I was even less quiet senior year. I felt much more comfortable. And also, being a part of the clubhouse made it easy to be close as a team. We had a clubhouse right on the field that Malc [Coach Malcolm] had built, with real lockers, and we had our nameplates on our lockers and foot boxes and a fridge and an Xbox.

"I do have to say, I was still always nervous for practice. Probably until I played club baseball [as a college student at UC Berkeley], I don't think there was ever a time that I wasn't nervous for practice. It has to do with being a girl and playing on a boys' team, because no matter what, as comfortable as you feel and as close as you are with your teammates and as much confidence as the coach has in you, you know that people are always looking, people are always watching you, and you're the different one."

She was hypervigilant about being perceived as "the girl," who must prove that she deserves to play her sport. "I don't think I ever thought I was at an athletic disadvantage. I mean everybody has their own capabilities, but I think it was my concern about how it looked in other people's eyes. Having them think, 'Oh, she screwed that up because she's a girl trying to play with boys. As an athlete, you never want to be the one that fucks up, but I felt like if I was the one that fucked up and I was the only girl, for some reason it has bigger implications."

She never took her future in baseball for granted. She thought about only one year at a time. "My goal had been to play high school baseball. That was a big thing, to be the only girl that didn't get shoved into softball and to be the first girl in Nevada to play high school baseball. I didn't have goals beyond that because I didn't think about college baseball that much. If you think about that in the context of boys, it's ridiculous. Boys assume that they are going to play high school baseball. Especially someone with the amount of talent that I had and the amount of hard work that I put in, based on my skills, it should have been an assumption that I would play high school baseball, but it wasn't. So I accomplished that, and I didn't think too much beyond that. Especially because I'm also very into school—I'm a good student. So I wasn't thinking about college in terms of sports; I was thinking about college in terms of academics. I wasn't willing to sacrifice my brains for baseball."

When asked whether she might have felt differently had she been a boy who was a baseball player with high academic aspirations, she responds that such a situation is nearly impossible for her to imagine. "It's really hard to do those kind of hypotheticals because I only know my experience as I had it. I've never been just a guy on the team. So definitely, as much as I would like to be able to play and not have anybody say, 'That's weird. Why is that girl playing?' being the only girl is a huge part of my baseball identity. Which is why in college I really thought it would be nice not to be different. I almost didn't want to play because I wondered what it would be like to go to school and not be 'the girl that plays baseball.'"

During late spring of Lilly's senior year in high school, Jim Glennie contacted her to suggest that she try out for the 2006 Women's National Team in June, just a few days after she graduated high school. The western regional tryouts were to be held at Phoenix Municipal Stadium, spring training home of Lilly's beloved Oakland Athletics. She was thrilled by the opportunity to even step onto that field, much less try out for the Women's National Team, although she hadn't even heard of the women's national baseball team. At first she actually thought it would be less nerve-racking to compete against other girls who played baseball, but when she got her first look at a Major League field full of women baseball players, she felt even more pressure. There were over sixty women at this regional tryout, and most of them were very good ballplayers.

Lilly remembers, "Oh, it was shocking. I mean I just assumed that I was one of the few girls in the country playing baseball with boys in high school, which automatically meant that I must be one of the best in the country. But these girls were good. I expected to just come out there and walk all over everyone. I expected there would be a bunch of softball players who wouldn't know how to hit a baseball and who wouldn't be able to pitch. But they were good. I mean, there was some stiff competition. So it was kind of shocking, and it took me a while to get over that. Having always had that kind of 'exceptional' identity, you think, 'Wait, what? No, *I'm* the girl baseball player. Who are you?' You feel like such a badass; you feel so cool when you're that girl that plays baseball. You learn to kind of love that exceptional quality, and you learn to love the fact that you've fought so hard for what you love. And when you find other girls that have done that, you have this inherent bond. Being with other girls who played baseball felt like what I imagined it would be like to be a guy on a baseball team. [. . .]

"Tryouts are a very weird emotional situation anyway, because usually you're in groups and you're competing against people, but you're also meeting them and trying to be friendly. You don't want them to do that well, and you want to be better, but then you're also cheering them on, especially if they're on your team during a scrimmage. Actually, in the second round of tryouts, when Team USA invites you back and you're rooming with somebody, there is even more camaraderie. You think, 'Oh, this is cool. There are other girls, and they play, and I'm not the only one.' You switch from thinking, 'I'm the only one,' like it's a really great thing, to realizing 'I'm not the only one' and that's even better. You also still want to be the best, but that's with any athlete. But the experience made me transition from valuing that exceptional identity to valuing even more the fact that I wasn't that exceptional.

"You have people out there that are way more like you than you've ever realized. Especially with the girls that have played high school baseball. You can share these stories about being the only girl and about having those awkward moments where you're walking on a baseball field with a new group of guys and they just look at you like, 'What are you doing here?' and you have to prove yourself. Finding people that can share that with you is really exciting. And once I made the team it was also exciting to be on a team and not be different—to not think that everybody is watching you. They're watching the team, and you're a part of it."

The difference between baseball and softball culture had always bothered Lilly as much as the differences between the sports themselves, but after the players had been selected and became a team, her objections to softball players subsided. "[Before Team USA] when I would hear softball teams cheer and stuff, it would always drive me crazy because I was like, 'That's not what you do. You don't yell and scream like a bunch of cheerleaders when you're on a field.' So I never thought being on a girls'

FIG. 31. (*above*) Lilly Jacobson, hitting for Team USA 2008. Courtesy of USA Baseball.

FIG. 32. (*left*) Lilly Jacobson, Team USA 2008, All-Tournament Outfielder. Courtesy of Jennifer Ring.

FIG. 33. (*top*) Jacobson lays out for a line drive, New England Women's Red Sox, 2011. Courtesy of Patricia Wagar.

FIG. 34. (*bottom*) Lilly Jacobson hitting for New England Red Sox, 2011. Courtesy of Patricia Wagar.

team would be that great because, I don't know . . . I don't want a bunch of girly girls doing stupid shit. But then I saw that they're not: these are women baseball players and some of them are softball players, but they are seriously competitive athletes. You think they haven't fought the same fight that we [baseball players] have. But that's not fair: they're doing the exact same thing that we're doing right now, they're our teammates, and they're playing baseball when a bajillion other softball players are not playing baseball, so they've got their own story."

Lilly's sense of exceptionalism about being a baseball player was stilled when she first played right field with USA center fielder Tara Harbert. "Tara is one of my favorite people in the world, and she is definitely a softball player. But I've never played better with another outfielder: I know how she moves, and I know how we communicate. And we just work together in the outfield. I think she is fantastic: she is an absolutely incredible athlete. So I would never be disdainful of her for being a softball player. And Veronica [Alvarez, USA Baseball catcher] was a softball player, but there's no way in hell anybody is going to say that she isn't the toughest person you've ever met and that she wouldn't fight for what she wants and that she isn't a fantastic baseball player and a fantastic leader. So I mean you get over the softball thing once they're your teammates, because at that point they are baseball players, and it doesn't matter anymore."

Team USA 2006 traveled to Taipei, Taiwan, to play in the second IBAF Women's World Cup Tournament. They were coached by Julie Croteau, the first woman to play NCAA baseball and the first woman to coach a men's Division I NCAA baseball team. With Team USA in 2006, Croteau achieved another first: she became the first woman to coach a women's baseball team to the gold medal in international competition. Lilly was one of the younger players on the team. There were four teenagers, as well as several former Silver Bullets players in their mid- and late thirties. Lilly was a relief pitcher, but when Julie Croteau saw Lilly hit, she made her the designated hitter (DH) for the tournament. Croteau was Lilly's role model: besides being a trailblazer in collegiate women's baseball, Croteau was of similar size and build as Lilly, and she is a left-hander who played first base and was a good hitter. Her prediction that Lilly would have a great future with USA Baseball made Lilly glow with pride. She was one of the young guns.

Immediately after the 2006 Taiwan tournament, Lilly moved to Pough-keepsie, New York, for her freshman year at Vassar College. At Wooster High Lilly had lettered in golf and skiing as well as baseball and was named one of ten Northern Nevada Student Athletes of the Year. Vassar had recruited her to play golf, a game she had been playing for only three years. She decided to forgo baseball for the first time in her life. Her baseball experience at Wooster had been so gratifying that she didn't think she could equal it in college.

"I actually was pretty excited about playing golf at Vassar and not play-ing baseball because I just wanted to be a regular girl. I thought it would be nice to just be a normal college kid and be an athlete, but not have the pressure of always being 'the girl that plays baseball.'" But when spring came around, the absence of baseball was painful. Lilly missed it too much. "It was the first time in my life that it was springtime and I wasn't playing baseball. I just missed it a ton, and everyone could tell. I'd been working out with the [Vassar] baseball coaches a little bit. Golf is just a frustrating sport in general, but what was even more frustrating is that I had a lot of talent and probably could have been really good, but I wasn't passionate about it, so I didn't want to put in the work. I realized that at one point when we were on the driving range . . . I like the driving range because it's not frustrating. But we [the Vassar golf team] were complaining about something, because we were always complaining about something, and my coach said, 'Come on, you're on a golf course right now. You're on a driving range! Where would you rather be?' And I said, 'In a batting cage.' And he said, 'I don't want to hear that.' But it made me realize that I really would have rather been working on my swing, my baseball swing, and golf was not my passion. And also, I noticed that my golf swing started to affect my baseball swing. In high school golf was a fall sport, so I could separate them and it didn't mess with my baseball at all. But at Vassar it started to affect my baseball swing, and I have great pride in my swing, so I was very upset by that."

She approached the baseball coach at Vassar, Jon Martin, about trying out for the team, and he told her she could try out the next fall. "Then I told my golf coach that I was going to try out for the baseball team, and I was really nervous to tell him, but he was not at all surprised and was, in fact, supportive. 'You know,' he said, 'you should be doing what you love.' So I did. I trained really hard all summer, came out for the team in the fall. It just so happened that my father passed away shortly after I got back to Vassar in the fall, which . . . I don't know . . . baseball might have been a good distraction from that, but it was also just a really emotional time. I played really well in the fall. The guys on the team were totally accepting of me. Actually, when I was hitting with the coaches the previous year, working out with them while I was still playing golf, the guys on the team saw me hitting, and one of them—this was a junior at that time—said, 'Dude, come out for the team. Are you kidding me? Come play with us.'"

During the most emotionally difficult time in her life, the young men on the Vassar baseball team embraced Lilly and helped take her mind off her grief. "It felt really nice that they just immediately embraced me and made me feel welcome and made me feel like I was immediately a part of the team. I still felt like I had to prove myself, and I was still nervous before every practice and every scrimmage and everything, but the guys were just fantastic, and initially it seemed like the coaches were pretty supportive too. I made the team."

When Lilly returned to Vassar in January after winter break, something had changed. The coaches no longer seemed supportive. Her foot had been bothering her for much of the fall, but she had made the team while ignoring the pain. She had seen one of the athletic trainers at Vassar, but he had failed to identify the stress fracture that was causing the difficulty. When she was home in Reno for winter break, her conditioning coach, Rob Conatser, sent her to Reno Orthopedics for an X-ray. This time the doctor found the stress fracture, which by then had become a full fracture in one of the bones in her foot and was not yet fully healed. Lilly had made the Vassar baseball team on a broken foot. The Reno orthopedist put her in a boot and instructed her to stay off the foot for four weeks and then to have it rechecked at Vassar.

It was only January. But when she had the foot rechecked and got the go-ahead to play again, the coaches were uninterested. "I'm not really sure what happened between fall and spring. I mean, I broke my foot, which made it so I couldn't do some of the preseason. I don't know what happened with the coaches, but suddenly, I got no playing time. The coaches wouldn't talk to me at practice. The Vassar coach wouldn't let me throw bullpens, and if I asked to throw a bullpen, he would finally say, 'Okay,' and then he wouldn't watch me. Growing up, I had never talked to a coach about playing time ever because that's not the player's role. The coach makes the decisions, but it just seemed unfair that . . . like, my teammates were saying, 'Why won't he put you in?' You know, I was working harder than everybody else . . ." Her voice quavers and she can't go on. "Sorry, I don't know why I'm crying."

When she regains her composure, she picks up the story, speaking in a strong voice, with tears still flowing freely down her cheeks. "But this isn't even the bad part. You know, I pushed him about it because I just wanted to know why. Like, what could I do to get some playing time? What could I do to get a shot at being on the field? And I should also mention that this is a pretty bad Division III men's team. It's not like we were a great team.[3] We had less than ten wins all season, so I don't really know what was at stake, and I had as much talent as anybody out there, and I worked harder, and all my teammates said that too. But he just basically told me the same shit that the Reno High coaches told me when I got cut from that first high school team: I wasn't big enough, fast enough, or strong enough to compete with college guys. And it's very hard not to take that seriously when your coach tells you that.

"So you know, it was devastating to me, and that season was the worst season I've ever had playing baseball. I hated it. I hated every moment of it because I had no confidence in myself, and I put so much pressure on myself because I not only had to prove myself to the coaches now, but I had to prove myself for, like, all women athletes, because I *am* big enough, fast enough, and strong enough. Every at bat, the weight of women's baseball, and the weight of women athletes everywhere, was on my shoulders. Obviously that's not reasonable, but whether or not it's just me putting pressure on myself doesn't matter, because that's how it was. It's impossible to play for a coach that doesn't have confidence in you.

"So I had four at bats all season. One of them I walked and scored our only run of the game. We lost that one 22–1. One of them I got a hit. It was the first hit that a female had gotten in college baseball since Julie Croteau.[4] I think I got the hit in the game right after I had talked to Coach Martin about playing time and after he had said he didn't think I could compete with college guys. You know, I got to first base, and the coach is standing there. The coach always gives you a high five when you get to the base, but Coach Martin didn't even look at me, let alone high-five. It was a legit hit. This wasn't like a little bitch hit, you know, a blooper that happened to fall or, like, a weak ground ball. This was a line drive over the shortstop, and I felt so great after that hit. I was like, 'All right. Maybe he'll give me a chance now.' But he didn't.

"I think I grounded out my other at bats. You know, you're coming in for a pinch hit late in the game when we're probably losing by ten or twelve runs, and it's just a courtesy, a 'put-the-shitty-players-in' type of pinch hit, which is . . . it's utterly impossible to do. Maybe some people can do it, but I hate pinch hitting, because you're cold. You've been jogging down to the fence and back [to keep loose]. Your head's not in the game. Usually I was just really angry because yet again I wasn't going to get a chance. And then I would put this pressure on myself like, 'You have to get a hit because otherwise you're just proving them right. I would just be depressed after these games no matter what. If I didn't play, it was depressing, and if I did play, every time I didn't succeed, I felt like was failing everyone. I was failing myself. I was failing women's baseball. It was awful. I hated baseball, absolutely hated it, and had no confidence in myself at all. And it was embarrassing to me to be on that team and not play at all because it does feel like then you're just a token. If you don't even have a chance to prove yourself, and you have to go and shake the hands of the guys on the other team after the game, it's like, 'What is this girl doing on the team?'"

A reporter from the *Poughkeepsie Journal* came out to interview Lilly and the Vassar team during one of their games. He stayed for the entire game, and Coach Martin didn't even put her in the game.

In the summer of 2008, after that traumatic sophomore year, Lilly returned to the Bay Area. That summer brought another Women's World Cup Tournament, and tryouts for the USA Baseball team were held at the end of July. Vassar had ruined pitching for Lilly, but she was learning to play the outfield. She found a men's junior college team to practice with (Mission College in Santa Clara, California, about forty miles south of Berkeley) and also commuted regularly over the Sierra Nevada to Reno, where Jay Uhlman continued to fine-tune her batting and was now also teaching her to play the outfield.

"So yeah, I was all over the place driving to hell and back to get some access to training. I was practicing an hour and a half away with the Mission College team, working with their pitching coach, even though I didn't want to pitch . . . I totally lost pitching after Vassar. And I was working at the city planning office in Albany [where she had a summer internship] and going to Reno to hit with Jay and work on outfielding. On my own, I was running sprints in the morning and lifting and things like that. Then we had [USA final] tryouts in LA, and I made the team. In 2006 I had been the DH mostly because we had three veteran outfielders and I was a rookie, but this year I was starting left fielder. We went to Matsuyama, Japan, and I played every inning of the World Cup, and it restored my confidence in myself and my love of the game. I hit—the coaches showed their confidence in me and put me in every situation. My teammates had confidence in me, and that's why I played as well as I did, and I ended up winning the 2008 All-Tournament Best Outfielder Award. One of three, I should mention, because they have three All-Tournament outfielders. I think it was really fortunate that I had that experience after Vassar because, if I didn't, I would have just quit and been like, 'Why do I keep doing this sport? I just keep getting beat up, and I'm not happy playing it anymore.' But Japan was an amazing experience, and I loved that for three weeks of the year, my only job was to play baseball. I didn't have to think about anything else."

After the tournament Lilly traveled directly from Japan to Vassar to begin her junior year. "I was miserable. I didn't want to go back to school. I didn't want to go back to that coach, but I said I was going to go back because, I mean, it's a good education, and I would have the opportunity to play college baseball, and I was one of two women in the country playing, so in my mind, being a pioneer in the sport was not something to take lightly. I got back and played the fall season, and at the end of the season, in our only fall scrimmage with another college, I got a hit. The next day, I got a call from the coach saying that I was cut. He didn't want me to play anymore.

"I was the only returner he cut, and at that point I was just like, 'I'm done with this place. This is awful. I just came back from playing international baseball, winning an award for being the best woman left fielder in the world, hitting great in the women's baseball World Cup, and you, the coach of a terrible Division III men's team, are going to tell me that I can't play, that I'm not good enough to play with a bunch of guys who have no future in baseball?' The ridiculous part was that he was saying the best female outfielder in the world cannot compete with any level of collegiate male baseball, even a terrible Division III team. So I thought, 'I'm done.'"

Lilly applied to transfer to UC Berkeley, where she hoped she could play club baseball. While she finished the fall semester at Vassar, she tried to come to terms with what appeared to be the end of her baseball career.

But baseball wasn't quite done with her: it found her again. Several of her USA teammates invited her to join them on a tournament team to which many of them belonged: the New England Women's Red Sox, coached by Kevin Marden. The team played against other women's teams in the United States and Canada and had a remarkable winning record under Coach Marden.[5] They were scheduled to play at a tournament in Arizona in November, and Lilly agreed to let Marden fly her there to join her USA teammates. It was the baseball catharsis she needed before she finished fall semester at Vassar and moved back to California in December.

Lilly was accepted as a junior at the University of California, Berkeley and would begin classes the following fall, 2009. Before she started classes at Berkeley, she found the courage to email the president of the club baseball team, Will Smelko, to ask him if she could try out. She wasn't sure how serious the club team at Cal was—sometimes at Division I schools club teams consist of the players who did not make the NCAA baseball team, and they are very competitive. Others are much more laid back. The Cal club baseball team had some very good ballplayers, but the feeling on the team was relaxed. Smelko, who was also the University of California student body president, responded to her email and was welcoming and enthusiastic. He told her the date of the team's first meeting in the fall semester and said he was eager for her to try out.

Lilly was startled by the club's unproblematic, welcoming attitude. "I emailed them and actually got a response back. I got the email from the president of the club baseball team at Cal saying, 'Yeah, come on out. Of course. Sounds great.' I started classes at Cal in the fall, and just a few weeks into the fall semester, we had tryouts. I made the team and had some of the most fun I've ever had playing men's baseball. They were just a group of guys that loved playing baseball, and we organized our own practices and organized our own travel to get places. We had a spring trip to Arizona, and it was super fun. It sort of restored my faith in men's baseball because it was just like, 'Yeah, let's go play.'

"Even if it was a club, it was like, 'I'm playing for Cal, and I'm in school. I've always played baseball while I'm in school. I need a team to play on. Let me play.' And I also think it was sort of a way to prove something to myself. Like, 'Fuck you, Vassar. If you're going to tell me I can't play with college-level guys, I'm going to find baseball somewhere else.' I guarantee you that our club team at Cal could have beaten the Vassar team."

When Cal played against the Stanford club baseball team that season, Lilly endured some heckling from Stanford players who presumed she could not hit a fastball. She let it get under her skin and didn't hit well. But no sooner was that tournament over than she grabbed a friend of hers who played on the NCAA varsity team at Cal and asked him to let her face the fastest pitches that the varsity pitching machine could throw.

"I was struggling on the club team to catch up to the pitching. At first I thought it was because I was a girl. I thought, 'Physically I can't. Physically I'm a girl. I just can't hit that speed pitching. I can't hit that.' So my friend and I went in the batting cages and just cranked up the pitching machine as fast as it would go, ninety-whatever. And my first twenty swings, I would completely swing and miss. It was past me before I swung. But you keep going, you see it regularly, you start to hit it. Your body makes an adjustment. You have no time to think about anything. You just see it and swing.

"It was just repetition, repetition, repetition, and you know, eventually I would foul them back, and then eventually I would foul them off the other way. So I was still a little bit late, but I was hitting it. We kept coming to the cages to practice, and eventually, I was able to hit a ninety-mile-an-hour ball up the middle, and I was like, 'Oh, I can do this.' It was a revelation to me that I could actually touch something that was coming at me at ninety miles an hour, and I thought, 'Oh. That's why I couldn't do it. It's not because I'm a girl. It's because I don't see it regularly and I haven't seen it.'[6]

"I should also mention that when I was going into the Cal varsity batting cages, one of the guys who was watching me said, 'You have the best fast-twitch hand-eye coordination I've ever seen of any girl ever.' Which he meant as a compliment, but I heard it like I'm an anomaly, right? I'm always an exception, and I'm always an anomaly. But I was thinking, 'Well, no. If we got girls to see this regularly, I bet they could hit it. I know I'm a good athlete, but there are a lot of good female athletes, like the girls that hit softballs from, you know, two feet away or whatever the mound is at for the college softball players . . . why do they even call it a mound? It doesn't go up. Don't put this in the book. I don't want softball players to get mad at me. But you know, if they can hit that, I think that's as much crazy fast-twitch hand-eye coordination as any baseball player has."

There are differences between men and women athletes that Lilly recognizes. But she does not believe those differences are definitive in baseball. "Obviously, size-wise on average, girls are smaller, so we're not going to be hitting as many home runs, but there are also girls that are bigger than the guys who play college and professional baseball now, and so to make the argument that it's because of these biological differences between women and men, and to make sweeping generalizations about size and strength and not think about the fact that especially in baseball, there are very small men that play, and some very large women that can probably compete with them . . . It's really hard to get that into people's heads, including your own. [. . .]

"Athletes are always exceptions because they're great at a specific thing. To use averages and generalizations as a method for discrimination is just that. It's discrimination, and it doesn't take into account individual ability, individual training. I didn't believe I could hit a ninety-mile an hour fastball because society has told me, 'On average, you can't.' But I'm not average."

The women on Team USA who have played both softball and baseball all mentioned adjustments required when moving from one sport to the other. None found the differences insurmountable, but most focused on the speed and distances in the two sports and what they found to be the slower pace of every aspect of women's baseball. Even though Lilly never played softball, she found it necessary to make similar adjustments when moving from men's to women's baseball. Like her teammates, she regards the adjustments as something any good athlete can accomplish with patience and training.

"When I'm playing with women versus when I'm playing with men, the differences are noticeable. Like, the men are just throwing harder. There's no denying that. And as an outfielder, the ball comes off the bat quicker. That's true. But that doesn't mean that women can't adjust to that, that they can't train at that level and compete with that. Okay, if you're talking about football or something, for the most part a girl is probably going to get crushed. But for baseball, it's a game of finesse. You don't need big huge strength. If you *learn* to hit a ninety-mile-an-hour pitch, you'll be able to hit a ball coming ninety miles an hour. I mean, it's true that there are some physical differences. Obviously, not every woman is going to be able to make those adjustments. If you get a shitty female athlete, she's not going to be able to do it, but neither is a shitty male athlete."

Lilly realizes that she has unwittingly internalized some of the biases against the women's game: rather than acknowledging the slightly different paces of games, she assumed that because she has played with men for so long, she should be finding women's baseball easier. "When I play with women, if I'm not playing perfectly, it's like, 'What's wrong with me? What's wrong with my swing? Something's wrong, because I should be dominating right now.' But I realized that when I switch from playing with men to playing with women, I have to make an adjustment too . . . like that split second that is the difference between eighty-five and seventy-five [mile-an-hour pitches] gives me too much time to think. So in the past tournament I played with women, I felt like I was overthinking my at bats."

Her years of experience playing with men have not been easy, and she bears some battle scars. It hasn't yet destroyed her love of the game, but it would have been much easier if she could have played with women all along.

"My love of baseball is always there. But it hides sometimes. It's kind of in hiding right now because I've had, whatever, twenty years of building up of pressure. When I love baseball, it just so happens to be when I'm playing with those girls on the U.S. team. The competition is right in line with where I am, and I don't feel like an exception. I can just play, and I'm playing with the best of the best, and I love those girls. They're my family. When I think of when I'm happy playing baseball, it's when Tara is next to me in center field and we're talking to each other, not just chitchat (although sometimes we do that too), but you know, communicating. We communicate really, really well in the outfield. Having Tara say, 'Hey, I'm over a couple steps.' And I'll be, 'All right,' so then I know she's a couple steps away from me so if there's a ball hit between us, then I might have to get it. Or running back for a ball that's over my head and having Tara say, 'Look, you got it, Lil, you got it,' and laying out and getting it. And hitting, because I have a pretty swing. When you connect on the sweet spot—I know everybody says this—but it's the best feeling in the world when you know you just hit a double. When I'm playing with the girls on the U.S. team, that's this very special feeling of a team at its finest."

Lilly Jacobson has played baseball with boys and men and with champion women athletes. She has been chased away from the national pastime more times than most people could tolerate being rebuffed and rejected at any endeavor. Still, every time she was shut down, she managed to recover her sense that she belongs and has what it takes to play the game she loves. She won't go away. Why? She answers simply, "It still is my sport."

14

Meggie Meidlinger

PITCHER/FIRST BASE

"In my mind it was baseball or nothing."

Meggie Meidlinger has been a baseball player since she was four years old, and she was a member of the 2006 and 2008 Women's National Teams.[1] She occupies a unique place in this book because she was not a member of the 2010 Women's National Team, and her athletic career vividly reflects the contradictions faced by all the women who play baseball in the United States. Passionate about baseball from her earliest memories, Meggie is a talented athlete with a six-foot-two Division I stature that could probably have gotten her serious consideration for an athletic scholarship in any sport except baseball. But as a serious student, she reached that fork in the road after playing high school baseball and chose academics instead of continuing to play with college men. She was away from baseball for five years while studying architecture at Virginia Tech and has paid an athletic price for it. Her skills as a pitcher did not develop as they would have had she been playing during those prime athletic years. Her story demonstrates just how tenuous the connection with competitive baseball is for a woman with responsibilities that prevent the game from being the center of her life.

Girls who play high school baseball are in a double bind: college choices are limited for a woman who wants to play baseball, and college without baseball makes it difficult to stay trained for the sport. Meggie chose the high-powered architecture program at Virginia Tech because it would best prepare her for her chosen career. Of the four high school baseball players on Team USA, only one, Marti Sementelli, allowed baseball to determine her college choice.

Meggie continues to play baseball as a regular member of the American women's amateur baseball circuit, where she was recruited while still in high school by Adriane Adler of the East Coast Yankees. She has also played on the Chicago Pioneers and the New England Women's Red Sox. She and Lilly became good friends through Team USA and have spent many hours together discussing their baseball experiences. So when Lilly was preparing to travel to Baltimore for the 2011 Eastern Women's Baseball Conference Tournament and was to be picked up at the airport by Meggie, who lives in Washington, I asked her to interview her friend and teammate.

When she was a senior year at Dominion High School in Sterling, Virginia, Meggie pitched a perfect game. She was featured in *Sports Illustrated*'s "Faces in the Crowd" for that accomplishment. Lilly saw the article about Meggie in May 2006, when she too was a high school pitcher intending to try out for Team USA. She was intimidated and wondered how she could she compete against Meggie's size and accomplishments. Lilly worried that her own sixty-mile-an-hour curve ball would be no match for Meggie's heat. Not to worry: They both made Team USA in 2006, and their friendship grew.

Meggie is the younger of Rick and Terri Meidlinger's two daughters. The family lives in suburban Sterling, Virginia, where Rick works for Johnson & Johnson and Terri is a CPA. The family is close-knit, loving, and religious. That supportive home base has allowed the girls to be adventurous and accomplished. Meggie's older sister, Jenny, is a dancer and dance instructor who moved to New York City and then Los Angeles.

Meggie discovered baseball early and enlisted her father's support. "Well, I basically got into baseball when I was about four years old. I grew up playing with the neighborhood boys . . . they'd play baseball out in the street, and I wanted to play too. Then I started playing T-ball when I was about five. We went to a clinic, and they announced that they needed more coaches. My dad says that I just tugged on his pant leg and asked him to be my coach, and he ended up being my Little League coach all the while I was growing up."

Meggie played baseball from Little League through high school and never considered changing games. "In my mind, it was baseball or nothing. I really had no desire to switch to softball, and I still do consider them two different sports. I never even thought about playing softball. All my guy friends were playing baseball, so why would it even cross my mind to play softball if all my friends were playing baseball?" There were a few other girls playing baseball in Little League, but they switched to softball when they were twelve. Aside from the occasional coach who would yell from the dugout to his batter, "Don't let a girl strike you out!" she felt she had plenty of support and encouragement to play baseball.

When Meggie entered high school, her physical education teacher spoke to the baseball coach to see if Meggie could try out for the team. "She was very supportive of my playing baseball, and with women's sports in general, and she even had a conversation with the head baseball coach for me, and he said, 'Yeah, come on try out. You are welcome to try out.'" In spite of the invitation, Meggie was overwhelmed with anxiety. "My stomach was in knots for months before tryouts. Leading up to it, I played women's high school basketball during the fall, and then I didn't play any sport at school in the winter, so I could focus on preparing for the baseball season. The head baseball coach held winter clinics to condition and prepare us for the season, and I wanted to focus on that." Meggie was in that conditioning program with some of the same boys she had played baseball with all her life. She was also on a travel basketball team in the winter. But none of it distracted her from her nerves about high school baseball.

"We had a whole bunch of snow that year, so the tryout kept getting pushed back, and pushed back one week and then another. The knots in my stomach just kept growing. Part of me was grateful that it was getting pushed back, but then it was almost like nausea, I had so much such nervousness building up. It's a wonder I was able to do anything during tryouts." Lilly asks Meggie if she thought the nerves had to do with being a

FIG. 35. Meggie Meidlinger straps on her catcher's gear, age seven. Courtesy of Terri Meidlinger.

girl or just with the tryout itself. Meggie responds, "I don't remember feeling the weight of all women, or of all women in baseball on my shoulders during that time because honestly I didn't even know that there were other female baseball players out there. I just felt, 'I've been playing baseball my whole life, and I don't want it to end here. I want to keep playing.' Yeah,

I was a girl, so I didn't know how that would pan out or how I would do. Our varsity team was winning district, and the senior guys were jacked, huge. I thought, 'How am I even going to compare to them, especially when our varsity team was doing well?' There were a lot of people trying out even just for the JV team because our high school doesn't have a freshman team . . . just a JV team."

It was a tough, competitive tryout, and many players were cut. Meggie made the JV team as a freshman and then made the varsity team the following year as a sophomore. During that first freshman tryout, her childhood baseball teammates helped to calm her down, and she also felt encouraged by the older boys. "The majority of the players were guys I had grown up with, which made it comfortable. But then a lot of the senior guys were these six-foot-something buff guys, and that was a little intimidating. But even those guys were supportive. One guy . . . he was the strongest guy on the team . . . came up and talked to me, and that meant a lot."

Meggie was also sustained by her faith. She is a religious Christian, and she prayed a lot before the tryouts. "The tryout itself was kind of a blur. Obviously, it went great because I made the team. I remember all the moments of the day leading up until the tryouts. I was a nervous wreck, but once I got my mitt on—I would throw with [her friend and baseball teammate] Kevin every day—that warm-up time with him calmed me down, settled me down. And I remember praying a lot about it. Just, 'Lord, if this is your will, let it be done. Whatever happens, happens. Just give me peace about whatever happens.' And yeah, I was pleasantly surprised when I found out I made the JV team my freshman year. Or, maybe not surprised so much as just very, very proud of myself. To me it was just a huge accomplishment because, in the face of adversity, I had proved myself."

Lilly turns the conversation to issues that she and Meggie faced as high school girls playing a boys' sport. She prompts, "What I am interested in is how gender issues affect your identity. For me, I very much identify with being a girl that plays baseball, and in high school I was 'the girl' who played baseball. That set me apart, but it also gave me a different perspective on being a girl and what it meant. Like I wasn't concerned with being skinny. I had to compete with guys, so I wanted to get bigger, and . . . I don't know . . . just kind of taking pride in being able to compete with guys but also as a straight girl having to find a balance between being quote 'feminine' versus being on the field and just being one of the guys, you know?"

The theme echoed with Meggie: "Yes. I can definitely, strongly relate to that. I think I hadn't been able to realize a lot of things until I got to college. I like being away from the high school boys scene because, honestly, you know, as a girl on a baseball team, you hear things that most girls don't hear." Lilly adds, "Or want to hear."

"Or want to hear. Exactly. And so, you know, dating in high school was not a priority on my mind. I had other things that were my priority. And I'm trying to think about how best to phrase this because . . . nothing against any of the guys . . . but there are some things that females just should not hear. And some of the things I heard from the guys' perspective about how girls were viewed or treated made me think, 'Why do I want to get in a relationship when I see that this is how females are treated?' Did you have an experience like this?"

Lilly responds, "You know, I had crushes on guys in high school, and I would go on dates and stuff, but when you hear how they talk about girls, I guess that maybe deterred me from drinking and partying because all their stories were just ridiculous. You don't want to hear these things about whatever girl they hooked up with at a party. And yeah, I think it definitely changes your perspective on how guys are."

Meggie believes her experience being the only girl on a team of boys fostered a deep sense of independence, as she had to prove to herself and everybody else that she belonged. She felt compelled to do every-thing the boys on the team could do and was never willing to take help or make excuses for anything. She still carries that attitude of independence, although she occasionally wonders if she has taken it to extremes. "You know, like when we were doing foul poles [strenuous running exercises in the outfield], I would be thinking, 'I gotta be keeping up with these guys. I cannot be the last one. I have to be at the forefront or the middle. I just can't be last.' And I still have that attitude. In college, even a couple of years away from playing with guys, I still had this mentality that 'No, I can do it on my own.' I still felt the need to throw a ball farther than one guy I know on my college campus. Or, 'No I don't need a guy's help. I can do it on my own.' Because I was able to play baseball with the guys, I refuse ever to hear that I can't do something because I am a girl. It comes down to even walking in a strange city at night or camping alone or just with one other girl. It really irks me when I hear, 'No, you can't do that; it's just two girls.' I refuse ever to hear that I can't do something because I'm a female."

Lilly agrees that playing baseball with boys has improved her self-confidence in some ways and also created conflict about what it means to be the "exception girl." "It's like I'm the different kind of girl . . . I don't need anyone's help. I can do it. In the weight room I want always to be the strongest girl. I'm not going to go to the weight room wearing tight clothes and whatever because you know what? That's not what I'm here for. I'm here to get big. The guys on my team always treated me not like a regular girl. They treated me like a teammate or like a sister. Actually, one of my club teammates [at Cal on the university club team] said at our barbecue—and he is this big guy who thinks he is super badass and tough—he is like six foot four, and he definitely is one of those guys that says lots of things about girls that I don't want to hear. . . . I said to him, 'Can you please not call all girls sluts?' and he was like, 'No, you're different though. You know like you and my sister are like the only girls that aren't sluts.' And I was like, 'Really, Mackenzie?? Really?!' But he was affectionate and sweet and a total gentleman to me. When I was cold in the dugout, he would take off his sweatshirt and give it to me, but then he treats other girls just like crap. So what does it mean that I'm 'different'? Is it that these guys are just idiots and they don't actually see that girls cannot, should not, just be looked on like objects? But that because I play a sport with them, they think of me as an actual human being rather than something else?"

Meggie has also struggled with wanting to be respected as a teammate—not a "girl teammate" but simply a teammate—but not wanting that to imply that she isn't a girl, like other girls. "It's hard because you so desire for them to see you as a teammate, you know. Not as the girl on the team but as a teammate. So are you losing something when you finally get that?" Lilly echoes her thought: "Yeah, are you denying part of your identity as a girl because you want to be a teammate, like one of the guys?" Meggie expresses some tentative hope: "I definitely feel like there is that balance somewhere. Just to be treated with the respect that we deserve as females. And it's almost like I need to let down a wall and allow others to serve me for once rather than always saying, 'No, I can do it myself! I stand alone!'"

Meggie and Lilly avoided being thought of as "sluts" by their teammates, but the price they paid for that respect was being made to feel that if they were not "sluts," they were probably also not really women. Obviously, there is work to be done here on the cultural mentality that permits adolescent boys to think of girls as sexual objects. This might be the strongest argument for the gender desegregation of sports: it may enable boys to think of girls as human beings. The flip side of the adolescent mind-set is equally debilitating: the assumption that if girls can't be regarded as sexual objects, they are probably lesbians. Either way, the price of being on a boys' or men's baseball team is experienced by female athletes as an attack on femininity. As they continue their sensitive dialogue about feminine sexuality and athletics, Lilly and Meggie are completing each other's sentences:

"I don't know if you are scrutinized in terms of your sexuality just because you're a girl playing a guys' sport . . ."

"Everybody just automatically assumes . . ."

"Yeah, automatically assumes that you're . . ."

"Just because you are playing a guy's sport . . ."

"I think it is more on them than on us if they want to think that 'Oh, you must be less of a woman if you're playing a sport. And if you can compete with guys and keep up with them, then you must be a lesbian. Because they think that makes you less of a woman. They want to think that it can't possibly be that a female can just compete with a guy because we can."

The choice to leave competitive sports after high school was painful for Meggie, but rational. "I realized in high school that I won't be playing on the Baltimore Orioles. Why not pursue a career that I can do something with for more than a few years? I'm not saying that there's not a chance for women to play in the pros, or in college, but I was just making a choice that was realistic for me. I was applying to architecture schools. I saw that if I wanted to play college baseball, I'd have to go to a small school, like of only a thousand people. I wanted to go to a big school, and I knew I wouldn't get the same architecture education if I went to a small school. So I guess I chose my education over baseball. But you know, right when I got into college, right away I missed sports. I'm grateful I got into club basketball, so I got to travel and play in tournaments for Virginia Tech. But I really did miss baseball."

Meggie's opportunity to play baseball was kept alive by Adriane Adler, who runs the East Coast Yankees. Adriane read an article written about Meggie when as a sophomore she won her first high school baseball game, which was also the first high school baseball game won by a girl in Virginia's history. Adriane called Meggie's parents, and Meggie recalls, "Adriane has been involved in women's baseball for a number of years now and is just hands down a wonderful woman. There was a newspaper article written about me when I was a sophomore in high school because I was the first female in the state of Virginia to win a varsity men's baseball game. She saw it, and she called my parents and said, 'Hey, there is this whole women's baseball league. Every year we play in the Roy Hobbs tournament in Florida, and we'd love for Meggie to come play with us.'

"I had never heard jack squat about any women's baseball; I never even thought or imagined that there was another girl who played baseball. I mean, I guess maybe I thought, 'Oh, there might be one other . . . ' But I honestly thought I was the only one on the face of the earth who played guy's baseball. Because all the girls who I knew who played baseball switched to softball, so I just assumed that was everybody. [. . .]

"I went down to Florida with my family for that Hobbs tournament, and there were eight other female baseball teams with fifteen women on each. We got introduced to this whole world of women's baseball. I played in that Hobbs tournament my junior and senior years of high school and was connected with the East Coast Yankees and with Adriane. Then—I think it was through Adriane too—that Julie Croteau gave me a call to let me know there was a U.S. team. I was like, 'Okay. One year I find out that there is women's baseball, and two years later I find out there is this whole USA women's baseball. What the heck is this??'"

Meggie played with Team USA in 2006, right out of high school, and again in 2008. But her choice to pursue architecture at a first-rate university meant that she didn't have the time she needed to pursue baseball on that elite level. Baseball needs to be all consuming for a woman who wants to continue to play at the top. Meggie still wants to keep playing but is now focused on giving baseball experiences to children. "I'm definitely not hanging up my cleats anytime soon. I'm going to play as much and as often as I can. I have this passion to move overseas to a third world country and do third world housing there. But along with that, I would love to coach kids in a third world country. I'd love to give other girls an opportunity as well."

She also says she became aware, after all the publicity about her perfect game during her senior high school season, that other little girls were looking up to her and gaining courage from her experience. "Senior year when the perfect game happened, I remember my athletic director coming to me and saying that he'd gotten an email or a phone call from a few little girls who wanted to play Little League and their dads called in to ask about it. And I thought, 'Oh, other girls know about this, and they have hopes too.' Then I felt some responsibility about it. It was cool to see that."

In the end, Meggie tries to maintain a sense of balance: "I feel it's so dangerous when you put all your worth in baseball. My worth is not me as an athlete. Our worth is in God. Everything in this world is just going to fail, you know. It's a full-on rule: it's just going to fail. So I don't want people to see my identity in baseball, but my identity in Christ. Because that is where my worth is from."

Meggie's worth is indeed much more than baseball, and that is true for the other women on Team USA too. But it would be nice for these good women to have an easier time playing the game that is a part of each of them.

FIG. 36. Meggie Meidlinger, Team USA 2008. Courtesy of Terri Meidlinger.

PART 5

Gender Segregation,
Equality, and
Women's Baseball

15

America's Team

This is America's baseball team. These are the American kids who have loved the game from the moment they picked up a baseball. Baseball is one of their earliest memories in life. They played catch with their dads, or mothers, or brothers and with the boys in the neighborhood. They played stickball, home run derby, keep-away, and two-on-two, with Wiffle balls, tennis balls, half balls, and baseballs. They broke windows, played indoors and outdoors, and played Little League. They thought they would be Major Leaguers up to the moment when they didn't, like every American kid who has ever played baseball. Most didn't play on elite tournament teams, take lessons from private coaches, or put a lot of time into being recruited for college baseball or a professional career. In this sense, they are much more like the traditional twentieth-century all-American baseball kid than the current crop of specialized, preprofessional baseball boys whose parents have the resources to pay big bucks to give their son a chance at a scholarship or the pros. If these ballplayers had been boys, they might very well have gone that route, but it might have robbed them of what makes them special. They are exceptionally talented baseball players who play for pure love of the game, without the danger of being spoiled by wealth and celebrity.

Like America's ideal team, this team is diverse racially, ethnically, religiously and politically. It comprises one African American (Tamara Holmes), one mixed-race African American (Malaika Underwood), one Cuban American (Veronica Alvarez), one Italian-Irish American (Donna

Mills), one Italian–Puerto Rican American (Marti Sementelli), one Australian American (Tara Harbert), one partly Mexican American (Sarah Gascon), one Mormon (Jenny Dalton Hill), one Jew (Lilly Jacobson), four Catholics (Mills, Gascon, Alvarez, and Sementelli), two devout Christians (Jenna Marston and Meggie Meidlinger), some not-so-devout Christians, a couple of Bay Area liberals, one Southern California conservative, a few who don't talk about politics at all, some straight women, some lesbians, a Cardinals fan, a couple of A's fans, a couple of Dodgers fans, a couple of Red Sox fans, a Rockies fan, a Braves fan, a Marlins fan, and an Orioles fan. The only major difference between this team and the iconic American hometown baseball team is that this team is all girls—the crowning touch of diversity in baseball that nobody ever thinks about.

All of them have expressed the desire to make a living playing their sport, but they have different ideas about what should happen to make women's baseball, and women's athletics in general, more robust and accessible. All have found other ways to make a living in the meantime.

Love of the Game

All knew that they were athletes from their earliest memory. Not one had to be coaxed or pushed to sports; they all felt they were doing what they were born to be doing. The majority use the word "love" to describe their connection with baseball from the moment they first held a ball or a bat. Sarah Gascon knew she was born to be an athlete by age two; Marti Sementelli thought of herself as a baseball player by age two; Lilly Jacobson knew she was born to be a baseball player by age three; Tamara Holmes fell in love with the first baseball uniform she saw. Malaika Underwood and Lilly Jacobson each used the identical phrase to describe their lifelong connection with baseball: "Baseball found me." Veronica Alvarez describes a "passion" for baseball more intense than any she felt for softball. Donna Mills, Sarah Gascon, and Tara Harbert mentioned that they cannot muster the same love for softball that they have always felt for baseball, although Tara is grateful she didn't taste that love until she finished her college softball career, and Sarah felt sorry for hurting her high school softball coach's feelings when she told him the love wasn't there. But she also

FIG. 37. Underwood, Holmes, and Alvarez. Courtesy of Veronica Alvarez.

knew, "I don't think I ever fell out of love with baseball. *This* sport—*this* is what it is. *This* is how it's supposed to feel when you get on a ball field." Jenna Marston loves both games but quietly admits, if you listen very closely, that she liked baseball just a little bit more. Holmes says it's "the love" that brings her out to baseball tryouts again and again, even when she knows she doesn't need to be putting herself through that anxiety.

FIG. 38. Members of Team USA on the New England Red Sox after winning the 2012 Roy Hobbes Championship. *Standing*: Underwood, Sementelli, Jacobson, Gascon. *Kneeling*: Harbert, Alvarez. Coach Kevin Marden can be seen to the left. Courtesy of Jennifer Ring.

Sementelli says that baseball is quite simply "who she is." And for Jenny Dalton Hill, although baseball was never her first love, USA Baseball has allowed her to reconnect with the Superman within her that empowered her during her softball glory days.

Mentors

All the players had supportive family members, and most also found a coach or a mentor who enabled them to stay in the game when they were being pressured to leave baseball. And all were pressured to leave. Tamara Holmes was sustained by her coach and baseball mentor Dave Krone. Donna Mills had Pine Hill Little League, her grandparents, Linda Reyes, and Pati Kane. Malaika Underwood had her dad and Jasiah's dad, Tim Neff. Marti had her dad, Jenny had her dad, Meggie had her dad, Sarah had her dad and her family's athletic legacy, Jenna had her whole family, Veronica had her whole family, Tara had her whole family, and Lilly had her parents and her coach, Jay Uhlman. This is not meant to diminish the supportive roles of the moms and siblings but to shine the spotlight on the people who were most important in sustaining the players' love of the game. It takes a village to raise a baseball girl.

Outsiders and Exceptions

All the members of Team USA are exceptionally smart and highly educated women. That's a necessity, because none of them is going to get rich playing baseball. All have (or are getting) college degrees at highly regarded academic institutions: Cal, Villanova, North Carolina, Arizona, Missouri, Hawaii, Colorado State, the University of Massachusetts, Southeastern Louisiana State, Virginia Tech, Montreat College. The women are all "superachievers," if that term is understood to mean motivated, disciplined, and accomplished students and athletes. All received some sort of scholarship to attend college, whether athletic or academic. But most have battled the feeling that they don't entirely "fit" in some fundamental way. In spite of their accomplishments, all feel, or have felt, like outsiders.

Most struggled with feelings of being outsiders in adolescence. They were "tomboys" or not quite what an American girl is "supposed" to be. Sarah Gascon remembered, "I was the only girl playing with boys during lunchtime or recess. [. . .] Nobody could really say that you're wrong. It's just how I viewed it, what I felt internally." Malaika remembered, "In school I wasn't girly enough. I had crushes on boys, but the boys liked the pretty girls and the girly girls and not me, because I was the tomboy." Malaika was also a mixed-race kid attending a wealthy white high school, although she identifies her feeling of being an outsider more with gender—with being an athletic girl—than race. At Berkeley High Tamara Holmes dealt with both gender and race issues. Of her experience with high school baseball, she remembers, "It was just about me being uncomfortable, even though the guys were [comfortable with me]. [. . .] At the time, you are the only one. There's no one to talk to; your female friends don't play. [. . .] They don't understand. So you are just all alone trying to figure it out."

Holmes had the additional feeling that she wasn't "black enough" when she got to Berkeley High because she had friends from many different races, because she speaks standard English, and because she was raised by her family not to focus on group identity. Lilly Jacobson grew up not only as the only girl on her baseball team, but as the only Jew, until she played at Vassar and Cal, where many of the men on the team were Jewish. But she was still the only girl, and it was gender and being an athletic girl that caused her to wonder what was "wrong" with her. Her baseball teammates treated her as one of the guys, which she liked, except for those moments when she wondered if that meant she really "was" a guy. I have heard her say, mostly in jest, but with an edge, "Maybe I really *am* a boy. . . . I don't do the things that normal girls do!" Lilly, Marti, and Meggie recalled, with some hilarity, that they heard so much bad stuff coming out of the mouths of their high school baseball teammates, whom they otherwise loved, that they didn't know for a while if they could ever possibly date a boy. They knew too much about what high school boys are like to ever trust one romantically.

Lilly and Meggie discussed the unsettling conflicts high school girls face when the activity that they love most, at which they excel, and which defines who they are for themselves, is labeled "wrong." All adolescents search for what makes them feel most at home in order to anchor themselves during tumultuous years of change. But what happens when a baseball-playing girl is made to understand that she *should not* feel at home where she has felt most at home her entire life? What happens to a girl when the boys with whom she has played baseball since childhood become confused by her presence, because they have been taught to think girls can't and shouldn't play baseball and because they've forgotten that they indeed played with a girl for most of their life? This presents some serious cognitive dissonance for the boys: "Yes, she *can* play baseball, but girls can't play baseball. So she must not be a real girl." The girls receive a deeply hurtful message: they are respected by the boys they play with, which exposes them to adolescent misogyny about "other" girls. As "exceptions" to that disrespect, they are led to doubt their own femininity.

The feelings expressed by the ballplayers do not correlate with whether they are gay or straight. Their sense of being an outsider or "wrong" correlates with athletic, more than sexual identity: "You're an athlete, and girls aren't athletes, so which one are you? A girl or an athlete?" Sarah Gascon heard that message from her first grade teacher. As soon as she showed up in school she was told that she was "wrong"—by a nun, a teacher, an authority figure. Luckily, her parents gave her a stronger message about how "right" she is.

Issues about sexual identity plague nonathletic adolescents too, of course. But the conflicts described by the players in this volume have more to do with gender identity than sexuality. None of the players interviewed described sexual orientation as central to their athletic lives. The straight women resent the assumption that all women athletes are lesbians, and the lesbians prefer not to be the only lesbian on the team, but basically all just want to be left alone to play ball. All remarked that sexual identity had nothing to do with what they felt like when they were actually on the playing field. If there were conflicts between gay and straight women on a particular team, it had to do with individual personalities. On this particular team, Team USA 2010, sexual identity was not a factor in the team chemistry, and all said that they wished people would stop asking them about it or making assumptions about their preference for sexual partners.

The sense of being an outsider because you are an athlete is much more prevalent among the girls who played baseball with boys than among girls who played softball with girls, regardless of sexual orientation. Adolescent softball players also struggled with self-image problems because of their athleticism, but they were buffered somewhat by the fact that they were on teams with girls who were all facing the same American hostility to female athletes. In that sense, Veronica Alvarez is utterly correct about self-confidence being easier to come by if you are on a girls' team, rather than the only girl on a boys' team. But as Malaika, Marti, Lilly, and Meggie make clear, while there are problems for girl baseball players, there is also a sense of pride, accomplishment, independence, and difference as a source of strength. Every woman interviewed described moments of feeling "not normal." Even Jenny Dalton Hill, who was very much at home on a softball field, felt that she didn't entirely fit with the culture of Arizona softball because she is a religious woman who doesn't drink or curse and who went to church in a dress and heels each Sunday before her Arizona softball games. Jenna Marston expressed the least conflict about her two-sport athleticism, although she did note that she was different from her teammates at Missouri because she didn't grow up dreaming of playing softball and because she had a baseball attitude toward dugout culture.

Race and Sex Segregation in U.S. History

The sense of being outsiders or exceptions, experienced by all the ballplayers, prompts comparisons between sexual exclusion and racial exclusion. Baseball has had a history of racism, at least up to the mid-twentieth century when Jackie Robinson "broke the color barrier" and opened the doors to the Major Leagues to other men of color. In American life, exclusion by sex has been more tenacious than exclusion by race. There is a wealth of scholarship on this, and a suggested reading list follows at the end of this volume. The task of this book is not to "prove" that sexism is more entrenched than racism in sports or to "prove" that sex and race are equivalent categories when it comes to privilege and discrimination. Rather, the hope is to shed light on the consequences of segregating women from men, girls from boys, in sports in general, and baseball and softball in particular. Is enforced segregation and exclusion ever "natural" or appropriate?[1] Can separate ever be equal, sexually or racially?

In the United States, race segregation has been addressed legally, if not socially and economically. It is recognized as a problem, even if American society still remains racially segregated in many aspects of life. Since the middle of the twentieth century, racial segregation in public life has been illegal, although dismantling segregation economically and socially has lagged behind the law. Sex segregation is not viewed as an equivalent problem. Scholars of women's history often trace the neglect of sexual discrimination back to the political battle over passage of the Fifteenth Amendment to the Constitution in 1869. The South had been defeated in the Civil War, slavery had been abolished, and an amendment to the Constitution that gave the freed black men the right to vote was proposed by the Republican Party in control of the federal government. The amendment did not include freed black women or any other women. Nineteenth-century women's rights activists, both white and black, became embroiled in political battles, with each other and with the male political establishment, over the question of whether the Fifteenth Amendment should include women as well as black men. In the end, congressional leaders determined that including suffrage for women of any race was too radical a concept to pass and would jeopardize the enfranchisement of black men.[2] The former slaves needed legal and political rights to protect them from the rage of their former masters in the South, and votes for black men were granted in light of this necessity. (It didn't work because whites in the South found ways to keep black men—and black women too—from voting for almost a century.)

Throughout the century and a half since the Fifteenth Amendment became law, there has been debate about the relationship between racial and sexual equality in the United States. The battle between the "radicals," who believed that women should gain the right to vote in 1869 at the same time as black men, and the "moderates," who believed that the pragmatic course of action was to settle for what was "realistic" at the time, still characterizes movements for civil rights in the United States, including arguments for sexual equality.

A second moment in American history when women's equality appeared as an afterthought to racial equality came during the civil rights movement of the 1950s and 1960s. The major legislation of that era was the Civil Rights Act of 1964, which was intended to secure racial equality and was seized upon by women's rights advocates as well. Title IV of the Civil Rights Act, "Desegregation of Public Education," was intended to provide racial equality in access to education. Title VII, "Equal Employment Opportunity," was intended to establish racial equality in the workplace.

Women legislators and activists from the "second wave" of the women's rights movement in the 1960s and 1970s leveraged the proposed equal employment act (Title VII) to include equal opportunities for women and protection from sexual harassment. The education amendment, Title IV, required a separate amendment to ensure sexual equality in education. It was for that purpose that Title IX was passed in 1972, extending the definition of discrimination in education to include girls and women. Title IX was intended to desegregate institutions of higher education, including elite institutions such as the Ivy League schools, which provided the most prestigious, but sex-segregated, degrees in the country, along with accompanying access to wealth and power. As that legislation was being debated, athletics unexpectedly became the focus of attention. Title IX scholars McDonagh and Pappano assert, "Any discussion of Title IX, then, [must] begin with the Civil Rights Act of 1964 and the omission of 'sex' in Title IV. It was that glaring absence that the Educational Amendments, including Title IX, sought to correct in 1972. The major purpose of Title IX was to gain for women the educational access that the GI Bill paid for and secured for economically disadvantaged men and that Title IV of the Civil Rights Act of 1964 guaranteed successfully to African American men."[3]

Title IX and Sex Segregation

Title IX contains no explicit reference to sports. Sports emerged as the center of the debate because the NCAA became concerned that Title IX would desegregate sports and threaten men's football programs. The NCAA lobbied hard for the continued right to segregate sports by sex. McDonagh and Pappano observe, "Congress's first concern in passing Title IX was not athletics but equal academic and educational access. Sports were an all but invisible component of that concern—and an unintended one at that. Secretary of Health, Education and Welfare Caspar Weinberger was not alone in expressing surprise when sports leapt to the fore of the Title IX debate. 'I had not realized until the comment period [for Title IX regulations] that athletics is the single most important thing in the United States,' Weinberger quipped during a Senate subcommittee hearing."[4]

Title IX opened the doors to women's sports in school and college and has proved an enormously important piece of legislation in helping to "normalize" athletic achievement for American girls. It does not, however, "desegregate" sports, and it has indirectly contributed to the exclusion of American girls and women from baseball by allowing softball to serve as a culturally sanctioned alternative for girls. The Fourteenth Amendment to the Constitution is the legislation that has been used more often to integrate sports and been more useful in granting girls legal access to baseball. It became law in 1868, guaranteeing equal protection under the law for all American citizens.[5] The Little League lawsuits of 1973 and 1974 made use of the Fourteenth Amendment to allow girls to play with boys in Little League.

The tenacity of sex segregation in sports bears some resemblance to the tenacity of racial segregation in American history. Segregating sports by sex is socially and culturally accepted in the United States, and many would argue that it is not an equivalent to racial segregation. It is sometimes referred to as "natural," a term that implies it is impossible to change. Racial equality, marriage equality, sexual equality have all been labeled "unnatural" by their detractors at one point or another.

Most of the women interviewed in this book would prefer sex-segregated baseball: they would rather play with women, if women's baseball teams and leagues were competitive. But the virtual nonexistence of women's baseball keeps them banging at the door of men's baseball, not because they prefer to play with men, but because there is so little competitive women's baseball available. Nobody's baseball dream is to be a solitary, marginalized girl playing on a boys' team. For most, Team USA is the first elite women's team they have played on, and although most enjoy it more than any other baseball they have played, the tournaments are not frequent enough to satisfy the need to play regularly. With that desire to play as the common denominator, opinions differ among the players about the benefits of playing baseball with men and softball with women.

Some of the women believe that differences in size, strength, and speed mean that women will never be able to play at the top of their game so long as they are a minority on men's teams. Truly gender-integrated baseball teams would be preferable because being the only woman on a men's team means that they are unlikely to be among the best players on the team. That perspective is expressed by Veronica Alvarez and Jenna Marston when they assert that it was more important for their development as athletes and as women to play softball rather than baseball in high school and college. The challenges faced by Lilly, Marti, and Meggie during high school and afterwards seem to support the advantages of playing with women, if possible. But Donna, Veronica, Tara, Sarah, and Jenna had to forgo baseball to succeed at softball, and that is not a choice Malaika, Lilly, Marti, and Meggie were willing to make. In sticking with their sport, and refusing to switch to softball or another sport, Lilly, Marti, and Meggie sacrificed their chance of an NCAA Division I athletic experience. They paid a stiff price, both emotionally and financially when they chose to forego the Division I athletic scholarships they might have been awarded in another sport. Malaika is the only player in this group who developed in an alternate Division I scholarship sport while remaining on the high school baseball team.

There is another side to the debate: if girls playing baseball with boys were the norm, would girls gain the confidence and experience needed to play with boys and men? Lilly believes that women *can* play baseball with men, given encouragement and training. If enough are willing to put the effort in, more will succeed than currently do. If nobody tries, girls' baseball will continue to languish, and women's baseball will continue to draw primarily from women's softball. From this perspective, the women who stand their ground and stay in the sport they prefer are path breakers for the future of women's baseball. Their sacrifice of conventional rewards in the present is simply the price that path breakers are called on to pay for future generations.

Breaking down the gender barriers and enabling girls to play with boys, and women to play with men, is within the realm of the athletically possible in baseball because it is not a sport where size is definitive, and it is not a contact sport. Lilly notes, "Okay, if you're talking about football or something, for the most part a girl is probably going to get crushed. But for baseball, it's a game of finesse. You don't need big huge strength. If you *learn* to hit a ninety-mile-an-hour pitch, you'll be able to hit a ball coming ninety miles an hour. I mean, it's true that there are some physical differences. Obviously, not every woman is going to be able to make those adjustments. If you get a shitty female athlete, she's not going to be able to do it, but neither is a shitty male athlete." Lilly learned to hit a ninety-mile-an-hour fastball, and she learned to get a jump on a line drive hit by a man. "When I'm playing with women versus when I'm playing with men, the differences are noticeable. Like, the men are just throwing harder. There's no denying that. And as an outfielder, the ball comes off the bat quicker. That's true. But that doesn't mean that women can't adjust to that, that they can't train at that level and compete with that."

Tara disagrees: "You just can't compete with boys because they are bigger and stronger. It's not any sexist thing. It's just the fact of life that, genetically, men are bigger and stronger and faster, and so I think at about age twelve they just need to start a girls' baseball league where you can really hone your skills of baseball." According to Tara, baseball for girls and boys in adolescence should be separate, but baseball should be available to girls, just as it is in Japan, Canada, and Australia. Malaika agrees with that: "Ideally we should have Little League Baseball, where boys and girls could play together until a certain age and then, instead of having high school baseball and high school softball, have high school boys' baseball and high school girls' baseball, just like we have boys' basketball and girls' basketball. [. . .] Why not baseball? I mean, ask anybody . . . baseball is America's pastime, right? So why can't girls play it?"

If, in baseball, you don't segregate girls from boys at a certain age—twelve? fourteen?—you open the door to what Sarah, Lilly, and Jenna experienced when they were that age: the boys get more playing time because they are beginning to get much bigger and stronger than the girls. Even Tamara Holmes, who is unquestionably the biggest, strongest woman on Team USA, might have avoided the insecurity she felt in high school baseball if she had had an opportunity to play on a competitive girls' baseball team instead of being the only girl on a boys' team. Currently (in part because of her involvement in Olympic weight lifting), Holmes is as strong as many men who play professional baseball, and as her teammates say, "She has as much pop as a man." But she didn't have that developed body or the self-confidence when she was fifteen and playing baseball with boys in high school.

Without access to baseball leagues of their own for adolescent girls, it's back to the chicken and egg dilemma: if girls want to get the best athletic experience they can while they're young, it's probably going to be playing competitive softball with other girls. But if girls don't grow up playing baseball, there will never be enough of them to compete in world-class baseball tournaments, and the need to draw from softball becomes a self-fulfilling prophecy, created because there are no opportunities for girls to learn to play baseball. There is something counterintuitive about insisting that the best way to develop competitive women's baseball is through competitive women's softball. A good athlete can move from one sport to the other, but why should that be a requirement for girls and women?

Baseball and Softball: Batting, Fielding, Throwing, Thinking

It is misleading to say that softball is an "equivalent sport" for baseball. To those who know both sports best, they are different games. But softball has achieved a legitimacy and institutional power as "baseball's equivalent for women" that forces girls out of baseball, even when baseball is the game they want to play. Both softball and baseball players agree that baseball and softball are very different games, requiring different skills.

The players on Team USA who have played softball describe it as a much faster game than baseball. The players who were accustomed to collegiate softball pitching found it a challenge to adjust to a baseball pitched by a woman. Even if pitched at the same speed as a pitched softball, it seemed slow, coming from almost twenty feet farther away and with different movement. Tara Harbert recalls standing in the batter's box, waiting for a baseball pitch, and wondering, "Is it ever going to get here?" When Tamara Holmes, who had only played baseball, tried her hand in Division I fast-pitch softball at Cal, her instinct was to stand as far away as possible: "I don't want any part of that pitch! That is too close!" Lilly spoke of the fast-twitch response needed to hit a softball arriving from "two feet away or whatever the mound is at for the college softball players." Yet all three women commented that when they play baseball and face men who throw in the mid eighty-mile-an-hour range, that's the pitch they want to see. "Yeah, throw the fastball!" they all recalled thinking, when men doubted their ability to hit it.

Different players had different challenges making the adjustment to baseball pitches. Tara had trouble in the beginning because she had learned to be a slap hitter in softball. Veronica and Jenna did not experience much trouble at all switching from softball to baseball because they were power hitters in softball and had kept their baseball swings when they switched to softball in college. Veronica shared her basic truth about hitting a ball—any ball—with a bat: "The ball's coming. You should hit it!" But in spite of that truism, she admitted that in softball your weight is always forward, and in baseball, your weight is back. All softball players have to adjust their swing to that. Jenna Marston observed, "The pitch just looks different. If you give a good athlete enough time, they'll figure it out and make adjustments. So the swing really isn't different. If you can hit one, you can hit the other. It's just figuring it out." Jenny Dalton Hill, who had never played baseball, was a softball power hitter who had no trouble adjusting to baseball hitting. If fact, she enjoyed how far the smaller ball traveled: "Hitting it was fun. It went a long ways, and that was really fun." But Lilly, who has only played baseball, has also had to make adjustments when switching from the men's to the women's game. Even with the same baseball swing, batting against women requires different timing than batting against men. "I realized that when I switch from playing with men to playing with women, I have to make an adjustment too . . . like that split second that is the difference between eighty-five and seventy-five [mile-an-hour pitches] gives me too much time to think. [. . .] I was overthinking my at bats."

It's not that softball is "too fast" or that women's baseball is "too slow." They are simply different games. One is not more "masculine" or "feminine," except by social convention. One is not more difficult than the other. For me, Tara Harbert's description of the difference between the games gets to the heart of the matter: it's mental. Tara found that she loved baseball after a lifetime of softball because baseball requires more thinking and independence. Jenny Dalton Hill doesn't like baseball as much as softball for precisely that reason. "The thing I hated about baseball was there was so much time to think." Tara was excited by baseball's complexity and infinite learning curve: "Baseball is a much more challenging game for me, and that's why I love it: because I still don't know all that I need to know about it. [. . .] I love baseball because I'm always learning something new. [. . .] It actually requires more thinking and initiative than softball." Malaika observed something very similar: "[Baseball] was also, quite honestly, a game that was at my pace. You have a chance to think about what to do and then the opportunity to make the play and then reset. I was really drawn to that. I like to think about things before I do them [. . .], and baseball is the type of sport where I get to do that." The difference between the sports has less to do with the dimensions of field or the strength of the players than with aesthetics. In the final analysis, why shouldn't anybody be able to play the game that most appeals to them?

16

Grassroots Women's Baseball

Major League Baseball is "The Show." It is the league every Minor League Baseball player in the world and every promising college, high school, youth league, and Little League Baseball player in the country aspires to play in. There is no "show" for girls. There's softball, a game many players on Team USA came to love or at least respect. But even college softball's "show"—the Women's College World Series—is a closing act on a run that didn't last nearly long enough, rather than an opening act for a lifetime in the spotlight. There is the possibility of playing professional softball after college, but the salary is unsustainable for an adult with responsibilities, not the wealth and celebrity of baseball players' dreams. College softball players hope to play for the USA Softball National Team. However, USA Softball has slipped out of the spotlight because softball is not currently an Olympic sport, and even when it was an Olympic sport, it provided a moment rather than a career for softball's best players. USA Baseball has provided a showcase for women's baseball and recently provided a venue for women's softball players as well. But without a nationwide infrastructure for women's *baseball*, it remains a showcase without a show.

Can American women have a baseball show of their own? There are models for women's baseball leagues that most of the ballplayers on Team USA admire: In Japan, Canada, and Australia, girls and boys play baseball together until adolescence. After that there are separate baseball leagues available for girls and boys, as well as mixed-gender teams available throughout adolescence. Americans have declared girls' baseball "unrealistic," "not cost effective," or just plain impossible. As a consequence, there is no opportunity in the United States for girls to choose baseball and develop into elite players in a nationally supported context.

To thrive, girls' and women's baseball needs both high-profile and grassroots organizations. Without a shining goal, such as wearing USA on their jersey and playing against the best teams in the world, there is nothing to encourage little girls to dream about their future in the sport. Without little girls dreaming about playing baseball in the future, there is no future for women's baseball. But there is a crippling disconnect between the not-so-well-groomed fields of American grassroots baseball for women and the pristinely beautiful diamond offered by USA Baseball, borrowed for a few weeks every two years from the boys.

Off Broadway

The sprawling, scattered, on-again, off-again network that is girls' and women's baseball in the United States is not easy to document. Since the 1990s women's leagues and teams have appeared and disappeared on all levels from recreational to professional, from youth to adult. There is the Eastern Women's Baseball Conference, with teams from Washington DC to New England, organized by Bonnie Hoffman and JoAnn Milliken. It hosts a tournament in Baltimore, Maryland, every Memorial Day weekend that has become one of the centerpieces of the women's baseball season. There is the California Women's Baseball League, organized by Melanie Laspina, with teams in both Northern and Southern California. There was the Great Lakes Women's Baseball League, organized by John Kovach and Jim Glennie, with teams in Chicago, Lansing, Fort Wayne, Battle Creek, and South Bend. Several teams from the league now play independently, although the league itself is no longer in existence. Kovach's South Bend Blue Sox participates regularly at women's tournaments throughout the nation.

There are currently teams in Seattle, New Jersey, Chicago, Boston, Washington DC, Philadelphia, Indiana, and Florida, organized by Jennifer Liu, Adriane Adler, Mary Jo and Greg Stegeman, Kevin Marden, John Kovach, Tiffany Brooks, and others, fueled by their own passion and funded by themselves and the players, who pay for uniforms, baseballs, travel expenses, and tournament fees. The most important amateur tournament in the nation, held for both men and women, is the Roy Hobbs World Series, organized by Tom Giffin and usually held in Fort Myers, Florida, around the time of the Veterans' Day holiday. Baseball programs for girls have emerged in recent years in Arizona, organized by Richard Hopkins, and Chicago, organized by Mary Jo Stegeman. Justine Siegel is also active in creating baseball opportunities for girls. Recently many websites and Facebook groups have emerged to provide a means of communication for the increasing number of people expressing an interest in girls' and women's baseball. The national publicity focused on thirteen-year-old Mo'ne Davis, star pitcher for the Taney Dragons of Philadelphia, who played in the 2014 Little League World Series, energized advocates for girls' baseball in the United States. Mo'ne was the first Little League Baseball player to appear on the cover of *Sports Illustrated* (August 19, 2014), and the subject of public discussion throughout the nation for a couple of weeks. The fact that she is an African American girl from a modest neighborhood in Philadelphia seems to reflect a growing acceptance of girls who play baseball. Every little step helps. Appendix B lists leagues, teams, and individuals affiliated with girls' and women's baseball in recent years.

Professional baseball teams and leagues for women—some more competitive than others—have also appeared and disappeared since the 1990s. Kim Braatz, Bridget Veenema, Tamara Ivie, Tamara Holmes, and Julie Croteau, members of the Silver Bullets from 1993 to 1997, are still involved in women's baseball. Ila Borders and Justine Siegel are two well-known individuals in women's baseball circles, although neither of them have played on women's teams. Borders is probably the most famous woman to play college and Minor League ball with men. She pitched for Southern California College from 1993 to 1997 and then played professional baseball with a Minor League team, the Madison Black Wolves of the Northern League. Siegel has practiced with and held exhibitions with men's professional and Major League ballplayers and has been involved in sponsoring teams and advocating opportunities for girls' baseball.[1]

The women's professional leagues and teams that have flickered in and out of existence may have hoped to break even financially, but nobody deluded themselves that the ventures would make a fortune, either for the owners or the ballplayers. Something like "love of the game" or "my daughter or niece or granddaughter or girlfriend wanted to play and there was no team for her to play on" is what has prompted most of the people who have been involved in "grassroots" women's baseball to enter the game.

Two individuals in particular are mentioned consistently by the ballplayers in this volume as important providers of access to the game. Jim Glennie and Kevin Marden are two men who have enabled the ballplayers interviewed in this book to keep playing baseball.[2] Glennie and Marden are both in their sixties: Jim is a retired assistant attorney general for the state of Michigan, living in Lansing, and Kevin is the president of a logistics company, living in Boston. Each has his own perspective on what is needed to further women's baseball in the United States and what role USA Baseball should play in that project. Their insights shed light on the challenges of developing an infrastructure that will build a pool of players for USA Baseball to draw on in the future.

Jim Glennie

Jim Glennie was the contact person for most of the women who have played on Team USA from 2004 to 2010.[3] I first heard his name when I was writing *Stolen Bases*. I expressed surprise when I learned of the existence of a women's national baseball team and was told, "You need to talk to Jim Glennie at the American Women's Baseball Federation." When I called Jim, he told me about the upcoming Phoenix tryouts for the 2006 USA team and urged me to convince Lilly, who was a senior at Wooster High at the time, to attend. I soon became aware that nearly every teenage girl playing baseball in the United States since the 1990s has sought out Jim to direct her to teams to play on. It sounded like an underground network, with the clandestine and somewhat romantic aura of a speakeasy during prohibition: A girl wants to play baseball and can't find a team to play on. Her parents make inquiries, and finally, they hear: "Psst! Over here! Call Jim Glennie . . . here's his number. He'll take care of you. Tell him I sent you!" Jim was singlehandedly acting as a clearinghouse for little girls

FIG. 39. Jim Glennie. Courtesy of Jim Glennie.

who wanted to play baseball. If the girls were too young to be looking for their own teams, their parents had found Jim and approached him for help finding a team for their daughter to play on. He served as the main conduit for most girls' and women's baseball in the country during the late 1990s and early 2000s.

Jim had an informal link to USA Baseball and the Women's National Team, something like a scout or a player development coordinator. That relationship was formalized from 2006 to 2008, when he was named director of player development by USA Baseball's CEO, Paul Seiler. But when Seiler hired Ashley Bratcher as the first director of the Women's National Team and the team stabilized under Ashley's leadership, Seiler decided that a player development coordinator for the women's team was unnecessary, especially since there was no similar position for the boys' and men's teams. But the boys' program doesn't need a player development coordinator: an extensive feeder system for boys' baseball throughout the country ensures that the talent pool is enormous and that the best players get noticed. That infrastructure is entirely lacking for the girls, and with Jim no longer funneling his ad hoc network of women ballplayers to USA Baseball, a major talent pipeline dried up.

After having communicated by email throughout 2006, I finally met Jim Glennie at a USA Baseball women's tournament that was being held at the National Training Facility in Cary in 2007. In 2009 we spent a day chatting about women's baseball during a rainout at another women's tournament in Huntingburg, Indiana. Finally, I asked him for an interview for this book, to discuss his relationship with USA Baseball and to get his ideas for building girls' and women's baseball in the United States. We met at his brother's house in Santa Ana, California, on February 18, 2011, and talked for several hours. Jim is a veteran of the political struggles that have undermined women's baseball in recent decades, and he shared his perspectives about how the ragged and tattered women's game has become a political football (mixed metaphor notwithstanding).

Jim had a vision for women's baseball. It featured a national team and, ideally, Olympic women's baseball, with a feeder network grounded in local teams and leagues so that American girls and young women could develop their skills. His older daughter, Kristen, a softball player through-out her youth, first urged him to start a girls' team. In 1988, when she was twenty-one years old, Kristen read an article about a girls' baseball team in Chicago and said, "Dad, let's start one!" It took a few years, but by 1992 they had a team, and Jim began exploring local leagues for them to play in. "Having the girls showed me what lousy coaching was out there. My daughters appreciated my game so much and wanted to learn so badly. I thought they deserved a chance."[4]

Jim began to make phone calls and met with the organizers of the American Women's Baseball Association in the Chicago area. They forged a cooperative relationship with each other, and Glennie organized the American Women's Baseball Federation, with two teams and a few players that he was training himself. He soon became frustrated with the lack of competition, the low level of play available, and the expense the players had to incur. The players were working women, some with family respon-sibilities, and they had to take entire weekends off to travel and had to pay for uniforms, equipment, and travel expenses. "After I started this team in 1992, I quickly realized that it's going nowhere because there's no ultimate goal for the women to visualize and to wake up and dream about each day, like boys do. There would have to be a national team or, preferably, a professional baseball organization like Major League Baseball. But there are a couple of steps before that, and the most important one was to develop a national organization for girls' baseball."

His dream of a national organization was fueled by the reemergence of men's Olympic baseball. "About that time [early 1990s], men's baseball had been brought back into the Olympics. I realized that women's baseball also needed a dream of a playing at the very top, visible level. Without that dream, this was just going to fizzle out, because as I looked around me those first couple of years, I saw a lot of very recreational efforts being put in place, but mostly to allow the people who had started to play to continue to play—not to find the very best players and develop a national team."

Jim's baseball vision grew organically: from Kristen's inspiration, to his first team, to his dream of a national organization and a women's national team. Many people would have been discouraged by the poor quality of girl's recreational baseball, but Jim thought that American girls just needed a baseball dream, like boys have, and then the league would improve and attract great athletes. But a year after he organized a small women's league in his hometown of Lansing, Michigan, Jim became convinced that the local league would flounder without a higher visibility goal, to inspire the players. "The difficulty was that to get to an elite team, we had to build a recreational structure to find baseball players. From 1993 on, that was my goal: I've got to develop this somehow to be a national dream for girls. In 1997 Jim switched his efforts to developing an elite women's national baseball team.

Two events accelerated his work toward that goal. "1992 was the year the *A League of Their Own* movie came out. In 1994, equally important and maybe more so, the Colorado Silver Bullets started with a name behind them. Phil Niekro and Joe Niekro were going around the country looking for ballplayers to play against the men in a 'battle of the sexes.'" The fact that two Major Leaguers would be coaching the team made it credible and attracted a lot of exposure. Manager Phil Niekro took his responsibility to coach the women seriously. The unexpected result was an opportunity to play real baseball. "Niekro respected the women, taught them baseball, they learned from him, and he didn't try to dumb it down or anything like that. So it was a wonderful experience for them, and it developed a crop of women who became exposed to baseball."

The Bullets' coaches traveled around the country, held tryouts, and picked a roster of twenty-five women. The team lasted four years, which was all that was intended. The Colorado Silver Bullets were part of an advertising campaign for Coors Light beer, but because Phil Niekro treated the women seriously as athletes and baseball players, it turned into something more. "The players were paid a pretty decent amount. I forget what they made, but it was more than Minor Leaguers made. This was not an altruistic thing. It was an advertising campaign for Coors, which turned into a kind of wonderful opportunity for women to play baseball."

The Silver Bullets differed from the World War II leagues (The All-American Girls Professional Baseball League) because they were a single team playing against men's teams. They were a barnstorming team, whereas the All-American Girls were a league, with women's teams playing each other. The similarity between the Bullets and the AAGPBL teams was that both lasted a few years as a company's publicity gambit and then folded.[5] The women themselves had never been at the center of either plan, but they were able to take away an important few years of professional baseball experience at a job that paid better and was more interesting than what the working-class players could have found elsewhere. It was glamorous and fulfilling. "It was just like *A League of their Own*: Suddenly these players were put into the spotlight where they had never been before, and then it went away. Wherever the Silver Bullets had tryouts, there was an interest in developing leagues around the country. We had a whole bunch of little leagues pop up that disappeared almost immediately."

Jim organized national tournaments to bring together the scattered local leagues. "The first truly national tournament was in 1994, when I got together with a person out in Phoenix. I had the Michigan league. We held a tournament in Phoenix, and seven teams came up for it. They loved it. It was successful; they went back to their homes with the knowledge that there were other teams playing in other parts of the country. They all started networking, and that was good."

The overall quality of play got better every year, although it was uneven. "A couple of good teams could be put together, and then the rest just wanted to play baseball. Some were terrible, some were above average, and some were very good. We had these national tournaments in 1994 and in 1995. About that time we also started spring tournaments down in Florida. There was a strong Florida league, the South Florida Diamond Baseball League . . . and they were a nice partner because they had access to fields. So we had spring and fall tournaments. People started to network; then, of course, the Internet got a little stronger, and I started a website and started reaching out that way."

In 1996 the women's baseball tournaments began to attract the attention of some men's organizations. The National Sporting Goods Association gave a grant to Stan Musial Baseball, part of the American Amateur Baseball Conference in Michigan. Stan Musial Baseball sponsored a women's team for a year and then gave up on the project.

"The next year was when USA Baseball first got involved, in 1997. They gave me a grant for my organization, I think it was only $7,000, but it seemed like a fortune then, to run a tournament. And we held that tournament in Washington DC. That's what really kicked off the Eastern Women's Baseball Conference." The league was operated by two women, JoAnn Milliken and Bonnie Hoffman, in the Washington area. The tournament Glennie organized with the USA Baseball grant money helped to consolidate Milliken and Hoffman's ongoing efforts. They formed a more competitive tournament team, drawing from the various recreational teams that were a part of their league. The Eastern Women's Baseball Conference is still one of the strongest in the country, and they host a major women's tournament every Memorial Day weekend in the Baltimore–Washington DC area.

In 1998, the year after that first Baltimore-Washington tournament, USA Baseball invited the teams to come to their National Training Center, which was located in Tucson before the new center was built in North Carolina. "A couple of good teams came, and four or five above average or average teams. USA Baseball saw that this really wasn't developed. So next year they said, 'Jim, we're not going to do this next year.' They had a men's team playing in the Olympics and were focused on that. I said, 'Okay.'"

Glennie didn't give up. Building a women's national team from the ground up was now his baby. He was invested in the process, and he could see that if he didn't take the lead, it wasn't going to happen. Jim went to Tom Giffin at Roy Hobbs Baseball, and Giffin agreed to include a women's tournament along with the men's. The Roy Hobbs World Series is the major annual tournament for men's amateur baseball teams of all age groups, usually held for a week in mid-November at the Minnesota Twins' and Boston Red Sox's spring training facilities in Florida. "I went down [to Fort Myers] and directed the women's tournament for the first couple of years, and after that Tom ran it for many years, from 1999 on. The women loved it, but it stayed static at a certain level again. Tom did a wonderful job, but he was losing money all the time on this."

Jim ran one final national women's tournament, in Huntingburg, Indiana, in 2009. A local businessman in that small town was interested in hosting the tournament and staging it in the town's historic baseball stadium, where the movie *A League of Their Own* had been filmed. Jim was getting ready to retire and feeling the burden of not having enough help in organizing the women's tournaments. When he stepped down in 2010, there was no national women's baseball tournament anywhere.

USA Baseball was interested once again in women's baseball, but the organization had a vision different from Jim's. Jim believed that the only way to develop a national team was to hold a series of national tournaments in which many local teams could enter and showcase their players. The national team would be culled from the best players in those tournaments. USA Baseball was not interested in a farm system, or a feeder system, that would develop players to be chosen at a national tournament to play on a national team. The organization preferred, following the model for the boys' and men's teams it sponsored, to select players directly for a women's national team that it would sponsor. USA Baseball's job, as the organization sees it, is not to develop players but to showcase talent. But where would the women's talent come from if no one put effort into development? There is no girls' or women's equivalent to the enormous network of baseball for boys in the United States.

Jim Glennie and USA Baseball went their separate ways in 2010. From Jim's perspective, USA Baseball was not really interested in developing women's baseball. "When USA Baseball put together that Tommy Lasorda team that won the Olympics, that was their bread and butter right there. Their whole budget was from the Olympic committee. USA Baseball was focused on Olympic baseball, and the women's team was being put on the back burner, in my opinion."

In Glennie's opinion, USA Baseball's focus on men's baseball so overshadows its obligation to support a women's team that it has led the organization to try to put together a championship women's team with as little investment as possible. The plan is to use NCAA softball to supply the team with elite athletes, to identify recent graduates, and to quickly train them for the women's national baseball team. "That's why they want to invite the softball players now, because they've already got trained athletes. They saw Jenna Marston, and they're licking their chops. They said this is going to be like taking candy from a baby. We'll just get a bunch of Jenna Marstons, and we won't have to put up with Glennie and those other fools bringing us all these baseball players that we have to look at. That's a little bit of ad lib there. So Mary Jo Stegeman and all the others around the country can blab and bark at USA Baseball all they want [about the talent they have on their local teams], but it's not going to do any good until USA Baseball comes up with an alternative to just selecting softball people."

Jim's frustration has momentarily gotten the better of him, and he asks for time to calm himself: "Let's turn the recorder off for just a second. I need a break."

He is steaming mad. His wife, Jannel, serves us coffee. We sip quietly, thinking. It is upsetting to both of us to imagine that the organization that represents the baseball dream of American girls is preparing to field a softball team to send into international competition against countries, like Japan, Canada, and Australia, that have real women's baseball. I'm hoping that what Jim is saying is not true.

Then Jim says he's ready, and I turn on the recorder again. "I think where we left off is we were talking about USA Baseball's role as an organization that accepts elite players and is just looking to showcase the elite players who come to them. Lately, we've seen that they put one of the top softball players ever, Jenny Dalton Hill, on the 2010 team, and now they have made her the women's baseball representative on the board of directors. But her pedigree is in softball. And this just shows that I think their new vision, their new development threat is going to be to look for top collegiate softball players who have graduated, because they can't interfere with the active players on a college softball team. That would just anger NCAA softball. So they'll wait until the softball players are done with their softball careers. Then they'll bring in those already developed athletes because they are much easier to train. Even though the question still remains whether you can train them into a baseball players in time to play in the World Cup since they have them only for a week."

Jim thinks the Canadian and Australian systems are much more promising for the future of women's baseball and that the United States should follow their lead. "It would be wonderful if there were lots of girls that wanted to go into Little League Baseball and play there, and they accepted them willingly and developed them. Eventually when they get to high school, a few of them can play with the boys, probably quite a few after a while. But the majority of them would continue playing against other women. If there were separate leagues for girls in high school, then USA Baseball would have trained league players to look at in tournaments and leagues around the country."

A large pool of girls playing baseball with boys as younger children and later in their own leagues would enable USA Baseball to compile scouting reports on girls who play baseball, just as they do for boys. "On the boys' side they're looking at the twelve-year-olds, and they're starting a book on them when they're young. And they follow them right up to the age when they can be called to the national team. USA Baseball doesn't have a scouting system as such. The coaches of boys' teams around the country will tell them about players, and they hold showcases where already developed players can come and display their skills. With the boys they hold monthlong trips to other countries [to prepare for the World Cup tournaments]. With the girls, it's three days ahead of the tournament."

For nearly two decades Glennie had been scouting and compiling a book of girls and young women in the United States who play baseball. He knew the players because he was on the ground: organizing tournaments and working with the coaches and organizers of the local teams and leagues. His database grew over the years, and when USA Baseball got involved in sponsoring a women's national team for the first time in 2004, Jim willingly gave them the names of the players he had been tracking. He was excited at the prospect of USA Baseball finally sponsoring a women's national team. It was actually his dream come true. But, from his perspective, USA Baseball took his database and told him his services were no longer required. "Right now they have a database because I've given them all these names. And so they don't need me anymore, they are just going to keep everything in house and develop it because they are the gatekeeper. They think they don't even need baseball scouts. If they just develop a relationship with softball, all they have to do is keep an eye on the top softball players and have [NCAA Softball] coaches throw names at them of those who have graduated. [. . .]

"It's just frustrating because we've been trying to differentiate ourselves from softball for twenty years. Now they suddenly have this brainstorm, or brain fart, or whatever you want to call it, that they are going to develop a national women's baseball team through softball."

Kevin Marden

Kevin Marden is currently the most successful coach in women's baseball in the United States.[6] He is, like the players he coaches, utterly unknown beyond the small circle that is American women's baseball. All of the women interviewed in the book who have played for him mention his importance in keeping them in the game. If Kevin and the members of Team USA who were on his New England Women's Red Sox hadn't reached out to Lilly after her experience with Vassar baseball, she very likely would not be playing baseball today. Tara Harbert credits Kevin with convincing her that she had the makings of a good baseball hitter and patiently working

FIG. 40. Kevin Marden gives Lilly Jacobson advice at the 2012 Roy Hobbes Classic. Courtesy of Patricia Wagar.

to help her lose her softball habits at bat. Donna Mills emailed me with an addendum to her interview: "I feel I should mention Kevin Marden and the NE Sox empire that he built and how supportive of women's baseball he's been. Since the late '90s, he's done nothing but support us. That's where I fine-tuned my baseball skills and learned about baseball. Base-running, hitting, pitching, fielding, and my approach to the game all came from Kevin and the Sox. That is our extended family. And that's what I was doing during the off seasons from USA Baseball and World Cups."[7] Jim Glennie knows and admires Marden and remarked, "You can't dislike Kevin. He's only done good things for the women's game."

Kevin Marden's New England Women's Red Sox are indeed extended family for many of the best women baseball players in the country. Nine of the eleven women in this book are regular members of the Sox, playing in two or three major women's baseball tournaments a year for Kevin's team. (Jenny Dalton Hill and Jenna Marston are the only two who have never played for Marden.) While meeting and playing together three times a year is not much for a baseball team, it has permitted the women to practice together, to know and trust each other as teammates, and to build a wonderful team chemistry. They live scattered across the country, but they find ways to plan weekend visits with each other in the off-season, away from baseball, just for fun. The players' parents have also become good friends, having traveled together with both the Sox and Team USA to watch their daughters play. The members of this multi-generation extended baseball family have on occasion expressed their belief that if only USA Baseball would invite Kevin Marden to coach the national team, the elusive gold medal could be theirs.

Women's baseball would surely benefit if the Red Sox had more competition. It would be good for the Sox and everybody else and would make for better games at the tournaments. There are some first-rate ballplayers on other teams who play against the Sox, including other members and former members of the national team. Team USA members Ashley Sujkowski, Lindsay Horwitz, and Stacy Piagno have played for the Chicago Pioneers. Laura Brenneman, who was on Team USA in 2004 and 2006, plays on the DC Thunder.[8] But no other team has come together in the same way as the New England Women's Red Sox. The team is not always popular with the other coaches and players, and others involved in this competitive women's circuit have grumbled that Marden "raided" Team USA to put his team together. But the women who accepted Kevin's invitation to join his team were looking for good baseball, supportive coaching, and nothing else. They pay their own way to the tournaments, sleep three to a room in the hotels, and nobody is forcing them to be on the team. Kevin's record of 112 wins and 5 losses speaks for itself: he's a great coach, if for no other reason than he knows how to pick a team and let his ballplayers play their game.

How does he do it? And why does he do it? Kevin Marden is a sixty-three-year-old Bostonian of Irish decent, is CEO of a logistics company, and has been an amateur baseball player and coach for decades. On a visit to Boston in 2011, I asked him for an interview to talk about his experiences coaching women's baseball. He invited me, Lilly, player Janet Miller, and her mother (originally from New York) to dinner at a Jewish deli in Boston's

Brookline neighborhood. We talked for several hours about women's baseball and his years of coaching both men and women. The meal ended with two desserts—Boston cream pie and New York cheesecake—and a lot of wisecracks about the Red Sox and the Yankees.

Kevin became involved with women's baseball through his friend, Janet Miller. Janet is an accomplished softball and baseball player and was playing in the newly formed New England Women's Baseball League when she asked Kevin if he would like to help coach in the league. Kevin had been coaching his men's amateur Red Sox for several years when the director of the New England Women's Baseball League asked him to coach the team that Janet played on. "Ironically, it was only because of my relationship with Janet that they brought me in to coach. Those women could really play the game. Sixty women, four teams of fifteen players, and they were extraordinary players. From my perspective it was really amazing. Probably forty-five of the sixty were the best athletes I've ever worked with. So it was a really good league. People came from California, Florida, and even Japan . . . they actually came to play in this league."

It wasn't Kevin's first experience coaching women. His sister-in-law had been a serious softball player, and in the 1970s she joined a women's flag football league. She asked Kevin to coach her team because he had been a football coach. "These were just great athletes who could adapt to the sport. I taught these girls how to play football. We won seventy-five straight football games! That was my first experience coaching women, and I thought, 'I love this!' I just love the whole aspect of it . . . of coaching somebody who listens to you and doesn't get in your face. That's basically how it all started. So when Janet asked me to coach her team I said, 'Yeah! I love coaching women.'"

He finds women to be more coachable than men: eager to learn and to improve. They don't take good coaching for granted, and they don't assume they know everything already. He doesn't overcoach and stays focused on the players and what they need to succeed. During one baseball tournament I told Kevin how much the women love playing on his team. It's hard not to be effusive about a team that has enjoyed so much success, but there is something more to the players' affection than just basking in all those wins. They really enjoy learning and becoming better ballplayers under Kevin's guidance. Kevin responded to the compliment, "You know what I do? I find good players, I put them out on the field, and I let them play. It doesn't take much to coach these women." There is undoubtedly a lot more to it than that, but that's what it feels like to the ballplayers. They have fun when they're playing for Kevin because he conveys his utter confidence in them as ballplayers, and they learn more about the game when they're having fun. He teaches them, and he knows what plays to call. He outsmarts the other coaches, and the women play at the top of their game.

While Kevin is not above enjoying the Sox's extraordinary success, his goal is not to prove something about his expertise or his prowess as a coach. He gets annoyed at the territorialism and egoism of many of the coaches he encounters in women's baseball and dislikes self-promoters who diminish the women's game. "When I got involved I said, 'Listen, let's just teach all these women how to play the game of baseball. Don't get into All-Star games; don't get into 'We need to go professional'; don't get into all this upper-level stuff. When I started playing baseball, I was eight years old. I wasn't going to be a professional until I was twenty years old. So you're not going to have a woman walking onto a field on day one and going immediately from being an amateur baseball player to being a professional. It doesn't work that way. So I kept trying to say these things, and the guys who were putting the [New England Women's Baseball] league together didn't want to hear a lot of that stuff."

The president of the New England Women's Baseball League was a man named Jerry Dawson. Kevin didn't think much of him: "He was a promoter, looking for recognition, not for the women but for him. I was all about the women; he was all about himself." Kevin wanted to expand their level of play gradually. "I really felt we should work to go to the next level, eventually get an All-Star team and then get an All-American team, but let the players develop. But these guys [Dawson and his partners] wanted an instantaneous reaction. Like, 'Get it all, fast.' Plus all the recognition came back to the guys. It was never about the women. It was all about the guys."

Kevin and Janet's team did well in the four years they played in the

New England women's league. "Once we got past the initial phases of this league, my team finished first or second each year, 1999–2003." Then another women's league was started: the North American Women's Baseball League, run by a man, named Nick Lopardo, who was prepared to sponsor and promote it. The new league was based in Lynn, Massachusetts, just outside of Boston. Lopardo was involved with a men's team named the Nashua Spirit, and he began a women's Spirit too. Janet Miller was on his team. Kevin remarks, "Nick Lopardo was the guru. I was not part of this, but I was watching. I went to their first national championship game in Fort Myers, Florida. I say to the coach, who's a pretty good guy, 'I can tell you some secrets of how to win this tournament.' Because I won the men's tournament eight times. The coach was okay with it, but the upper echelons said, 'Get out of here.'"

Kevin was banished from the field and told to stay far away. Janet was told by the tournament officials that if her boyfriend was seen on the field, she would be asked to withdraw from the team. "So fine, I go off by myself in the tournament. And they [the Nashua Spirit] lost. Even though they were clearly the best team in the tournament. After, the tournament the guy who ran the team said, 'Sorry I didn't involve you.' I said, 'Listen, you don't have to say anything to me because I am going to put my own team together and I am going to come down here and win this thing all by myself, and you will regret the day you ever didn't let me on the field.' And the rest is history." Kevin's Irish temper and his competitive nature launched the New England Women's Red Sox.

After that tournament, Janet and three of her teammates—Donna Mills, Keri Lemasters, and Judy O'Brien—left the Nashua Spirit and asked Kevin to start a new team. They even had the roster all ready for him: the four of them and five softball players. Kevin was dubious: "I said, 'Oh no . . . I don't think we can do this. This is a national championship. The level of play is pretty high. The softball players haven't played enough baseball.'" But he remembered his good experience with the women's football team and reneged: he would coach the women's team, along with his men's New England Red Sox. The new team trained together for a few months under Kevin's direction to prepare for the Hobbs tournament. Once again Kevin found that coaching talented women athletes was a gratifying experience. Although inexperienced at baseball, the players were "gutsy athletes" and willing to take instruction. "From a coaching standpoint they did every single thing I asked them to do. That's the greatest thing about coaching women. It's not like guys. They just do it. And these kids did it. So we went down to the Hobbs tournament the first year and . . . we won the damn thing! We pulled it out!" They've been winning ever since.

Marden knows that he's a good coach and a very competitive guy. That much is obvious from the delight he took in showing up the coaches on the Nashua Spirit when he was exiled from the ballpark. But he gives most of the credit to the talented, hardworking athletes and to team chemistry on the Sox. That's what he's looking for when he invites a baseball player to join the team: "It's chemistry. Any team game is played with chemistry. I have a thousand players [perhaps an exaggeration—JR] who want to play on this team. And there's a screening process. Because I don't want anybody on this team who will foul up the chemistry. I can teach anybody how to play, but I don't want just anybody."

There are also a few simple secrets of his coaching technique that he is willing to reveal and that he believes are neglected by some of the coaches of other women's teams. For example, after an out is made, Kevin insists that the Sox throw the ball around the infield. This is basic baseball: the team stays connected, and that opportunity is lost when the ball is simply returned to the pitcher after an out. Another simple but important coaching technique is making sure that every infielder is backed up by an outfielder on every play. "We keep the players moving," says Kevin. That is also basic baseball, but he sees many of the fielders on other women's teams letting a teammate make a play without backing her up in case there's a mistake. Making sure that every play is backed up also forces the team in the field to stay alert and involved, rather than standing there watching their teammates make a play. Fielders play with more confidence and can make more daring plays when they know there is a teammate backing them up. It's utterly obvious, but some of the coaches in women's baseball don't even have this level of experience.

Also, Kevin talks to his players in the dugout all the time. "Every single time they come off the field, we'll sit on the bench, and we'll watch, and there will be a situation, and I'll say, 'Lilly, what would you do in that situation?' And it's feedback for me, but I'll also give feedback to her. I've been playing this stupid game for fifty years, but I still always think, 'Oh my God, I didn't do that. I should have done that.' You're always thinking about how to improve your game." He lost a game to the Chicago Pioneers, Greg and Mary Jo Stegeman's team, in 2011 at the Hobbs tournament, and it cost the Sox the championship for the first time. He is still annoyed at himself for failing to call a suicide squeeze that he believes would have brought home the winning run. He is always thinking about how to win, and that competitive energy is contagious in the dugout. His admiration for the women's baseball skills is repaid by their admiration for his coaching. It's a happy situation for all. They need better competition and in Kevin's view, that will only happen when the overall quality of coaching in women's baseball improves. There are great athletes playing baseball on these few scattered women's teams, but there are not enough really good coaches to turn them into contenders and improve the overall quality of the game.

The New England Women's Red Sox is the best women's baseball team in the United States. Many of the players on the Sox have said that they learn more about baseball from Kevin than from any other coach they've known and that they enjoy playing with their Sox teammates more than those on any other team they have played on. It would be nice to see this combination, enhanced by the best players from other teams in this tournament circuit, on the field playing for USA. But a disconnect between grassroots baseball and the national team has interfered with any pooling of resources lately.

Jim Glennie and Kevin Marden are unusual men in their dedication to women's baseball for the sake of the game itself. Neither of them are easygoing fellows, and their tempers may have aggravated a few people over the years. But they have much in common: their tireless efforts to sustain and develop women's baseball are pure hearted and centered on their belief that women can play world-class baseball. They also share views about developing the women's game that are remarkably simple in the face of all the nonsense about women's baseball being an impossibility in the United States. Both see the need for steady, persistent player development with more opportunities to play under the guidance of knowledgeable, experienced baseball coaches. Kevin has been successful because of this mentality, and many of the venues that are available for his women's teams are the result of Jim's patient efforts to build an infrastructure. Yet USA Baseball is not availing itself of the resources that Jim, Kevin, and others in the grassroots women's baseball community have worked to establish. The heartbreak is not only that the pool of women's baseball players is being ignored. More than that, the emphasis on a quick gold medal rather than a slower, more patient development strategy undermines the resources that are available to build a successful women's national baseball program.

17

USA Baseball

Team USA is the best hope for a "show" for women's baseball. USA Baseball has the National Training Complex; the financial backing of Major League Baseball; the Majestic USA uniforms;[1] USA equipment bags and gear; sponsorship agreements with Nike, Under Armour, Rawlings, and other Major League equipment manufacturers, shoe companies, airlines, and hotel connections; and the international infrastructure from their boys' programs to facilitate organizing World Cup tournaments for women. Wearing a USA jersey is the biggest thrill most American athletes, male or female, dream of. It is certainly the highest profile experience available to women ballplayers. On top of it all comes the honor of representing the United States of America. USA Baseball's member organizations include Little League Baseball, Babe Ruth Baseball, Pony Baseball, American Legion Baseball, the American Coaches Organization, the NCAA, the National Interscholastic Athletic Administrators Association (NIAAA), the Amateur Athletic Union (AAU), and nearly every other baseball organization in the United States.

The United States Baseball Federation Inc., or USA Baseball, is a 501(c)(3) not-for-profit, tax-exempt corporation, incorporated on January 6, 1965, in the state of Michigan. It has served as the official governing body for amateur baseball in the United States since 1978, when the Amateur Sports Act of 1978 (36 U.S.C. § 220501 et. seq.) was signed into law by President Jimmy Carter, establishing the U.S. Olympic Committee and mandating national governing bodies for each Olympic sport. Before adoption of the Amateur Sports Act, the AAU had represented the United States in international competition and had often clashed with other amateur sports organizations, such as the NCAA. The 1978 act charters the U.S. Olympic Committee, which in turn charters the national governing body (NGB) for each sport. Each NGB establishes the rules for selecting the U.S. Olympic Team and promotes amateur competition in its sport. The Amateur Sports Act was revised in 1998 to reflect changes in Olympic rules, such as the fact that amateurism is no longer a requirement for competing in most international sports.[2]

USA Baseball's funding comes from its relationship with Major League Baseball, which provides 24 percent of its budget. The rest of the money is raised by merchandise sales, events that are "pay to play," and sponsorship from sporting goods and clothing manufacturers. USA Baseball executive director and CEO Paul Seiler explained, "There are a number of different ways that we generate revenue. We have hotel rebate programs. Some of it is VIK [value in kind], so you have a relationship with a sponsor. Instead of having to buy Majestic uniforms, as an example, Majestic is the official uniform supplier to USA Baseball, and we get X amount of uniforms as a part of that relationship."[3]

USA Baseball's first priority, as stated in the organization's constitution and bylaws, is "to develop, foster and encourage interest and participation in baseball throughout the United States" (Article V, Sec. 1). Among its other duties is "to provide equitable support and encouragement for participation by women where separate programs for male and female athletes are conducted on a national and international basis" (Article V, Sec. 7).[4] This is the single mention of women in the bylaws, and it is the basis for the existence of the Women's National Team.

USA Baseball first fielded a women's national team in 2004. That decision was prompted by several international tournaments held since 2001 in which a national women's team had participated. The participating team had been assembled and the tournaments organized by individuals in the United States and Japan. The two American organizers were Jim Glennie, who had been organizing women's baseball tournaments since 1992, and Nick Lopardo, who had funded several women's baseball teams and leagues, including the Nashua Women's Spirit and the North American Women's Baseball League. Glennie had entered a team in a 1999 tournament in Fort Lauderdale. A Japanese organization had seen his American Women's Baseball Federation website and contacted him to ask if they could also enter a team in the Florida tournament. Glennie recalls, "In the spring of 1999, the Japanese came over and brought television crews, their top guns, and a great team. The purpose of this was to show how good they were, and of course we were all impressed. They were very good, even though my little entry beat them 3–2. I had a very good team too."

At the end of the tournament, the directors of the Japanese team talked to Jim about organizing an international women's baseball league. "They had an interpreter there, and a Major Leaguer from Japan, Murakami. He was the manager. He was their show guy, and he got a lot of publicity."[5] Glennie and the representatives of the Japanese Women's Baseball Program agreed to organize an international women's baseball tournament and to invite teams from Canada and Australia to join them. To administer international women's baseball, they formed the Women's International Baseball Association (WIBA), with Jim serving as chairman. The Japanese offered to fly an American team to Tokyo for an exhibition game with a Japanese women's team the following summer, 2000. The Japanese group publicized the exhibition game and arranged for it to be held in one of their national professional baseball stadiums, with more than four thousand spectators in attendance. Jim had uniforms made that said "USA" on them and contacted USA Baseball to inform them of what was in the works. At that point USA Baseball chose not to be involved.

The 2000 exhibition game between Japan and the USA was successful, and the WIBA planned a tournament for the following year, having expanded the pool of teams with commitments from Canada and Australia to participate. The tournament was to be called the Women's World Series and would take place in Edmonton, Canada, in 2001. The series was also successful, and in 2002 a second Women's World Series was planned for Florida, at Tropicana Field, where the Tampa Bay Rays play. Jim had been negotiating with Major League Baseball about donating the field, but at the last minute the organization declined and Jim provided $20,000 of his own to rent the stadium. The following year, 2003, another Women's World Series was held in Australia at the national training center, and a fourth Women's World Series was planned for Japan in 2004. By then, the International Baseball Federation, the governing body for international baseball, had become aware of the tournaments and began organizing its own tournament in Edmonton, Canada. They called it the Women's World Cup Tournament and scheduled it for two weeks after the WIBA Women's World Series in Japan.

The IBAF's involvement meant that the Women's World Cup was an officially sanctioned international tournament. The privately organized, funded, and marketed WIBA Women's World Series already scheduled and planned for Japan was, by default, downgraded to unofficial status. The IBAF, as baseball's official international organization, only recognizes teams affiliated with the national federations, such as USA Baseball, Baseball Canada, Australian Baseball League, and so forth. To participate in the official IBAF Women's World Cup Tournament, the Americans needed a team sanctioned by USA Baseball. Paul Seiler explains, "The IBAF will only recognize National Teams that come under the direction of the National Federations (USA Baseball, Baseball Canada, etc.)."[6] That is, individuals may organize all the baseball they want, but only the IBAF makes it an official event.

USA Baseball had become interested in a women's national team and was prepared to sponsor its participation in an international tournament. But why, when the IBAF threw its hat in the ring with the Women's World Cup Tournament, did it schedule it at nearly the same time as the fourth WIBA Women's World Series? The same teams would have to play in Japan and then travel to Canada to play again the following week. The women were astonished at the sudden surplus of baseball, but they were game. Donna Mills was on the team and recalls the daunting logistics: "The travel time was awful, poorly planned, but we were so grateful to have a competitive team to play on that we didn't complain."[7] The Americans did well, winning the silver in Women's World Series in Japan and the gold at the first official Women's World Cup Tournament with the players that Glennie had been molding into a team over the years.

Jim Glennie did not accompany the team. He was gratified that the national team he had dreamed of and worked to make a reality was finally recognized by the IBAF and USA Baseball. But he felt that he was being pushed out. "The same team played in the World Series and the World Cup. I was beginning to train the team, and when the Women's World Cup was announced, they said they were going to have tryouts and field a team. I said, 'Great, I want you involved, you can do a better job than I am in a position to do. I'm going to defer to you. So I was glad that USA Baseball was finally going to be involved in doing a women's baseball team, but I was sad that I was kind of dissed and booted out of the process. But we all had in the back of our mind the goal of getting women's baseball into the Olympics, and the only way to do that was to get the IBAF involved. They're the gatekeeper, they saw I was at the gate, and they allowed everyone in but me."

Jim is not happy that he and USA Baseball have parted ways. It's a story of the politics of sports, perhaps with a little David and Goliath thrown in. Jim ruefully notes, "This is what bothers my wife so much, is that I let other people take my power so many times. But, it would have been worse for me to fight this. I had to remember all the time that my goal was to get women playing baseball in the Olympics, or something like that. And we were all struggling to make this happen."[8]

The national team gained some things and lost others by the conflict over its leadership and direction. The team had finally been acknowledged as a part of the national baseball program, sanctioned by USA Baseball and indirectly supported by Major League Baseball. This was an unparalleled development, promising real recognition on an international stage for the athletes and the sport they had sacrificed to stay with. Because of USA Baseball, the Women's National Team has gained funding, recognition, and stability. The price of that security and enrichment has been a loss of autonomy. The team's survival is ensured for the time being, but its growing pains currently involve a struggle for its soul and future direction.

FIG. 41. Team USA 2010 in Caracas, Venezuela. Courtesy of USA Baseball.

Is the U.S. women's national baseball team a baseball or a softball team? Is softball the inevitable talent pool for women's baseball, or is softball a stopgap measure until more baseball players can be developed and identified? And if USA Baseball does not develop those ballplayers, who will? There is, as we have seen, longstanding interest women's baseball at the grassroots level, and now there is also USA Baseball's national showcase. All the pieces are falling into place for success. So why is there still such a lack of communication between the shining star of USA Baseball, and the grassroots efforts of the local girls' and women's baseball leagues? Why can't the folks interested in developing girls' and women's baseball with local teams and national tournaments bring the young players along until they are ready to try out for the national team? To begin to answer these questions, I interviewed Paul Seiler, CEO of USA Baseball, and Ashley Bratcher, the director of the USA Baseball Women's National Team.

Paul Seiler was appointed executive director and CEO of USA Baseball in 1988. I interviewed him by phone on November 28, 2012, to ask him about the role the women's team plays in USA Baseball's program, his vision for the future of women's baseball, and the selection of coaches for the women's team. I was concerned with what I had been hearing from many players about the need for better coaching for the national team. Seiler explained that USA Baseball's mission is to identify the best baseball players in the United States and to showcase them in international competition. The institutional role is not to develop women's baseball, but rather to field a championship team when there are international tournaments. This is the same role USA Baseball plays for its boys' and men's teams, except that an extensive infrastructure for boys' baseball is already in place. In the United States, the challenges of scouting men and women are virtual opposites. Seiler notes, "One thing we're blessed with in the United States from a male perspective in the sport of baseball is a very, very broad base from which to choose. How do you scale that down to a manageable number? Conversely, on the women's side, you're really beating the bushes trying to find not just a good player but great players."

Seiler described the selection process for the teams USA Baseball sponsors, which include the (men's) collegiate national team, 18U boys, 17U boys, 15U boys, 14U boys, 12U boys, and the women's team. The various youth baseball programs—Little League Baseball, Pony Baseball, Dixie League Baseball—apply for membership in USA Baseball. "USA Baseball is an umbrella organization over those organizations. We can't tell them how to run their programming, what fees to charge for players to participate, all those things. We act more as a commissioner's office to address issues, procedures, protocol within the sport on a macro level." USA Baseball only sees the elite players that the youth organizations bring to their attention. "So the masses, if you will, are in various separate youth organizations. As the elite athlete rises, that's where USA Baseball as a governing body comes in and says, 'Okay, this player, that player is someone who needs to be considered and put into the pipeline of consideration for a national team opportunity.'"

But the problem for girls who want to rise into the elite bracket is that there isn't the equivalent set of baseball organizations to fill that pipeline. "Traditionally, boys and girls [in most youth sports] will play together up until a certain age. And then for a number of different reasons, physiological being one of them, the girls have been steered to softball while the boys continue to play baseball. And that's the dilemma we have in our country for the female athlete who wants to continue playing baseball. Now a seventeen-year-old girl playing with a seventeen-year-old boy may not be competitive in terms of physical ability as baseball players, but what about the seventeen-year-old girl versus a seventeen-year-old girl?"

Seiler, as a business executive, must view development in terms of market opportunity, and at the moment he sees no market opportunity in either girls' or women's baseball. The CEO of USA Baseball is obligated to guide his organization with an eye on the bottom line. "Part of the challenge is with the market, at least right now. The market is driving it, and there's not enough. This isn't something that the women who desire to play baseball want to hear.

"The fact of the matter is if there was enough energy, for lack of a better term, for impactful numbers of females to continue to play baseball, I can tell you right now that an organization like Pony Baseball or Babe Ruth or Little League would say, 'Hey, here's a market opportunity. Let's go ahead and create that vehicle so that those thousand, five thousand, ten thousand, hundred thousand girls can become members of our organization, and we'll provide that opportunity for leagues and teams and everything that goes along with running a baseball organization.' So that's the challenge."

From the perspective of USA Baseball then, the bottom line defines the opportunities for girls and baseball. USA Baseball's obligation to field a women's team creates a conundrum if no feeder system is available in the United States. As Seiler puts it, "What comes first, the chicken or the egg? If you provide the opportunity, will the girls come out? Or do you say, 'Hey, we're not there to provide an opportunity.' I'm not saying USA Baseball says that. I'm saying the market says that. If the demand isn't there, what are we doing? The other part of it too is from the demand perspective. If the demand was there, it would be in our schools as well, right? So do we provide opportunities and hope the numbers will come later? Or, do the numbers tell us that there isn't even a quantifiable need for this?"

It's a problem for women's baseball when the organization whose responsibility is to field a national women's team doesn't believe that women's baseball in the United States is viable. "If the demand isn't there, what are we doing?" surely reflects a less than enthusiastic commitment to building a women's national baseball team. From Seiler's business perspective, the most cost-effective way to put a competitive women's baseball team on the field is to recruit highly developed softball players. The position makes financial sense if it works, but the jury is still out on whether it is possible to develop an internationally competitive *baseball* team with softball players who are only together for a few weeks every two years.

Looked at from another angle, it might not be cost-effective to try to build a baseball team without baseball players. Each year that goes by without investing in developing women's baseball in the United States is another year wasted if the goal is to identify a women's championship baseball team to represent the United States. Every time USA Baseball selects a team of softball players in the hope of turning them into a baseball team, it loses time and opportunity that could be spent developing a team of athletes who have actually chosen to play baseball and are willing to push themselves to be the best women's baseball team in the world. It's not clear that the love of softball necessarily translates into the love of baseball that inspires athletes to do the work of becoming great at that game.

I asked Paul whether an explicit tactical decision has been made to look for the USA women's baseball team from the ranks of collegiate softball players. "It has. And here's the point. What's our responsibility in terms of fielding a national team? To put the best team we can on the field to win the gold medal. So where do those athletes come from? A lot of girls playing softball had a baseball start. Granted a softball pitcher's skill set isn't necessarily transferable back to the baseball diamond, but hitters and other position players, if given the opportunity. . . . You know, our job at the end of the day is to put a team on the field that has the best opportunity to win a gold medal no matter where that athlete comes from. Softball is a resource that we've at least explored and identified as a potential place to find elite-level athletes who are good in the sport or can be good in the sport. At the end of the day, the job of the team is to win a gold medal."

As Seiler points out, this is not the message supporters of women's baseball want to hear. Is it really the mission of USA Baseball to win a gold medal, no matter where the athletes come from? Or should a national baseball team actually be a baseball team? What's the point of winning a gold medal in women's baseball if there are no women's baseball players on the team?

Seiler is the father of a daughter and sympathetic to providing every opportunity for girls to pursue their dreams. His job running USA Baseball is not to provide opportunities for either girls or boys but to find players who can win a gold medal in baseball. "As a parent I want my daughter to have every opportunity to be successful no matter where her heart lies. But USA Baseball does not operate teams and leagues. That is not what we do as a governing body; that's not the way we're set up. We don't do it for men. We wouldn't do it for women."

I asked Paul about the process of selecting the coaches for the Women's National Team. He explained that each of the teams in USA Baseball has its own director, and Ashley Bratcher is the director for the Women's National Team. The actual logistics of that team, including selecting coaches, is her responsibility. The boys' teams have had excellent coaches, often retired Major League players and coaches with Major League experience. The women would certainly benefit from their expert guidance. But the current process of identifying players for the women's team from NCAA softball programs presents a conflict between coaches with access to women's softball and coaches with knowledge of baseball. If the decision has been made to recruit softball players, then softball coaches will have the best access to them. But even the best softball coaches don't necessarily have the right set of skills to convert the best softball players into a baseball team at short notice.

Seiler describes the process of finding coaches for the boys' teams: "We don't put coaches on national team staffs unless they've had previous exposure with us. So just as a player will show up to try out for a national team, we have coaches who we bring in to various programs to work on a task force, as an auxiliary coach, because we want to know about that person as well. We have an interview process, or a tryout process—maybe that's even a better term. We have a tryout process for coaches just like we do for athletes."

Often USA Baseball will consider coaches from the ranks of former USA Baseball players, many of whom have gone on to have Major League careers. A number of women have played on Team USA and have retired from active play. Donna Mills, Bridget Veenema, and Kim Braatz are examples of women with extensive experience in baseball who have played on Team USA. Julie Croteau led the team to a gold medal in 2006 as head coach. Seiler suggested Jenny Dalton Hill as a candidate for a coaching position with Team USA. His thinking was, "Okay, Jenny Dalton Hill, is it time for you to put on a different hat and start thinking about how you would feel about getting on the other side of the line? Let's see what you're like as a coach."

The coaches receive a stipend and the honor of being a part of USA Baseball. Seiler informed me that when USA Baseball budgets for the women's team, it allocates the same funds as it would for a boys' tournament. However, there is no question that the boys and men receive more experienced, qualified coaching, simply because there are so many experienced baseball players and coaches at the professional and collegiate levels. It would be interesting to see what the former Major League players and coaches, or former Division I baseball coaches, who currently lead the boys' teams could do for the women's program. Donna Mills expressed the frustration some USA players feel about the coaches who have led the team in recent years. "USA Baseball gives us the best cleats, the best gloves, the best equipment, beautiful uniforms, but I'd sacrifice all of that. You can keep it all. Just give us the best coaching available." Given the difficulty of recruiting a women's baseball team and the fact that at least some of the players will be relative novices to baseball, the women's team would seem to require the most experienced baseball coaches available.

Ashley Bratcher is hopeful about Team USA's future. She is the first director of the Women's National Team and is also director of operations for USA Baseball, with responsibility for overseeing all operational needs at the National Training Complex, USA Baseball camps and clinics, and the Women's National Team program. Bratcher graduated from the University of North Carolina–Chapel Hill in 2009 with a degree in exercise and sports science and a focus in sports administration. While a student at Chapel Hill, she was the team manager for the UNC women's soccer program and an administrator of the North Carolina girls' soccer camps. She interned at USA Baseball in the spring of 2009 and was invited to join full-time in October 2009. She is a rising star in the organization and very popular with the women of Team USA.

Before Bratcher's appointment, the Women's National Team was directed by Miki Partridge, who was the chief financial officer for USA Baseball. But Partridge's involvement with the Women's National Team was not a full-time responsibility; it was simply one of the duties assigned to her. The lack of a full-time director left the players on those early teams with a sense that they were just an afterthought to the boys' programs. Since Ashley has come on board, the women's program has been energized. A young woman, the same age as many of the players, she is easy for them to relate to and trust. She is sensitive to the politics of women's baseball, and her heart is in the right place. She wants to support women's *baseball*, although she also understands and supports the organizational needs and goals of USA Baseball.

I have spoken to Ashley several times by phone and gotten to know her in person at the National Training Complex in Cary. When Lilly was injured before Team USA departed for Venezuela in 2010, Ashley coordinated her care, which began with an on-field diagnosis from the USA team trainer, a drive to the Wake Forest emergency room by a USA Baseball intern for an X-ray and triage, and an invitation to Lilly to remain with her USA teammates until they left for Caracas and she returned home for hand surgery. Ashley even made sure that Lilly received her USA team jersey. She is a true professional.

On November 19, 2012, Ashley granted me a phone interview about the USA Baseball women's team. She preferred not to be recorded, so I took notes and there are no transcripts. The issues we discussed are the issues that concern the ballplayers: how to build the best baseball team and how to find coaches that can be effective for ballplayers of their caliber, experience, and age range.

I asked her whether there had been a policy decision to recruit exclusively from the ranks of NCAA Division I softball. Ashley assured me that was not the case, and there had been no explicit decision to recruit only from NCAA softball, although she acknowledged that the 2012 team could give one that impression. Ideally, she said, it would be best to find women who had extensive baseball experience in Little League and up to high school, like Jenna Marston, and who were easy to identify in Division I softball. In theory that seems like an efficient way to find elite women athletes who also know something about baseball. But as the oral histories of the eleven players in the book make evident, few girls who play Division I softball have also played high school baseball. Jenna, indeed, is the only one on the team with that résumé. The rest of the players on the 2010 team who played college softball also played high school or tournament softball to prepare for the NCAA recruitment process. The four players besides Marsten who actually played high school baseball are Underwood, Jacobson, Sementelli, and Meidlinger, and none of them played college softball.

Ashley and I had a frank conversation in which I expressed my concerns that USA Baseball was abandoning baseball players in favor of softball players. I also asked her about the quality of coaches for the women's team in recent years. From the players' viewpoints, after Croteau in 2006, the coaches have either had too much softball background with not enough high-level baseball coaching experience or had no experience coaching women and were bewildered by the very task of coaching women baseball players of such a range of ages.

Ashley responded that the boys' and men's programs do have a longer "breeding process" before a candidate is entrusted with a head coaching position. There are many more opportunities for men to coach the boys' teams and for USA Baseball to evaluate their coaching skills. This is another benefit of the boys' teams playing all summer long every year. Since the women's program consists of, at most, a few weeks of training and tournament play every year or two, USA Baseball doesn't have an opportunity to see the prospective coaches in action with the women for very long.

With regard to the ratio between softball and baseball players on the women's team, the USA Baseball coaching staff has the responsibility for selecting the team. Although the choice of the team is not the domain of either Ashley Bratcher or Paul Seiler, Ashley is eloquent and unequivocal about her commitment to the importance of building a team around baseball players: "The baseball girls will always be your core. There's no way we can field a team with 100 percent softball players, but awareness is our biggest problem. We need to find the lost girls. I know that they [the baseball players] feel as though 'We were the ones that broke down this barrier, and then the flood gates opened and softball players rushed in.' There is no way that we made a decision to undermine or replace them." She is aware of the sense of betrayal felt by the girls who have loved baseball since they were children and developed their baseball skills against stiff odds and outright opposition for years.

Although Ashley believes that the core of a baseball team should be built around baseball players, she also expressed her sense that a "fine line" needs to be walked between finding those girls who love and excel at baseball and finding accomplished competitive, highly trained athletes, even if that means drawing from the best softball players in the country.

One way to maintain balance on that line is with real baseball coaches. That, it seems, would be the easiest thing for USA Baseball to find and an important component of building a women's baseball program that is successful in the long run.

How to Build It

Building a "show" for women's baseball will take everything we have, beginning with a commitment to encouraging girls to play baseball if they want to. Canada and Australia have the right idea: boys and girls should play baseball together and have easy access to the game up until early adolescence. At a certain point—age twelve or thirteen or fourteen—the young ballplayers should have a choice about whether they prefer to play on same-sex or mixed-sex teams. The best players will rise to the top, as they always do, when given a chance. If women can play with men, they should; if they can't or don't want to, they should have the option to play with women. A pool of women who have played baseball from girlhood will emerge. Girls who have played baseball from a young age will want opportunities to play in high school and college, and by then, there may be enough of them to make that possible on either same- or mixed-gender teams.

The elite ballplayers that Paul Seiler, Ashley Bratcher, and USA Baseball are looking for will emerge and be brought to the attention of the Women's National Team, just as the boys' currently are. During a transition period when girls' baseball is growing in the United States, recruiting elite softball players who are interested in playing baseball is a wise choice. But when they identify those softball women who want to learn how to play baseball, they will need the very best *baseball* coaches available to prepare them for international competition. This will take a commitment on everybody's part: players, coaches, and USA Baseball. It will take more than a summer. There isn't a boy in the world who can be taught to play baseball in one summer and then move directly to international competition. Why should girls be any different?

Where will the coaches—who hold the future of American women's baseball in their hands—come from? Potential coaches are already out there. They include the women, now in their forties, who played on the Silver Bullets and Team USA and on other professional teams. They may also include Division I and other college baseball coaches and retired professional baseball players who want to coach a women's team and would value the satisfaction of teaching them and leading them into international competition. Adequate compensation for time away from their regular responsibilities is necessary. Coaching for USA Baseball is an honor that many would make sacrifices for, but paying the bills is a requirement that doesn't go away during baseball season.

Phil and Joe Niekro coached the Bullets; Kevin Marden coaches the New England Red Sox. There are scores of others who have devoted time to women's baseball, including Major League pitchers who have taught girls how to throw a knuckle ball and curve. There are, without question, many other coaches with deep knowledge of baseball who, out of love of the game and respect for women athletes, could be enlisted to help build a future for women's baseball in the United States.

Player Interview Questions

*These questions were presented to players in advance
of the recorded oral history interviews.*

These are questions I would like you to think about before we talk. During our interview we may or may not cover any or all of them. It's up to you. But I will begin by asking you these questions and seeing how our conversation goes. If there are any questions that you would rather discuss or that you think would be more descriptive of your life in baseball, please share them with me.

You will have the opportunity to review anything I have written that concerns you before it is published and to change any quotations that you would prefer that I edit, revise, or omit. You may also choose to remain anonymous, if you don't want your real name published.

I. Childhood

1. What was your first attraction to baseball? What made you want to play?
2. What role did your parents(s) or sibling(s) play in introducing you to baseball and supporting or not supporting your participation as a girl?
3. Were you the only girl on your team or in your league? Did you know other girls who played baseball? Did you experience any problems with teammates or coaches?
4. Did you get enough instruction and playing time as a girl? Did you play the position you wanted? Did you play on All-Star teams? Did your dad coach your team? Was that helpful to you?

5. As a girl (in Little League or on a traveling team) were you aware of any problems with coaches or teammates based on your gender? Did you feel comfortable playing with boys?
6. Did you have goals or dreams for your future in baseball?

II. Adolescence

1. Did you continue to play baseball after Little League? For how long and in what capacity? If you switched to softball, was it with any regret? Did you feel pressured to make the switch, or was it your choice?
2. If you stayed with baseball, what were the biggest struggles you faced to stay in the game? Were you able to get enough instruction and playing time to develop into the best ballplayer you could be?
3. If you played baseball, were there any specific issues about gender identity that you faced as an adolescent girl playing with adolescent boys?
4. If you played softball, were there any specific issues about gender identity that you faced as a female athlete in general or specifically as a softball player? Did those issues have an impact on your enjoyment of your sport?
5. If you played baseball in high school, what role did baseball play in terms of your sense of self as a teenager? Did it add to your self-esteem? Create difficulties?
6. If you played softball in high school, what were the things you gained or sacrificed being a high school softball player? How central to your life was your desire to play softball in college?
7. Did knowing that the chances were slim for a girl to become a college or professional baseball player affect your decision about whether to play softball or baseball?
8. Did you ever think about quitting your sport (either baseball or softball)? Why?

1. What choice did you make about sports in college? Has it been (or was it, if you've graduated already) a positive experience?

2. If you play softball, do you enjoy the game as much as baseball? Do you feel you were "forced out" of baseball at any point? Would you have chosen baseball if there were more competitive women's teams available to you?

3. If you play only baseball, what sacrifices have you made to stay in the game? What have you gained by staying with baseball instead of playing softball? Would you rather play baseball with women if there were more competitive women's baseball teams?

4. How did you discover the USA Baseball Women's National Team? What are the best things about being a member of the team? What is the hardest part of being in the USA Baseball women's program?

5. As an athlete who has achieved elite status in your sport, how do you think your life would be different if you were a man?

6. For the ballplayers who are also mothers, what are the challenges of being a mother (and/or bearing a child during your athletic career) and maintaining your life as an elite athlete?

7. What keeps you playing baseball now?

APPENDIX B

USA Baseball Women's National Team Rosters and Current
Women's Baseball Leagues and Teams in the United States

The following are the rosters of Team USA from 2004 to 2010 and a partial list of women's baseball leagues, teams, and players in the United States as of 2012. Rosters and coaches are included if they were available. The list was compiled by an Internet search and by contacting known coaches, organizers, and administrators to ask for rosters. It does not include high school players: there are no high school girls' baseball teams in the United States, although there are over one thousand girls currently playing high school baseball on various boys' high school teams. Only one American girl is playing college baseball as of fall 2014: Ghazaleh Sailors is a right-handed pitcher at the University of Maine–Presque Isle. Marti Sementelli was a right-handed pitcher at Montreat College in Montreat, North Carolina, during her freshman year and then switched to the softball team the following year. There have been two USA Baseball Women's National Teams and two Women's World Cup Tournaments since this book was written. Team USA won silver medals in the Women's World Cup Tournaments of 2012 in Edmonton, Canada, and 2014 in Miyazaki, Japan. Team Japan won gold medals in both the 2012 and 2014 tournaments and remain the world champions.

2010

Manager: Don Freeman

Assistant Coach: Sandra Wente

Assistant Coach: Ed Kurakazu

Pitching Coach: Tim O'Brien

ROSTER:

Karen Costes

Laura Espinoza-Watson

Sarah Gascon

Tara Harbert

Alex Hebert

Jenny Dalton Hill

Tamara Holmes

Nicki Holt

Lindsay Horwitz

Lilly Jacobson (unable to travel due to injury)

Anna Kimbrell

Jenna Marston

Wynne McCann

Clarisa Navarro

Ghazaleh Sailors

Marti Sementelli

Loren Smith

Christin Sobeck

Ashley Sujkowski

Malaika Underwood

2008

Manager: Brian Bright

Assistant Coach: Lee Ketcham

Assistant Coach: Ed Kurakazu

Assistant Coach: Kim Voisard

ROSTER:

Heather Brusokas

Kristin Caldwell

Karen Costes

Sarah Gascon

Tara Harbert

Alex Hebert

Lilly Jacobson

Anna Kimbrell

Keri Lemasters

Meggie Meidlinger

Donna Mills

Marti Sementelli

Christin Sobeck

Jane Uh

Malaika Underwood

Ashleigh Vargas

Bridget Veenema

2007

Manager: Brian Bright

Assistant Coach: Lee Ketcham

Assistant Coach: Ed Kurakazu

General Manager: Miki Partridge

ROSTER:

Laura Brenneman

Heather Brusokas

Kristin Caldwell

Sarah Gascon

Alex Hebert

Tamara Holmes

Lindsay Horwitz

Jen Hunter

Tamara Ivie
Lilly Jacobson
Anna Kimbrell
Keri Lemasters
Molly McKesson
Meggie Meidlinger
Donna Mills
Judy O'Brien
Lacy Prejean
Laura Rose
Christin Sobeck
Ashley Sujkowski
Jane Uh
Malaika Underwood
Ashleigh Vargas
Bridget Veenema
Kim Voisard

2006
Manager: Julie Croteau
Assistant Coach: Brian Bright
Assistant Coach: Lee Ketcham
Assistant Coach: Ed Kurakazu

ROSTER:
Laura Brenneman
Ashley Cook
Tamara Holmes
Jennifer Hunter
Tamara Ivie
Lilly Jacobson
Keri Lemasters
Molly McKesson
Meggie Meidlinger
Donna Mills

Lacy Prejean
Laura Rose
Trista Russo
Sabrina Sexton
Jane Uh
Malaika Underwood
Bridget Veenema
Kim Voisard

2004
Manager: Marty Scott
Assistant Coach: Julie Croteau
Assistant Coach: Lance Green
Assistant Coach: Ron Marfione
Assistant Coach: Al Melanson

ROSTER:
Laura Brenneman
Kim Braatz-Voisard
Dominisha Britton
Ashley Cook
Sarah Gascon
Keri Lemasters
Molly McKesson
Bonnie Mills
Donna Mills
Kristin Mills
Erin Mullen
Judy O'Brien
Laura Purser-Rose
Patti Raduenz
Alex Sickinger
Amy Stinton
Bridget Veenema
Robin Wallace

Comets
Coach: Chris Feyerherd

2012 ROSTER:
Joelle Balfe
Katie Cherry
Lauren Clister Salituro
Elizabeth Eschker
Lorena Hernandez
Flor Jiron
Peggysue Marlin
Kim Marrazzo
Jasmine Martinez
Missy Mulert
Amy Schneider
Annie Snider

Riveters
Coach: Bill Bernabei

2012 ROSTER:
Jill Bianco
Katie Bidstrup
Jamie Conachen
Dominique Gougis
Andrea Juracek
Jen Liu
Brenda Mendoza
Megan Oswald
Victoria Randall
Caroline Zuno

Skyline
Coach: John Kovach

2012 ROSTER:
Christine Devane
Yolanda Diaz
Tanya H
Shellie Hall
Irina Kovach
Marsha O
Tracy R
Jen Smith
Maria Villate
Kristen Vuchichevich

Turtle Rocks
Head Coach: Colin Cowden
Pitching Coach: Steve Cosme
Fielding Coach: Jason Milen

2012 ROSTER:
Alicia Borsa
Stephanie Dudek
Jennifer Griffith
Amy Jandek
Jaclyn Jones
Alicia Marcellis
Valerie Morse
Yumi Muso
Marie Ortiz
Hannah Solomon-Strauss
Megan Tolpa
Dawn Vana

Baltimore Blues
Manager: Bonnie Hoffman
No roster available.

DC Thunder
No roster available.

Montgomery County Barn Cats
Coach: Richard Bender

2012 ROSTER:
Kelly Frederick
Katie Fricke
Robin Gelman
Jenna Greenwaldt
Debbie Hofheimer
Lisa Laios
Rachel Laufer
Felicia Levine
Susan McCarthy
Jena McLellan
Stephanie Miller
Angie Ortiz
Gaby Richeimer
Della Romano
Lisa Scott
Colleen Shepherd
Diane Sweeney
Lisa Zifcak-Dunn

Virginia Flames
No roster available.

Virginia Fury
Manager: Jennifer O'Keefe
No roster available.

East Coast Yankees
Coach: Adriane Adler
Coach: Pete Hall

2012 ROSTER:
Hera Andre-Bergmann
Tess Brogan
Nicole Callahan
Amanda Grieco
Janice Halls
Leigh Howard
Stephanie Kung
Jennifer Liu
Emily McPherson
Meggie Meidlinger
Nicole Michel
Jennifer Pantalone
Samantha Rodriguez
Jenny Ross
Crystal Vargas
Vanessa West
Jan Yuvan

Chicago Pioneers
Organizer: Mary Jo Stegeman
Coach: Greg Stegeman
No roster available.

New England Women's Red Sox

Coach: Kevin Marden

Assistant Coach: Bobby Anderson

2012 ROSTER:

Veronica Alvarez

Megan Borgaard

Ashleigh Cook

Sarah Gascon

Tara Harbert

Alex Hebert

Tamara Holmes

Lilly Jacobson

Meggie Meidlinger

Janet Miller

Donna Mills

Judy O'Brien

Marti Sementelli

Brionna Skinner

Sara Strohl

Melanie Taylor

Malaika Underwood

Kira Wagar

Pat Wagar

Stephanie Wagar

American Women's Baseball Federation

San Diego Bandits

Manager: Richard Cosgriff

2012 ROSTER:

Michele Betti

Melissa Carter

Meghan-Tomasita

Cosgriff-Hernandez

Carin Elliott

Jordan Fingerle

Jennifer Gomez

Katie Gonzalez

Jade Gortarez

Jessica Perez

Sarah Strohl

Katie Walker

Kelsie Whitemore

Lacey Yahnke

Independent

Arizona Dream Team

Coach: Richard Hopkins

No roster available.

San Diego Legends

Manager: Kelly Deutsch

2011 ROSTER:
Jessica Marie DeLine
Kelly Deutsch
Lindsey Hollis
Mikalya Khramov
Cristina Metildi
Leeann Morrentino
Teresa Ruiz
Sabrina Sexton
Sandra Sexton
Melissa Scosta-Jenson
Melissa Surby
Jenelle Theone Frese

Long Beach Bombers

Manager: Jo Corone

2012 ROSTER:
Jo Corone
Trudy Dehmar
Elizabeth Gasper
Jade Gonzalez
Lisa Hughes
Hilda Flor Martinez
Becky McLean
Claire Mezzetta
Annette Moto
Michelle Proctor

Liz Ross
Rebecca Singer
Mel Taylor

Los Angeles Aces

Manager: Melissa Acosta Jenson
No roster available.

Harbor Hearts

No roster available.

San Jose Spitfires

Manager: Rhonda Staton

2012 ROSTER:
Rachel Gary
Shelby Jensen
Caroline Johanson
Sara Krenz
Susan Kyle
Melanie Laspina
Monica Macer
Nancy Moricz
Sandra Dawn Moy
Rhonda Palmer
Ashley Rameriz-Rico
Miali Reynoso
Rhonda Staton
Courtney Zobac
Whitney Zobac
Sandra

Peninsula Peppers

Manager: Claudia Li

2012 ROSTER:

Kitt Allenser

Michelle Bullington

Kayla Chambers

Rachel Freeman

Taylor Gomez

Dominque Gougis

Rachel Henley

Agatha Kruse

Claudia Li

Terri Martin

Katie Perry

Adrienne Raquiza

Amanda Sedano

Alison Wendler

Donna Williams

Amanda Yaquinto

San Francisco Fillies

Manager: Ed Sickinger

No roster available.

Alameda Oaks

Manager: Sal Coats

No roster available.

NOTES

A reference to each player interview, identifying the
date of the interview, is made in the first endnote of each
chapter. Interviews were each several hours long, and
transcriptions run from 100 to 175 pages. Unless otherwise
cited, quotations in each chapter come from the player's
oral history interview. Follow-up comments by email,
Facebook, or phone conversation are cited as necessary.

Preface

1. Title IX of the Educational Amendments (to the 1964 Civil Rights Act) of 1972 (20 U.S.C. §§ 1681–88 [1972], http://www.justice.gov/crt/about/cor/coord/titleixstat .php) states, "No Person in the United States shall, on the basis of sex, be excluded from participation in, be denied the benefits of, or be subjected to discrimination under any educational program or activity receiving Federal financial assistance." Eileen McDonagh and Laura Pappano note, "Where Title VII altered women's employment opportunities, Title IV of the 1964 Civil Rights Act did nothing to challenge sex discrimination in education. Any discussion of Title IX then begins with the Civil Rights Act of 1964 and the omission of 'sex' in Title IV. It was that glaring absence that the Educational Amendments, including Title IX sought to correct in 1972." Eileen L. McDonagh and Laura Pappano, *Playing with the Boys: Why Separate Is Not Equal in Sports* (New York: Oxford University Press, 2008), 101, 102.

2. See, e.g., Susan K. Cahn, *Coming on Strong: Gender and Sexuality in Twentieth-Century Women's Sport* (Cambridge MA: Harvard University Press, 1994); Allen Guttmann, *Women's Sports: A History* (New York: Columbia University Press, 1991); Jennifer Hargreaves, *Sporting Females: Critical Issues in the History and Sociology of Women's Sports* (London: Routledge, 1994); and Sheila Scraton and Anne Flintoff, eds., *Gender and Sport: A Reader* (New York: Routledge, 2002). See also the "Suggestions for Further Reading."

3. Wilma Rudolph and Althea Gibson are two African American superstars in individual sports in the pre–Title IX era.

4. See, e.g., Mark Hyman, *Until It Hurts: America's Obsession with Youth Sports and How It Harms Our Kids* (Boston: Beacon Press, 2009). See also the "Suggestions for Further Reading."

5. A full discussion of the New England Women's Red Sox and other women's baseball teams can be found in chapter 16.

6. I received grants from the College of Liberal Arts at the University of Nevada, Reno; the Society for American Baseball Research; and the American Women's Baseball Federation to enable me to travel to the homes of each of these players and interview them each for several hours, or however long they chose to speak. I used a small digital recorder and had the interviews transcribed.

Introduction

1. Albert Goodwill Spalding, *America's National Game*, rev. ed. (San Francisco: Halo Books, 1991), 9.

2. Spalding, *America's National Game*, 11.

3. In contrast to this perspective of baseball as Elysian and peaceful, however, Robert Elias, in *The Empire Strikes Out: How Baseball Sold U.S. Foreign Policy and Promoted the American Way Abroad* (New York: New Press, 2010), delineates American baseball's deep metaphorical association with war, as well as the historical reality of baseball's influence on U.S. militarism and imperialism: e.g., "In baseball the batting team pursues a constant war of maneuver. To make a successful advance it tries to put the ball out of its enemy's reach. A hit baseball challenges the opponent's defenses, drawing his troops out of position and giving the batter a chance to occupy enemy territory; that is, the batter tries to get on base" (34), and "In war, defense is accomplished when an army incapacitates the enemy, preventing him from carrying out his designs, rendering his strategy useless. In baseball, the defense tries to get the third out without allowing the offense to occupy even the first station on the road to the city it would hope to capture" (51).

4. In the 2008 Women's World Cup Tournament, held in Matsuyama, Japan, Team Japan had been followed by a round-the-clock television crew and a troop of print journalists.

5. Bill Plaschke, "These Girls Are Playing Hardball with the Boys," *Los Angeles Times*, March 6, 2011; Marx Saxon, "Female Pitchers Make It a Special Day," ESPN Los Angeles.com, March 6, 2011, http://sports.espn.go.com/los-angeles/columns/story?id=6185670.

6. Jennifer Ring, *Stolen Bases: Why American Girls Don't Play Baseball* (Urbana: University of Illinois Press, 2009).

7. See David Block, *Baseball before We Knew It: A Search for the Roots of the Game* (Lincoln: University of Nebraska Press, 2005), 22–31; Elias, *Empire Strikes Out*; Joel Zoss and John Bowman, *Diamonds in the Rough: The Untold History of Baseball* (Chicago: Contemporary Books, 1996); Harold Seymour and Dorothy Z. Seymour, *Baseball*, vol. 3, *The People's Game* (New York: Oxford University Press, 1990); David Quentin Voight, *American Baseball: From the Gentleman's Sport to the Commissioner System* (University Park: Pennsylvania State University Press, 1983), vol. 1.

8. Paul Dickson, *The Worth Book of Softball: A Celebration of America's True National Pastime* (New York: Facts on File, 1994), 51; Zoss and Bowman, *Diamonds in the Rough*, 206.

9. Spalding, *America's National Game*, 371–80; A. Burgos Jr., *Playing America's Game: Baseball, Latinos, and the Color Line* (Berkeley: University of California Press, 2006); Ring, *Stolen Bases*, 194n24.

10. Henry Chadwick earned the nickname "Father Baseball" and is credited with "rationalizing" the game with statistics. He invented the box score, among other vehicles for controlling uncivilized emotions that had previously dominated the game. See Block *Baseball before We Knew It*; Harold Seymour and Dorothy Z. Seymour, *Baseball*, 3 vols. (New York: Oxford University Press, 1960–90); Richard Crepeau, *America's Diamond Mind* (Lincoln: University of Nebraska Press, 2000); Zoss and Bowman, *Diamonds in the Rough*; Gai Ingham Berlage, *Women in Baseball: The Forgotten History* (Westport CT: Greenwood Publishing, 1994); Ring, *Stolen Bases*.

11. Zoss and Bowman, *Diamonds in the Rough*; Dickson, *Worth Book of Softball*; Ring, *Stolen Bases*.

12. Lance Van Auken and Robin Van Auken, *Play Ball! The Story of Little League Baseball* (University Park: Pennsylvania State University Press, 2001); Hyman, *Until It Hurts*, 5–14; Ring, *Stolen Bases*, 116–33.

13. Sarah K. Fields, "Cultural Identity, Law, and Baseball," *Sport in Society* 4, no. 2 (2001): 34; Berlage, *Women in Baseball*, 97–106.

14. Fields, "Cultural Identity," 23–42; Sarah K. Fields, *Female Gladiators: Gender, Law and Contact Sport in America* (Urbana: University of Illinois Press, 2005); Ring, *Stolen Bases*, 116–33. Judge Sylvia Pressler of the New Jersey Division of Civil Rights found excluding girls to be discriminatory. Her decision was appealed by Little League Baseball and upheld by the Supreme Court of New Jersey.

15. McDonagh and Pappano, *Playing with the Boys*; Cahn, *Coming on Strong*; Colette Dowling, *The Frailty Myth: Redefining the Physical Potential of Women and Girls*

(New York: Random House, 2001); Anne Fausto-Sterling, *Sexing the Body: Gender Politics and the Construction of Sexuality* (New York: Basic Books, 2000). See also the "Suggestions for Further Reading."

16. Indeed, this sentiment would be confirmed by most women who have played baseball seriously, even though they tend not to think of their desire to play ball in political terms. The interviewees from the All-American Girls Professional Baseball League in Carol J. Pierman's "Baseball, Conduct, and True Womanhood" (*Women's Studies Quarterly* 33, no.1 [2005]: 2), much like the women I have been interviewing who currently play elite baseball, would rather keep the conversation on baseball, rather than talk about their sexual behavior or gender expression.

17. McDonagh and Pappano (*Playing with the Boys*, 29) state that sports is the most segregated institution in the United States, including the military.

18. McDonagh and Pappano, *Playing with the Boys*, 223.

19. McDonagh and Pappano, *Playing with the Boys*, 108-10; National Women's Law Center, *Title IX and Women's Athletic Opportunity: A Nation's Promise Yet to Be Fulfilled* (Washington DC: July 15, 2008), http://www.nwlc.org/resource/title-ix-and -womens-athletic-opportunity-nations-promise-yet-fulfilled; Office for Civil Rights, *Annual Report to Congress, Fiscal Year 1997* (Washington DC: U.S. Department of Education, 2000), http://www.ed.gov./about/offices/list/ocr/AnnRpt97/edlite -index.html; Deborah L. Brake, "The Struggle for Sex Equality in Sport and the Theory behind Title IX," *University of Michigan Journal of Law Reform* 34 (2001): 13; Kimberly Bingaman, "Fourth Annual Review of Gender and Sexuality Law: Education Law Chapter: Title IX of the 1972 Education Amendments," *Georgetown Journal of Gender and Law*, Fall 2002, 329-72; Michael A. Messner, *Taking the Field: Women, Men, and Sports* (Minneapolis: University of Minnesota Press, 2002); Julia Lamber, "Gender and Intercollegiate Athletics: Data and Myths," *University of Michigan Journal of Law Reform* 34 (2001): 151-229.

1. The Dream and Its Challenges

1. Julie Croteau (b. December 4, 1970) attended St. Mary's College, NCAA Division III, and played first base for three seasons, 1989-92. Leslie A. Heaphy and Mel Anthony May, eds., *Encyclopedia of Women and Baseball* (Jefferson NC: McFarland, 2006), 82.

2. Laspina played for the San Jose (CA) Spitfire of Ladies' League Baseball in 1997.

3. Julie Croteau was the other woman in NCAA Baseball.

4. Club baseball, as compared to NCAA varsity baseball, is student run and nationally organized. It is not governed by NCAA rules nor funded by a university's intercollegiate athletic budget. It is funded by student fees and governed by the

National Club Baseball Association. Quality of play differs campus to campus. At a Division I school like Cal, the club team was made up primarily of former high school players who wanted to attend a high-quality university but were not up to playing the preprofessional game of NCAA Division I baseball. They were good ballplayers, were great students, and did not expect to go pro with baseball. Cal Club Baseball plays other Pac-10 club baseball teams and also other club teams from colleges on the West Coast. There is a Club Baseball World Series each year.

5. Marti Sementelli, conversation with the author, July 2, 2010.
6. Lilly Jacobson, conversation with the author, July 2, 2010.

2. *Cary, 2010*

1. USA Baseball (www.USABaseball.com) is the national governing body of amateur baseball in the United States and is a member of the U.S. Olympic Committee (USOC). The organization selects and trains the World Baseball Classic Team and World Cup Team (and all other USA Baseball professional teams); the Collegiate National Team; the 18U, 17U, 15U, 14U, and 12U National Teams; and the Women's National Team, all of which participate in various international competitions each year. USA Baseball also presents the Golden Spikes Award (www.GoldenSpikesAward.com) annually to the top player in college baseball.

2. USA Baseball, Constitution and By-Laws of the United States Baseball Federation, Inc., 2008, http://www.usabaseball.com/downloads/2008/constitution_and _bylaws.pdf.

3. Regional tryouts were held in late June and over the July Fourth weekend in Phoenix; San Francisco; Chicago; Orlando; New London, Connecticut; and Cary, North Carolina. This was a well-intentioned effort to reach out to all available ballplayers. Problems with the plan included the fact that not all the coaches could be present at all of the tryouts, which were spread across the country, and outreach efforts were only marginally effective. Only seventy girls and women showed up at all the tryouts, making for an inefficient first-round evaluation process.

4. Previous tournaments have been held in Edmonton, Canada (2004); Taipei, Taiwan (2006); and Matsuyama, Japan (2008). The twelve teams in the 2010 Women's World Cup were USA, Japan, Canada, Australia, Venezuela, Cuba, Puerto Rico, South Korea, India, Hong Kong, Chinese Taipei, and the Netherlands.

5. See the USA Baseball master schedule for the 18U and Collegiate National Teams at http://web.usabaseball.com/schedules.jsp.

6. Many of the veterans of the women's U.S. national team keep in touch with each other by playing on a women's baseball tournament team based in Boston. They play two to three tournaments a year on major American holiday weekends against a handful of other teams from major American cities. Most regular participants in these tournaments are teams from Boston, Chicago, Washington DC, Philadelphia, New York, Seattle, and San Francisco. Tournaments are generally held Memorial Day weekend, July Fourth weekend, and Columbus Day weekend.

7. The ballplayers whose photos flanked Marti's were Albert Almora (14U), Bryce Harper (16U), James Taillon (18U), Stephen Strasburg (college), and Justin Smoak (pro). All except Almora, who is still too young, are currently in the pros, with Strasburg and Harper picked in the first round of the draft in 2009 and 2010, and Taillon picked second in 2010.

8. See McDonagh and Pappano, *Playing with the Boys*, especially ch. 1 ("What's the Problem?") and ch. 4 ("Sex Segregated Sports on Trial").

9. Jim Glennie, interview by the author, February 18, 2011.

10. Paul Seiler, phone interview by the author, November 28, 2012.

11. Ghazaleh Sailors, phone interview by the author, September 15, 2010.

12. Clarissa Navarro, phone interview by the author, November 2, 2010.

13. Bill Marston, conversation with the author, August 2010.

14. Donna Mills, interview by the author, May, 16, 2010.

15. Lilly Jacobson and Veronica Alvarez, conversation with the author, May, 31, 2010.

16. Kathy Welsh and Katie Gaynor, conversation with the author, August 2010.

17. Kathy Welsh, interview by the author, August 3, 2010.

18. Katie Gaynor, interview by the author, August 3, 2010.

19. Taylah Welsh, interview by the author, August 3, 2010.

20. Andre LaChance, conversation with the author, August 5, 2011.

21. Ed Kurakazu, interview by the author, September 19, 2010.

22. Glennie interview.

3. From Cary to Caracas

1. The Colorado Silver Bullets were a professional women's baseball team from 1994 to 1997. They earned a reputation as the best modern women's professional team, although they were not a part of a league and had to find men's Minor League teams to play against. Former members of the team are still revered in women's baseball circles—and in the eyes of American girls who want to play baseball—as the elite women ballplayers of the late twentieth century.

2. Marston was so impressive at the tournament that she won USA Baseball's Sportswoman of the Year Award for 2010.

3. Malaika Underwood, phone interview by the author, September 9, 2010.

4. Tim O'Brien, phone interview by the author, October 14, 2010.

5. Sailors phone interview.

6. Ofelia Alvarez, email correspondence with the author, August 28, 2010.

7. Tamara Holmes, interview by the author, August 29, 2010.

8. Marti Sementelli, interview by the author, September 23, 2010.

9. Holmes would be successful in that ambition: she hit three out-of-the-park home runs in Venezuela, two of them with the bases loaded.

10. Kurakazu interview.

11. Marti Sementelli, interview by the author, September 24, 2010.

12. Holmes interview, August 29, 2010.

13. Holmes interview, August 29, 2010.

14. Sementelli interview, September 23, 2010.

15. Don Freeman, phone interview by the author, October 9, 2010.

16. Sementelli interview, September 23, 2010.

17. Sailors phone interview.

18. Underwood phone interview, September 9, 2010.

19. Jenna Marston, phone interview by the author, October 20, 2010.

20. Sailors phone interview.

21. Holmes interview, August 29, 2010.

22. Veronica Alvarez, phone interview by the author, November 15, 2010.

23. Malaika Underwood, phone interview by the author, September 6, 2010.

24. Holmes interview, August 29, 2010.

25. Underwood phone interview, September 6, 2010.

26. Navarro phone interview.

27. Tamara Holmes, unpublished account of her experience on Team USA 2010, September 19, 2010.

28. Underwood phone interview, September 9, 2010.

29. Tara Harbert, phone interview by the author, September 21, 2010.

30. Veronica Alvarez, phone interview by the author, November 16, 2010.

31. Alvarez phone interview, November 16, 2010.

32. Lindsay Horwitz, Facebook correspondence with the author, November 29, 2010.

33. Alvarez phone interview, November 16, 2010.

34. Horwitz Facebook correspondence.

35. Sementelli interview, September 23, 2010.

36. Alvarez phone interview, November 16, 2010.

4. Tamara Holmes

1. Tamara Holmes, interview by the author, April 10, 2011. I interviewed Tamara Holmes first because she lives nearest to me. This was before I developed the question prompts that I distributed to her teammates (see appendix A). As a result, the narrative flow of this interview is slightly different from the interviews that follow.
2. City of Albany, "History," October 29, 2010, http://albanyca.org/index.aspx?page =59.
3. Albany, California, "Albany Little League Scrapbook," June 25, 1986. Tamara Holmes supplied me with a scanned version of the article about the league championship.
4. She overcame the ADD, mastered the fire department classes she enrolled in after she graduated from Berkeley, and has been a firefighter for the City of Oakland Fire Department since 2004. She was promoted to the rank of lieutenant in the Oakland Fire Department in August 2013.
5. She hit him in the back while he was standing in the batter's box because her pitch was so far inside that he had to turn his back to get away from it.

5. Donna Mills

1. Donna Mills, interviews by the author, May 16, 2010, and July 6, 2012. The first interview with Donna took place before I developed the question prompts, and the second one used the prompts. Donna followed up the second interview with several email and Facebook messages to add to what she had discussed. Those messages are cited as necessary.
2. Donna Mills, Facebook correspondence with the author, July 9, 2012.
3. Donna Mills, email correspondence with the author, November 5, 2012.
4. Team USA won the Women's World Cup championship in Taiwan in 2006, and Donna won the Most Valuable Player Award.
5. Mills, email correspondence with the author, November 21, 2012.
6. For a full discussion of the two tournaments of 2004 and the first USA Baseball–sponsored Women's National Team, see chapter 16.
7. Former members of the All-American Girls Professional Baseball League from the 1940s and 1950s are now often present for Team USA tryouts and are very involved in furthering women's baseball in the United States. Even in their seventies and eighties, they are still sitting on the top edge of a dugout bench and talking baseball.
8. The "luck" was the Australians beating the more highly regarded Canadians for the bronze to set up a gold medal game between Japan and the USA and a rainstorm at just the right moment in that championship game. The United

States took a ten-run lead, which Japan then tied. Then in the fifth inning, a sudden deluge delayed the game for more than a half hour. Japan's momentum was interrupted, and the American pitchers regained their control and got out of the inning. When the United States came up to bat in the bottom of the sixth, Tamara Holmes lined a double with a runner on base and drove in what proved to be the winning run for the Americans.

9. In 2013 Donna was hired as (boys') varsity baseball coach for her former high school, Lynn Tech.

10. The coaches selected for 2012 were Ruben Felix, an assistant softball coach at Central Florida University; Jonathan Pollard, a former college baseball player at Salem State College who now runs a youth baseball academy in Woburn, Massachusetts; Jenny Dalton Hill, the former softball star from the University of Arizona and member of Team USA in 2010; and Ed Kurakazu, an assistant boys' high school baseball coach in Phoenix, Arizona, who has been an assistant coach with the Women's National Team several times.

11. Mills email, November 21, 2012.

12. Mills email, November 21, 2012.

6. Jenny Dalton Hill

1. Jenny Dalton Hill, interview by the author, March 20, 2012.

2. In 1995 UCLA beat Arizona for the championship but was then found guilty of rules violations and had its championship revoked. There was no official winner of the College Softball World Series that year.

3. Kim Braatz Voisard is a former member of the Silver Bullets and Team USA and one of the most accomplished women baseball players in the country. She is retired now, married and raising a family, but very involved in helping younger women baseball players to advance in the sport.

7. Tara Harbert

1. Tara Harbert, interviews by the author, May 25, 2012, and May 27, 2012.

2. University of Hawai'i Athletics, "Hawai'i Softball's Strong Finish Not Enough for NCAA Bid," May 15, 2005, http://hawaiiathletics.com/news/2005/5/15/SB_394821.aspx?path=softball.

3. Ichiro Suzuki is a star Major League outfielder who played right field for the Seattle Mariners and was traded to the Yankees in 2012. He is small, is extremely fast, and has an unusual run-up batting style for a Major Leaguer. He is also the first Japanese baseball player to have played his entire career in the American Major Leagues.

4. Hill interview.

5. Kevin Marden coaches the New England Women's Red Sox, a women's tournament team located in Boston. Many of the Team USA players also play on the Red Sox, and the team has been virtually unbeaten in its last one hundred games—although they don't have much competition. Marden's importance in furthering women's baseball and giving the best women in the nation a venue in which to shine and hone their baseball skills is discussed fully in chapter 16.

6. Tara's teammates Tamara Holmes and Lilly Jacobson have both made similar observations: when men assume women ballplayers can't hit their fastball, it makes it easy for a woman to tempt them to throw it, precisely because she knows she *can* hit it. Holmes enjoys bluffing men by letting them think she can't hit their fastballs. Then they throw her a fastball, and she crushes it. "I'm like, 'Oh, throw the fastball!' I like to pretend I can't hit the fastball because that's what I want. I'll light that up every time." Holmes interview, April 10, 2011. Tara's observation about elite men respecting women implies that men who are confident of their own ability are able to acknowledge that women also know how to play and know that it would be as foolish to throw a fastball down the middle to a woman as it would be to a man.

8. Veronica Alvarez

1. Veronica Alvarez, interviews by the author, April 20 and April 21, 2012.
2. Veronica Alvarez, phone conversation with the author, December 19, 2012.
3. Alvarez phone conversation.
4. Lilly Jacobson, in multiple conversations with the author over a period of several years.

9. Sarah Gascon

1. Sarah Gascon, interview by the author, February 11, 2012.
2. "Pickle" is a children's game played with a ball, two bases, and three players. It simulates a rundown in baseball: one player in the middle is the runner trying to reach one of the bases safely, while other players throw the ball to each other, trying to tag the runner before she can touch either of the bases.
3. "T-ball" is softball or baseball for very young children. Instead of hitting a moving ball pitched at them, the youngsters learn the sport by standing at home plate and hitting a ball resting on a tee. They run to base when the ball is successfully hit off the tee. It's slow and unexciting, but it is the safest way to encourage children to begin to play without the worry of getting hit by a pitch.
4. Sarah also plays on the U.S. National Handball Team.
5. "Laying out" for a ball is diving for it and hopefully catching it or trapping it before it gets past you. You end up lying face down on the field whether you are

successful or not. In this case Sarah caught the ball for the elusive third out and ended the inning for her team.

6. In other words, the starting third basewoman was recovering from knee surgery and could not play her position that year. But she was in the lineup as a designated hitter. This left the starting position at third base open, just as Sarah showed up to try out for the team.

7. Bridget Veenema, Laura Purser, and Kim Braatz, three former Silver Bullet players.

10. Jenna Marston

1. Jenna Marston, interview by the author, March 19, 2012.

2. Jenna's memory is correct: Manchester Athletic Association is indeed a public baseball and softball association in suburban St. Louis.

3. The players on women's softball teams do organized cheers for their teammates in contrast to the more understated dugout culture in baseball.

4. Statistics from Mizzou Tigers, "26 Jenna Marston," 2014, http://www.mutigers.com /sports/w-softbl/mtt/marston_jennajj00.html.

5. Jenna Marston, Facebook correspondence with the author, August 17, 2012.

11. Malaika Underwood

1. Malaika Underwood, interview by the author, April 19, 2012, and April 20, 2012. Malaika also sent me an email narrative titled "My Baseball Story" on July 12, 2009, which is quoted in this chapter.

2. Malaika Underwood, email correspondence with the author, June 8, 2012.

3. More recently, Malaika was asked to play first base for the 2012 USA Baseball Women's National Team. The transition to first base was much easier than moving to third base because the perspective is similar to second base. "I enjoyed the challenge of learning a new position. I will always think of myself as a second baseman, but if I can contribute to the team at first base then I'm all in." Malaika Underwood, email correspondence with the author, November 29, 2012.

4. Currently, softball is played on a diamond with 60-foot baselines (compared to baseball's 90-foot baselines); the softball outfield fences are set 195–225 feet from home plate, whereas the average full-sized baseball field has outfield fences between 300 and 400 feet from home. The softball is pitched underhand from 43–45 feet, depending on the level of play, whereas in baseball the ball is pitched overhand from 60.5 feet. The softball is about 12 inches in diameter and weighs between 6 and 7 ounces, whereas the baseball is about 9 inches in diameter and weighs a little over 5 ounces (the size of both the softball and baseball depends on the level of play and the age of the players). The different dimensions in all aspects of the game and different rules result in a different pace and feel to each game.

5. Malaika Underwood, "My Baseball Story" (unpublished manuscript, July 12, 2009), email.
6. The ball was hit to the shortstop, who threw it to Malaika for the force out at second base. She then turned the double play with a throw to first base to get the runner out.
7. Underwood, "My Baseball Story."

12. Marti Sementelli

1. Marti Sementelli, interview by the author, June 15, 2012.
2. Gary Sementelli worked in the administrative office at Sherman Oaks Recreation Park, so he was available when Marti attended the summer camps there and preferred his company.
3. In 2008 there was only one preliminary tryout. In 2006 there were three regional tryouts, and in 2010, six regionals.
4. Justine Siegel, quoted in Dave Krider, "California Girl Earns College Baseball Scholarship," *Maxpreps News*, May 13, 2011, http://www.maxpreps.com/news/NuRm EX2LEeCkhgAcxJSkrA/california-girl-earns-college-baseball-scholarship.htm. The other women were Ila Borders (Southern California College, 1994–96, and Whittier College, 1997) and Molly McKesson (Christian Brothers College in Memphis, 2005–8). A handful of other women have played the college game without scholarships: Julie Croteau was the first woman to play NCAA Division II baseball, at St. Mary's of Baltimore from 1989–92, and Lilly Jacobson was the first woman to play NCAA Division III baseball, at Vassar College in 2009. Croteau and Jacobson are the only women to have gotten hits on NCAA baseball teams. Croteau went on to be the first (and only) woman to coach NCAA baseball, at the Division I level at the University of Massachusetts–Amherst. She also coached the 2006 USA Baseball Women's National Team to a gold medal against Japan in the second Women's World Cup Tournament in Taipei, Taiwan. She is the only woman coach Team USA has had. Ghazaleh Sailors graduated high school the same year as Marti and also went on to play college baseball. She pitched at the University of Maine–Presque Isle of the National Association of Intercollegiate Athletics (NAIA) Sunrise Conference for her entire college career. Sementelli pitched for one season at Montreat College and then switched to the college's softball team.
5. Vincent Bonsignore, "Pitcher Is Armed and Ready for the Next Step as She Signs Letter of Intent with NC College," *Los Angeles Daily News*, June 1, 2011, http://www. dailynews.com/20110602/pitcher-is-armed-and-ready-for-the-next-step-as -she-signs-letter-of-intent-with-nc-college.
6. The fourth batter is the cleanup hitter, the power spot in the batting lineup.

7. In fact, Marti did not have the opportunity to play baseball her final three years at Montreat. At the start of her sophomore season, she was ignored by the coach and given no playing time. She tried to talk to him about what was wrong and received no encouragement to stay on the team. She withdrew from Montreat Baseball and was invited to play on the softball team, where she had many friends. Her academic scholarship at Montreat and her friends on the softball team were her motivation to stay at the school to finish college.

13. Lilly Jacobson

1. Lilly Jacobson, interviews by the author, May 16, 2011, and July 6, 2012. Lilly Jacobson is my daughter. I have written about the early part of her story before, in my previous book, *Stolen Bases*. Chapter 1 of this book gives this story from my perspective, with my recollections. This chapter is Lilly's recollection of her own experiences. My interviews with Lilly for this chapter took place in two segments, the first in May 2011 in Berkeley, California, and the second in July 2012 in Boston, Massachusetts. I interviewed her as I interviewed her teammates on Team USA 2010: same set of questions sent by email beforehand, same invitation to depart from the suggested questions and talk about whatever seemed most important to her baseball story. I tried to speak as little as possible throughout the interview, just as I did during the interviews the other nine players in the "starting lineup." However, the fact that this was a conversation between a mother and daughter undoubtedly influenced the dynamic of the dialogue. Obviously, my feelings are not neutral, especially with regard to the heartbreaking discrimination Lilly has endured. To the fullest extent possible, however, I have tried to let Lilly's voice come through this oral history in the same way I tried to encourage her teammates to tell their own stories in their own voices. I refer to myself in the first person throughout.
2. The girl was Andrea Lazzari. Andrea was a softball star at Wooster High School in Reno, Nevada, and later earned an NCAA softball scholarship to Wagner College in New York City, where she had a stellar career. Lilly played baseball at Wooster High School with Andrea's younger brother, Pete.
3. In 2008 Vassar won 8 and lost 22 overall in the season, were 3-18 in Liberty League play, and finished 7th in league (in an 8-team league). In 2009 the team that Lilly was cut from fared even worse: they won 6 and lost 29 overall and were 3-21 in league play, finishing 7th out of 8 again. Statistics from Vassar College Athletics, "Baseball Year-by-Year Records," 2009, http://www.vassarathletics.com/sports/2009/2/3/bb_0203091458.aspx?path=baseball.
4. Julie Croteau was the only woman to have hit successfully in NCAA baseball until 2008, when Lilly hit while playing for Vassar.

5. The New England Women's Red Sox, coached by Kevin Marden, are centered in Boston and draw many players from Team USA and the Silver Bullets. They have very little competition among other women's teams in the United States, and their record as of 2012 is 106-2. They hope to play against stiffer women's competition, but what really draws the Red Sox together is that they enjoy each other's baseball prowess and company and have the deepest respect for Coach Marden.

6. The next year that she faced Stanford on the Cal team, she hit everything they pitched to her, to the delight of her teammates and the consternation of the Stanford players. Stanford's sense of frustration was undoubtedly amplified by the fact that, not just any girl, but a girl on their historic rival's team was hitting their pitching. Cal won.

14. Meggie Meidlinger

1. Meggie Meidlinger, interview by Lilly Jacobson, May 26, 2011. Lilly interviewed Meggie in Washington DC while they were traveling together to the Eastern Women's Baseball Conference Tournament in Baltimore, Maryland.

15. America's Team

1. For an excellent discussion of the stages of sex desegregation in sports, see McDonagh and Pappano, *Playing with the Boys*, particularly p. 34.

2. The Fifteenth Amendment to the U.S. Constitution reads, "Section 1. The right of citizens of the United States to vote shall not be denied or abridged by the United States or by any State on account of race, color, or previous condition of servitude. Section 2. The Congress shall have power to enforce this article by appropriate legislation." For discussion see Eleanor Flexner, *Century of Struggle: The Women's Rights Movement in the United States* (Cambridge MA: Harvard University Press, 1959); Paula Giddings, *When and Where I Enter: The Impact of Black Women on Race and Sex in America* (New York: HarperCollins, 1984); and Mari Jo Buhle and Paul Buhle, eds., *The Concise History of Woman Suffrage* (Urbana: University of Illinois Press, 1978).

3. McDonagh and Pappano, *Playing with the Boys*, 101.

4. McDonagh and Pappano, *Playing with the Boys*, 80.

5. The Fourteenth Amendment to the Constitution, ratified July 9, 1868, reads, "All persons born or naturalized in the United States, and subject to the jurisdiction thereof, are citizens of the United States and of the State wherein they reside. No State shall make or enforce any law which shall abridge the privileges or immunities of citizens of the United States; nor shall any State deprive any

person of life, liberty, or property, without due process of law; nor deny to any person within its jurisdiction the equal protection of the laws."

16. Grassroots Women's Baseball

1. See Berlage, *Women in Baseball*, 89–110; Jean Hastings Ardell, *Breaking into Baseball: Women and the National Pastime* (Carbondale: Southern Illinois University Press, 2005), 86–101; Heaphy and May, *Encyclopedia of Women and Baseball*; Susan E. Johnson, *When Women Played Hardball* (Seattle: Seal Press, 1994).
2. The only three players on Team USA 2010 who did not come to the team through Jim Glennie were Tamara Holmes, Jenny Dalton Hill, and Jenna Marston. Hill was recruited to Team USA through Kim Braatz, and Marston through Ashley Bratcher, both of USA Baseball. Tamara Holmes learned of USA Baseball from the Silver Bullets.
3. Unless otherwise cited, all of Jim Glennie's quotations in this chapter are from his interview by the author, February 18, 2011.
4. See also Ardell, *Breaking into Baseball*, 97.
5. The Silver Bullets were funded by the Coors Brewing Company, and the All-American Girls Professional Baseball League was funded by Wrigley Chewing Gum.
6. All of Kevin Marden's quotations in this chapter are from his interview by the author, December 26, 2011.
7. Donna Mills, email correspondence with the author, November 20, 2012.
8. In the 2013 Eastern Women's Baseball Conference Tournament on May 25-28, two teams from Canada participated: Toronto and Quebec. For the first time in this tournament's history, there were ten teams, which required two brackets of play to determine which teams would play for the championship. The gold medal game was played between the New England Sox and Team Quebec. The Sox won, 7–6, in a thrilling game that ended in a seventh-inning walk-off hit.

17. USA Baseball

1. Majestic is the official manufacturer of Major League Baseball's uniforms.
2. Ted Stevens Olympic and Amateur Sports Act, 36 U.S.C. § 220501 (1998), http://www.law.cornell.edu/uscode/text/36/220501; Comm. on Commerce, Science, and Transportation, Olympic and Amateur Sports Act Amendments of 1998, S. Rep. No. 105-325 (1998), http://www.gpo.gov/fdsys/pkg/CRPT-105srpt325/pdf/CRPT-105srpt325.pdf.
3. Unless otherwise cited, all of Paul Seiler's quotations in this chapter are from his phone interview by the author, November 28, 2012.

4. USA Baseball, Constitution, Article V, Secs. 1 and 7.
5. Glennie interview.
6. Paul Seiler, email correspondence with the author, December 31, 2012.
7. Mills interview.
8. Glennie interview.

SUGGESTIONS FOR FURTHER READING

Books

WOMEN AND BASEBALL

Ardell, Jean Hastings. *Breaking into Baseball: Women and the National Pastime*. Carbondale: Southern Illinois University Press, 2005.

Berlange, Gai Ingham. *Women in Baseball: The Forgotten History*. Westport CT: Praeger, 1994.

Cohen, Marilyn. *No Girls in the Clubhouse: The Exclusion of Women from Baseball*. Jefferson NC: McFarland, 2009.

Gregorich, Barbara. *Research Notes for Women at Play: The Story of Women in Baseball*. Vol. 2, *Lizzie Arlington, Alta Weiss, Lizzie Murphy, Edith Houghton, Jackie Mitchell, Babe Didrickson*. N.p.: CreateSpace Books, 2013.

Gregorich, Barbara. *She's on First: A Novel*. Chicago: Philbar Books, 2011.

Gregorich, Barbara. *Women at Play: The Story of Women in Baseball*. San Diego: Harcourt Brace, 1993.

Heaphy, Leslie A., and Mel Anthony May, eds. *Encyclopedia of Women and Baseball*. Jefferson NC: McFarland, 2006.

Johnson, Susan E. *When Women Played Hardball*. Seattle: Seal Press, 1994.

Mills, Dorothy Seymour. *A Woman's Work: Writing Baseball History with Harold Seymour*. Jefferson NC: McFarland, 2004.

Ring, Jennifer. *Stolen Bases: Why American Girls Don't Play Baseball*. Urbana: University of Illinois Press, 2009.

Seymour, Harold, and Dorothy Z. Seymour. *Baseball*. Vol. 3, *The People's Game*. New York: Oxford University Press, 1990.

GENDER AND FEMINIST THEORY AND SPORTS

Cahn, Susan K. *Coming on Strong: Gender and Sexuality in Twentieth-Century Women's Sport*. Cambridge MA: Harvard University Press, 1994.

Dowling, Colette. *The Frailty Myth: Redefining the Physical Potential of Women and Girls*. New York: Random House, 2001.

Fields, Sarah K. *Female Gladiators: Gender, Law, and Contact Sport in America*. Urbana: University of Illinois Press, 2005.

337

Griffin, Pat. *Strong Women, Deep Closets: Lesbians and Homophobia in Sport*. Champaign IL: Human Kinetics, 1998.

Hall, M. Ann. *Feminism and Sporting Bodies: Essays on Theory and Practice*. Champaign IL: Human Kinetics, 1996.

Hargreaves, Jennifer. *Sporting Females: Critical Issues in the History and Sociology of Women's Sports*. London: Routledge, 1994.

Ireland, Mary Lloyd, and Aurelia Nattiv, eds. *The Female Athlete*. Philadelphia: W. B. Saunders, 2002.

McKay, Jim, Michael A. Messner, and Don Sabo, eds. *Masculinities, Gender Relations, and Sport*. Thousand Oaks CA: Sage, 2000.

Messner, Michael A. *Taking the Field: Women, Men, and Sports*. Minneapolis: University of Minnesota Press, 2002.

Messner, Michael A., and Don F. Sabo, eds. *Sport, Men, and the Gender Order: Critical Feminist Perspectives*. Champaign IL: Human Kinetics, 1992.

O'Reilly, Jean, and Susan K. Cahn. *Women and Sports in the United States: A Documentary Reader*. Boston: Northeastern University Press, 2007.

Osborne, C., and F. Skillen, eds. *Women in Sports History*. New York: Routledge, 2012.

Prettyman, Sandra Spickard, and Brian Lampman, eds. *Learning Culture through Sports: Perspectives on Society and Organized Sports*. 2nd ed. Lanham MD: Rowman & Littlefield, 2011.

Scraton, Sheila, and Anne Flintoff, eds. *Gender and Sport: A Reader*. New York: Routledge, 2002.

TITLE IX

Brake, Deborah L. *Getting in the Game: Title IX and the Women's Sports Revolution*. New York: New York University Press, 2010.

Hogshead-Makar, Nancy, and Andrew Zimbalist, eds. *Equal Play: Title IX and Social Change*. Philadelphia: Temple University Press, 2007.

McDonagh, Eileen L., and Laura Pappano. *Playing with the Boys: Why Separate Is Not Equal in Sports*. New York: Oxford University Press, 2008.

GENDER AND RACE SEGREGATION IN SPORTS

Cozzillio, Michael J., and Robert L. Hayman Jr. *Sports and Inequality*. Durham NC: Carolina Academic Press, 2005.

Scholarly Articles

WOMEN, BASEBALL, AND SOFTBALL

Petranek, Laura Jones, and Gina V. Barton. "The Overarm-Throwing Pattern Among U-14 ASA Female Softball Players: A Comparative Study of Gender, Culture, and Experience." *Research Quarterly for Exercise and Sport* 82, no. 2 (2011): 220–28.

Ring, Jennifer. "America's Baseball Underground." *Journal of Sport and Social Issues* 33, no. 4 (2009): 373–89.

Ring, Jennifer. "Invisible Women in America's National Pastime . . . or, 'She's Good. It's History, Man.'" *Journal of Sport and Social Issues* 37, no. 1 (2013): 57–77.

Ross, Sally R., and Kimberly J. Shinew. "Perspectives of Women College Athletes on Sport and Gender." *Sex Roles* 58 (2008): 40–57.

Shattuck, Debra. "Women's Baseball in the 1860s: Reestablishing a Historical Memory." *NINE: A Journal of Baseball History and Culture* 19, no. 2 (2011): 1–26.

Travers, Ann. "Thinking the Unthinkable: Imagining an 'Un-American,' Girl-Friendly, Women- and Trans-Inclusive Alternative for Baseball." *Journal of Sports & Social Issues* 37, no. 1 (2012): 78–96.

GIRLS AND BOYS: TRAINING, STRENGTH, ETC.

Faigenbaum, Avery D., et al. "Youth Resistance Training: Updated Position Statement Paper from the National Strength and Conditioning Association." *Journal of Strength and Conditioning Research* 23, no. 5 (2009): S60–S79.

Kanehisa, H., et al. "A 2-Year Follow-Up Study on Muscle Size and Dynamic Strength in Teenage Tennis Players." *Scandinavian Journal of Medicine & Science in Sports* 16, no. 2 (2006): 93–101.

Reynolds, Monica L., et al. "An Examination of Current Practices and Gender Differences in Strength and Conditioning in a Sample of Varsity High School Athletic Programs." *Journal of Strength and Conditioning Research* 26, no. 1 (2012): 174–83.

WOMEN AND MEN: TRAINING AND STRENGTH

Brown, Gregory A., et al. "Oxygen Consumption, Heart Rate, and Blood Lactate Responses to an Acute Bout of Plyometric Depth Jumps in College-Aged Men and Women." *Journal of Strength and Conditioning Research* 24, no. 9 (2010): 2475–82.

Buchman, Aron S., et al. "Effect of Age and Gender in the Control of Elbow Flexion Movements." *Journal of Motor Behavior* 32, no. 4 (2000): 391–99.

Evans, Rachel K., et al. "Sex Differences in Parameters of Bone Strength in New Recruits: Beyond Bone Density." *Medicine and Science in Sports and Exercise* 40, no. 11 (2008): S645–S653.

Magnusen, Marshall J., and Deborah J. Rhea. "Division I Athletes' Attitudes toward and Preferences for Male and Female Strength and Conditioning Coaches." *Journal of Strength and Conditioning Research* 23, no. 4 (2009): 1084–90.

Pincivero, Danny M., et al. "Angle- and Gender-Specific Quadriceps Femoris Muscle Recruitment and Knee Extensor Torque." *Journal of Biomechanics* 37, no. 11 (2004): 1689–97.

Poiss, Candice C., et al. "Perceived Importance of Weight Training to Selected NCAA Division III Men and Women Student-Athletes." *Journal of Strength and Conditioning Research* 18, no. 1 (2004): 108-14.

Vetter, Rheba E., and Matthew L. Symonds. "Correlations between Injury, Training Intensity, and Physical and Mental Exhaustion among College Athletes." *Journal of Strength and Conditioning Research* 24, no. 3 (2010): 587-96.

Yanovich, Ran, et al. "Differences in Physical Fitness of Male and Female Recruits in Gender-Integrated Army Basic Training." *Medicine and Science in Sports and Exercise* 40, no. 11 (2008): S654-S659.

GENDER AND FEMINIST THEORY AND SPORTS

Schell, Lea Ann, and Stephanie Rodriguez. "Our Sporting Sisters: How Male Hegemony Stratifies Women in Sport." *Women in Sport and Physical Activity* 9, no. 1 (2000): 15-34.

Sykes, Heather. "Transsexual and Transgender Policies in Sport." *Women in Sport and Physical Activity Journal* 15, no. 1 (2006): 3-13.

GENDER AND RACE SEGREGATION IN SPORTS

Anderson, Eric. "'I Used to Think Women Were Weak': Orthodox Masculinity, Gender Segregation, and Sport." *Sociological Forum* 23, no. 2 (2008): 257-80.

Dworkin, Shari L., and Cheryl Cooky. "Sport, Sex Segregation, and Sex Testing: Critical Reflections on This Unjust Marriage." *American Journal of Bioethics* 12, no. 7 (2012): 21-23.

Glennie, Elizabeth J., and Elizabeth Stearns. "Opportunities to Play the Game: The Effect of Individual and School Attributes on Participation in Sports." *Sociological Spectrum* 32, no. 6 (2012): 532-57.

Gooren, Louis J. "Olympic Sports and Transsexuals." *Asian Journal of Andrology* 10, no. 3 (2008): 427-32.

Love, Adam, and Kimberly Kelly. "Equity of Essentialism? U.S. Courts and the Legitimation of Girls' Teams in High School Sport." *Gender and Society* 25, no. 2 (2011): 227-49.

Mathewson, Alfred Dennis. "Black Women, Gender Equity and the Function at the Junction." *Marquette Sports Law Journal* 6 (1996): 239-409.

Walton, Theresa. "Pinned by Gender Construction? Media Representations of Girls' Wrestling." *Women in Sport & Physical Activity Journal* 14, no. 2 (2005): 52-68.

TITLE IX

Cohen, David S. "The Stubborn Persistence of Sex Segregation." *Columbia Journal of Gender and Law* 20, no. 1 (2011): 51-140.

Pickett, Moneque Walker, Marvin P. Dawkins, and Jomills Henry Braddock. "Race and Gender Equity in Sports: Have White and African American Females Benefited Equally from Title IX?" *American Behavioral Scientist* 56, no. 11 (2012): 1581–1603.

Stevenson, Betsey. "Title IX and the Evolution of High School Sports." *Contemporary Economic Policy* 25, no. 4 (2007): 486–505.

Yuracko, Kimberly A. "Title IX and the Problem of Gender Equality in Athletics." *Gender Issues* 20, no. 2 (2002): 65–80.

Research Foundation Reports on Title IX

Butler, J., and Lopiano, D. *The Women's Sports Foundation Report: Title IX and Race in Intercollegiate Sport.* East Meadow NY: Women's Sports Foundation, 2003.

Cheslock, J. *Who's Playing College Sports? Money, Race and Gender.* East Meadow NY: Women's Sports Foundation, 2008.

Cheslock, J. *Who's Playing College Sports? Trends in Participation.* East Meadow NY: Women's Sports Foundation, 2007.

Griffin, P., and Carroll, H. *On the Team: Equal Opportunity for Transgender Student Athletes.* East Meadow NY: Women's Sports Foundation, 2005.

Heywood, L. *The Women's Sports Foundation Report: Addressing the Needs of Female Professional and Amateur Athletes.* East Meadow NY: Women's Sports Foundation, 1999.

Sabo, D. *The Women's Sports Foundation Gender Equity Report Card: A Survey of Athletic Opportunity in American Higher Education.* East Meadow NY: Women's Sports Foundation, 1997.

Sabo, D., and Veliz, P. *The Decade of Decline: Gender Equity in High School Sports.* East Meadow NY: Women's Sports Foundation, 2012.

Sabo, D., and Veliz, P. *Progress without Equity: The Provision of High School Athletic Opportunity in the United States, by Gender 1993–94 through 2005–06.* East Meadow NY: Women's Sports Foundation, 2011.

Smith, M., and Wrynn, A. *Women in the 2000, 2004 and 2008 Olympic and Paralympic Games: An Analysis of Participation, Leadership and Media Opportunities.* East Meadow NY: Women's Sports Foundation, 2009.

Smith, M., and Wrynn, A. *Women in the 2010 Olympic and Paralympic Games: An Analysis of Participation, Leadership and Media Opportunities.* East Meadow NY: Women's Sports Foundation, 2010.

Tucker Center for Research on Girls and Women in Sport. *Developing Physically Active Girls: An Evidence-Based Multidisciplinary Approach.* Minneapolis: University of Minnesota, 2007. http://www.cehd.umn.edu/tuckercenter/library/docs/research/2007-Tucker-Center-Research-Report.pdf.

Women's Sports Foundation, comp. *Women's Sports & Fitness Facts & Statistics.* 2009. http://www.womenssportsfoundation.org/en/home/research/articles -and-reports.

Zurn, L., D. Lopiano, and M. Snyder. *Women in the 2006 Olympic and Paralympic Winter Games: An Analysis of Participation, Leadership and Media Coverage.* East Meadow NY: Women's Sports Foundation, 2006.

INDEX

Page numbers in italics refer to illustrations.

Robinson, Jackie, 22, 61, 262
Roosevelt, Theodore, xxx
rounders, xxviii, xxx
Roy Hobbs World Series, 189, 249, 273, 280

Sailors, Ghazaleh, 202, 313; at Caracas World Cup, 32, 35, 40–41; media coverage of, xxiv–xxv
San Diego Bandits, 318
San Diego Legends, 319
Sandoval, Pablo, xxxii
San Francisco Chronicle, 68, 70
San Francisco Fillies, 320
San Jose Spitfires, 319
Saxon, Mark, xxvii
scholarships, college: for Alvarez, 122, 128; for Gascon, 148, 149; for Harbert, 109, 110, 113; for Holmes, 54–55, 59, 62; for Mills, 72, 78; for Sementelli, 195, 203, 205; for Underwood, 182, 187; for women in baseball, 29, 118, 195, 203, 205, 332n4
Scott, Marty, 81
second base position, 95, 176, 331n3
Seiler, Paul: on USA Baseball funding, 294; on women's baseball, 298–303; and Women's National Team, 24, 275, 296
self-confidence, 143, 145, 261–62, 267; women in baseball, 246–47
Sementelli, Gary, 195–96, 197, 199–200, 201, 208–9, 259
Sementelli, Marti, xiii, 195–210; at Caracas World Cup, 36–37, 39–40, 44, 46–47, 48–49; collegiate baseball scholarship of, 203, 205; family of, 195–96, 259; in high

school, 201–3; in Little League, 196–200; love of baseball, 201, 256; media coverage of, xxiv–xxv, 197, 202, 206, 208; at Montreat College, 203–8, 333n7; negative reactions to, 205–6, 208; photos, *199, 204, 205, 258;* on "The Silence," 16–17; and switching to softball, 198, 200–201, 313; and Women's National Team, 12, 21, 31, 202–3, 305
Severino, Josephine and Ralph, 75
sexual discrimination, 22, 215, 218, 238, 262–64, 321n1. *See also* gender segregation
sexual identity, 58, 64–65, 245–46, 248, 261
sexuality, 179; female athletes and, 137–38, 192, 248
Sharpe-Underwood, Lynn, 174, 175, 181
shortstop position, 95, 149–50, 152
Sickenger, Alex, 82
Siegel, Justine, 273
"The Silence," 16–18
Silver Bullets. *See* Colorado Silver Bullets
slap hitting, 111–12
Smelko, Will, 235–36
Smit, Hunter, 221
Smith, Loren, 32, 43
Smoak, Justin, 21, 325n7
Sobeck, Christin, 31, 41, 43
soccer, xxxiii, 23
Society for American Baseball Research (SABR), xii–xiii
softball: Alvarez in, 126–33, 261, 266; baseball differences with, 23, 79–80, 98–99, 114–17, 128–29, 135–36, 163–64, 191, 201, 226, 229, 238,